| | | | |
|---|---|---|---|
| Thomas Blair Esqr. | Christ. Dunn | Moses Davis | James Cosgrave |
| | John Smith | James Lamb | John Mayne |
| | John Dempsy | John English | William Hill |

Newman's lithograph of Kingstown Harbour *c.*184[illegible]

# HISTORY OF DUN LAOGHAIRE HARBOUR

# HISTORY OF DUN LAOGHAIRE HARBOUR

JOHN DE COURCY IRELAND

CAISLEÁN AN BHÚRCAIGH
2001

ISBN 0 946130 27 2

British Library in Cataloguing in Publication Data
A catalogue for this book is available
from the British Library.

Dublin by Éamonn de Búrca for Edmund Burke Publisher
"Cloonagashel", 27 Priory Drive, Blackrock, County Dublin

Printed by Betaprint
Design and production by Dunbar Design

This book is dedicated to the memory of my wife
Beatrice (Bet) who spent most of her life in the vicinity of
Dun Laoghaire which she loved, and was the inspiration
behind the writing of this book

# CONTENTS

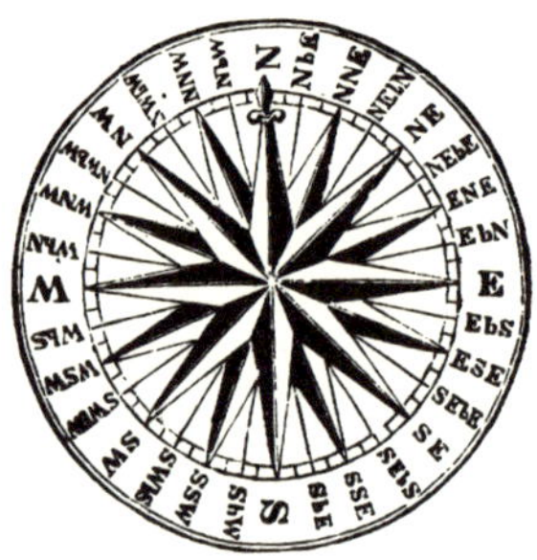

# LIST OF ILLUSTRATIONS

DUN LAOGHAIRE HARBOUR BOARD

Cllr Jane Dillon Byrne, Aine Elliott, David Redmond, Cllr Donal Marren,
Michael Hanahoe, Dr Tim Wilson, Arthur Byrne, Cllr Betty Coffey,
Alice Hayes, Philip Lynch, Eithne Scott-Lennon, Anne Joyce


## ACKNOWLEDGEMENTS

This book could never have been written without the patient and generous help so freely given by Brian Donnelly and Rena Lohan of the National Archives, Dublin; the valuable advice and documentation so kindly given by Captain James Carter, Harbour Master at Dun Laoghaire; and Tom Vaughan, the former Harbour Manager; together with the slides and other illustrations and references to numerous articles and publications cited in the Bibliography provided by Patrick Flood of the Maritime Institute of Ireland. The encouragement of Jim Love, Administrator (1994–1995) of the National Maritime Museum at Dun Laoghaire; the prompt and courteous dispatch of information by the National Maritime Museum, Greenwich, and its former Keeper of Manuscripts, David Proctor; the cheerful assistance of Dr Smyly Robbie Brennan and Philip Booth of the Maritime Museum at Dun Laoghaire, the patience, good humour and erudition of my publisher Eamonn de Burca and the patience and perseverence of my daughter Moneen and grand daughter Michelle, who typed the book from my manuscript.

For photographs, maps and illustrations: Andrew Bonar Law of the Neptune Gallery; Eddie Chandler, Joanna Finegan and staff at the National Library; National Maritime Museum, and Justin Merrigan. For proofreading and indexing Sonia Schorman and Grainne Farren.

Edmund Burke Publisher gratefully acknowledge the support of The Dun Laoghaire Harbour Company in making this publication possible.

# FOREWORD

IT WAS EAMON GILMORE, TD, Minister of State at the Department of the Marine, and Tom Vaughan, former Harbour Manager at Dun Laoghaire, who encouraged me to undertake the task of trying to write a history of our harbour. To them I shall always be deeply grateful. To plough through the acres of documentation about the harbour in the National Archives and the innumerable legends, myths and flotsam and jetsam of hearsay that have accumulated about the harbour's history proved no easy task and, in time, no doubt somebody else will make another and perhaps more effective effort. But for me, the task, whatever its problems, was always stimulating and rewarding. It was so because for more than half of a long life I have been a citizen of Dun Laoghaire, intimately connected most of the time with the port's famous lifeboat station, Ireland's oldest, and affected more and more with the passage of the years by the sheer elegant beauty of our harbour; but perhaps even more because the history of our harbour, as it unfolded under careful scrutiny, became a history of hope and optimism. Hope and optimism can hardly be said to have been very characteristic of the Irish scene in the centuries since the Tudor conquest of our country. But the port of Dun Laoghaire was built to satisfy the hopes and fulfil the optimistic forecasts of a great popular movement, one of the very earliest manifestations of true "people's power" in Ireland, before O'Connell or Parnell or Larkin, the greatest embodiments of popular will in our tumultuous history. And once a harbour, not only beautiful but eminently useful, had been successfully established by the pressure of the popular movement that started in 1808, stage by stage our harbour's problems have been solved through far-sighted optimism. This has been the optimism of forceful characters, like Harbour Master Hutchison, or the management of the shipping companies that brought prosperity to the port and the masters of their ships, or the seafarers of many kinds who sailed in and out of Dun Laoghaire, or the port workers who took pride in it, or the public of Dun Laoghaire. The public accepted the amenity of their harbour perhaps a little too casually right up to the new surge of "people's power" in the 1980s and early 1990s that seemed to guarantee that the alterations which changing times and conditions were demanding in the harbour would be beneficial to the widest possible spectrum of the harbour's users, respecting the claims of all and keeping open the fairway to greater progress for still more people in the future.

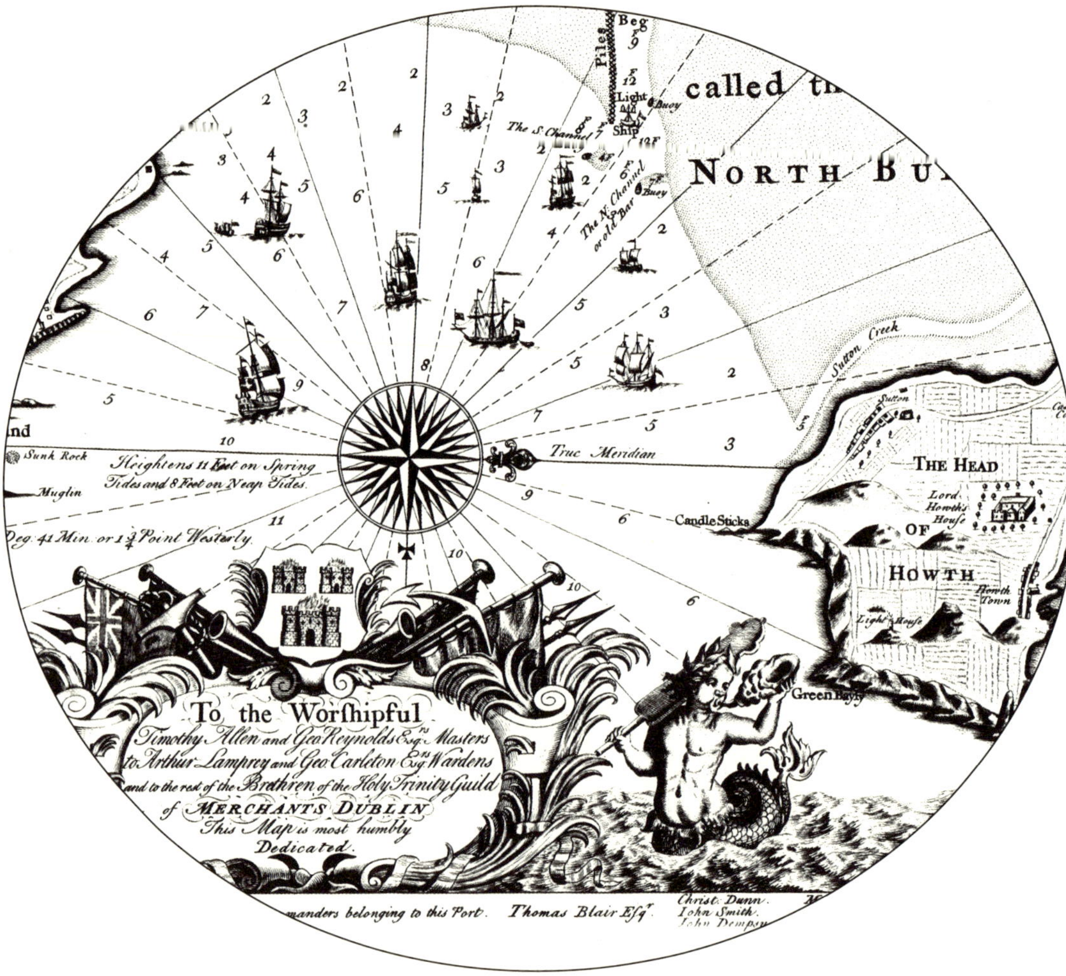


Detail of Gibson's Chart, 1756

# 1
# DUBLIN BAY BEFORE 1808

O God! have mercy in this dreadful hour
On the poor mariner! In comfort here
Safe sheltered as I am, I almost fear
The blast that rages with resistless power.
What were it now to toss upon the waves,
The maddened waves, and know no succour near,
The howling of the storm alone to hear,
And the wild sea that to the tempest raves;
To gaze amid the horrors of the night
And only see the billow's gleaming light;
Then in the dread of death to think of her
Who, as she listens sleepless to the gale,
Puts up a silent prayer, and waxes pale?
O God! have mercy on the mariner!

ROBERT SOUTHEY

Southey, an English poet and writer on maritime affairs, lived from 1774 to 1843 and must have heard with interest of the decision to build an asylum harbour at Dun Laoghaire. This poem of his helps to recapture the terror and utter helplessness of the people living around Dublin Bay when great storms blew up and there was no port of refuge for ships caught in them to enter.

CONSTRUCTION OF THIS PORT was undertaken as the result of the passage of an Act through the Parliament of the then United Kingdom of Great Britain and Ireland in London in 1815. Work began in 1816. The first stone of the port's East Pier, originally visualised as its only pier, was laid by the Earl of Whitworth, Lord Lieutenant of Ireland, on May 31st, 1817, and in that year a Scotsman, John Rennie, one of the best known engineers in Europe at the time, was appointed directing engineer of the works. Rennie insisted on the erection of a West Pier to prevent the accumulation of drifts of sand from Dublin Bay in the anchorage to be provided by the construction of the East Pier.

After Rennie's death in 1821 John Aird, as engineer on site and Rennie's son, also John, as directing engineer, supervised continuation of construction of the harbour, largely as Rennie Senior had proposed. By 1842 the two piers – the West 4950 feet long and the East 3500 feet – were complete, enclosing an area of 251 acres, and the harbour, already teeming with shipping, was a distinctive landmark on the south side of Dublin Bay, then, and for long afterwards, the largest artificial harbour in the world. Around it, in what had been a stony wilderness, a town was growing up which, with a population today of 60,000, is one of the four largest in the Republic of Ireland.

Dun Laoghaire is situated six and a half miles eastward of O'Connell Bridge spanning the River Liffey which flows through the centre of Dublin city, roughly from west to east. Three miles to the west of Dalkey Island, which marks the entrance of Dublin Bay from the south, and three and a half miles from the Poolbeg Lighthouse at the mouth of the Liffey, the point of entrance to Dublin harbour, which bears N.N.W. from the battery at the end of Dun Laoghaire's East Pier.

Why was an artificial harbour constructed at great expense so near to the ancient port of Dublin early in the nineteenth century? The clearest indication of the answer to this mystery is a statement made by one of the most eminent navigators in the British Royal Navy at the time, Captain (later Admiral) Charles Malcolm, Master of the Royal Yacht "William and Mary" of the British King George IV, who spent many months based in the new harbour which was under construction in the 1820s. Malcolm wrote:

> The Bay of Dublin has perhaps been more fatal to seamen and ships than any in the world, for a ship once caught in it in a gale from E.N.E. and S.S.E. must ride it out at her anchors or go on shore, and from the nature of that shore the whole of the crew almost invariably have perished.

Ships undoubtedly arrived at and departed from the Liffey estuary in prehistoric times, when "... the grey waters of the Irish Sea were ...", according to the famous archaeologist V. Gordon Childe, "... bright with Neolithic argonauts".[1] But it was the Norse who built the first quays at Dublin and built around them the town which became their most important commercial port. Dublin's commercial importance had remained through the Middle Ages, when it was the centre from which the English crown maintained a precarious influence over some areas in eastern Ireland. When, in the sixteenth century, the English laboriously and long-windedly undertook the conquest of the whole island, Dublin city and its harbour saw their importance further enhanced, and by the later years of the eighteenth century Dublin had become the second city of Britain's growing empire.

But the port of Dublin, on which the city largely depended for its living, had been growing more and more unsatisfactory, a situation made worse by the slow

1 V.G. Childe *The Dawn of European Civilization* London 1957, quoted in E.G. Bowen's *Britain and the Western Seaways*, London 1972, p34

but steady growth in the size of ships.

Dublin Bay is the seat of a series of sandbanks which, until the very end of the 18th century, not only changed shape and even location with the passage of time, but were uncharted in any scientific way, until the famous Captain Bligh in the winter of 1800 made a meticulously thorough survey of the Bay. This was done on the instructions of the Directors General of Inland Navigation, a body which in 1800 had, in view of the rapidly growing importance of Dublin as a canal port and the hindrance caused to canal transport owing to the unsatisfactory condition of Dublin seaport, been temporarily vested with the duty of trying to make Dublin port safer.

At that time the mouth of the Liffey was much wider and shallower than it is today. There was a dangerous bar across the main entrance channel and the passage upstream to where the port then was along quays in the city centre was obstructed by mud and sandbanks, and by ballast dumped from ships in the fairway.

Until 1708 control of Dublin port had belonged to the Dublin City Corporation, by an interpretation of the Charter given to the city by King John of England early in the 13th century. The Corporation had made fitful efforts to improve matters, such as placing a perch on the bar in the 1580s, which was quickly swept away, and anchoring a buoy on it instead early in the 17th century. The buoy was dislodged by the sea as early as 1609, and several times after replaced, and appears on the map of Dublin Bay made in 1685 by Greenville Collins, one of the British Navy's early hydrographers. From time to time efforts were made to remove obstacles to navigation, as in 1593 when the Corporation made two merchants remove "... the carcass of the ould Hulke ... from which great danger groweth to ships coming into the Pole of Clontarfe".

But right through the later Middle Ages and beyond, the masters of ships, particularly from other countries, approaching Dublin, had tended to make for the Sound between Dalkey Island and the mainland, and discharge their cargoes in Dalkey, then a fishing town protected by several castles. The goods discharged were then sent in shallow draft lighters when weather was fine to the Liffey, or to Dublin by cart or packhorse. Dalkey Sound provided shelter and a good anchorage, but the small harbours at Dalkey and neighbouring Bullock, another fishing village a mile nearer Dublin, were totally inadequate for the regular and careful handling of merchant shipping. The tide, moreover, creates a powerful current in Dalkey Sound.

So bad had things become that a series of agitations led to the passage of The Ballast Office Act of Parliament in 1707 that led to control over Dublin port passing in 1708 to a body called the Ballast Board. The chief achievement of this organisation was the construction of the South Wall along the lower reaches of the Liffey as far as Poolbeg, near the bar at the river's mouth, and the erection at its end of the Poolbeg Lighthouse, completed in 1768.

Nevertheless, conditions remained poor for merchant shipping. There seems little doubt that in the 18th century, as today, Dublin Bay experienced winds of gale force or more on thirty five days in an average year, some forty per cent of them blowing from the directions indicated by Captain Malcolm, as well as the short, steep waves characteristic particularly of the area round the Kish Bank, the great danger at the south-eastern entry to Dublin Bay (height/length ratio 1:40), and occasionally waves as high as 26.9 feet, recorded at the Kish light in 1964, or the 47 foot wave calculated by the Commissioners of Irish Lights as probable in Dublin Bay once in every ten years, or even the 64 foot wave believed to be likely about once each century.

While there is evidence that after three quarters of a century of Ballast Board rule ships of over one hundred tons and even up to three hundred were now regularly coming up the Liffey, and while there was now a full fathom (6 feet) of water over the bar even at low tides spring, many ships still grounded in the river at low tide and the number of shipwrecks in the Bay was horrific.

There is no full record of Dublin Bay shipwrecks before the 19th century, but knowledge has survived –

of January 1608 when a ship "… riding at ancre at Poole Begg … by great tempest was overthrown and its maariners and other shippemen therein weare lost …";
of November 1637 when "… ten to twelve barks were carried away from their anchor outside Dublin bar and never heard of since …";
of a similar disaster in November 1674; of the mail packet "William" driven ashore near Sutton with more than 80 aboard and "the master and a ship's boy alone surviving",
of January 24th 1724 when "… ships in Dublin Bay dragged their anchors and were wrecked …";
of January 1st 1726 when

> Thirty odd ships we hear are lost
> between our North and Southern coast …
> Near us was lost, on the South Bull,
> The 'Dublin Brothers' from Bristol;
> Twenty-two passengers were drown'd
> Many of them on strand was found;
> Another was on North Bull blown
> Loaded with Apples, Silk from Roan [Rouen];

of January 19th 1745, when "Faulkener's Dublin Journal" reported "ships lately cast on the North Bull";
of actor and dramatist Theophilus Cibber, with a group of actors, perishing in the wreck of the mail packet from Parkgate;
of a gale in Dublin Bay in January 1768 that "destroyed a number of ships";

of the wreck of a Philadelphia ship in October of (it seems) 1769 on Dublin bar with another vessel, the only survivors being two Philadelphians saved by a boat rowed to the bar by the daughters of the foreman of the South Wall construction works;
of the "Lovely", carried by wind and a strong spring tide in January 1792 through a breach in the South Wall, to where Merrion Square is now;
of the loss of a collier in the Bay in September 1807 with all twelve men on board;
of the Dublin bound New Bedford brig "Olympus" dismasted off Dalkey Island in February 1808, the last of a period of four years of exceptionally bad weather that thoroughly tested the newly established Dublin Bay lifeboat service. But there was worse to come.

In 1785 the Irish Parliament, freed three years before by its own endeavours and those of the Irish Volunteers from restraints imposed upon it by Britain, staged a lengthy debate on the condition of Dublin port. Expert witnesses were called before the Parliament to provide their opinions.

Captain Holloway, "... for twenty years conversant with harbour affairs ...", deposed that the harbour was worse than he had ever known it. John Dennis, forty years connected with the harbour, corroborated. So did shipwright Matthew Cardiff. Merchant mariner William Robinson swore that more seamen than ever were scared of entering Dublin because of its dangerous reputation.

The consequence of the general disquiet about the problems of shipping using the port of Dublin and of the lengthy discussion on the subject in the Irish Parliament was the enactment by that body in 1786 of a law which replaced the Ballast Office Act by a new one setting up the Corporation for Preserving and Improving the Port of Dublin, etc., predecessor of the Dublin Port and Docks Board. This body, popularly known as the Ballast Board, was given a good deal more power and authority than the former Ballast Office. After completing the North Wall, retaining the Liffey waters on the left bank of its estuary, repairing and strengthening the South Wall, and constructing the Bull Wall, with the object (in which it was successful) of constricting the Liffey water's outflow so as to ensure it gradually removed the notorious Liffey Bar as Bligh had suggested should be done (but according to a different plan), the new port authority began a series of dredging activities, established a lifeboat service round Dublin Bay and, for a time, even supervised the building of a series of lighthouses round Ireland.

But in spite of a new authority and enhanced activities in the port of Dublin, anxiety for the shipping approaching and leaving Dublin persisted. It was made worse by persistent delays in the mail service to and from Britain. The Dublin terminal had been Ringsend, then Poolbeg (where embarkation and disembarkation were by boat) and then from 1790 a new port at the Pidgeon House which, however, dried out at low tide springs and was not very viable on the neap tides. The sailing packets – yachts, a new Dutch invention in the late 17th and early 18th centuries – needed seventeen to twenty hours even in favourable wind conditions to make the passage, and often took two or three days. Bad weather not seldom delayed a mail packet's departure for as long as three weeks.

Dublin buzzed with projects for dealing with the problems of its port. One suggestion was the building of a new harbour at Howth to be linked with Dublin harbour by a canal built along the north side of the isthmus at Sutton, which would cut through to Kilbarrack and thence via Clontarf to Dublin port. Thomas Hyde Page of the Royal Engineers sent a memorial to the Directors General of Inland Navigation in which he proposed "… a short pier from the Rock of Sandygo [Sandycove] point to be carried about four hundred yards into the Bay nearly parallel with the tides …" and connecting "… the Codling Rock between Sandygo Point and Dunleary to the shore by a short pier". This, he maintained, would create a safe anchorage.

Separately, Page proposed the creation of a ship canal "through the Country to the New Docks at Dublin". This suggestion received a good deal of popular support, though Bligh and Rennie disapproved of it.

The Directors of Inland Navigation had on January 15th 1801 sent Bligh's chart to the Lord Lieutenant, together with two reports he had presented with it, one describing "the present state of the Bay and Harbour and of the several Harbours and Roads adjoined thereto", the other stating his "… Ideas of the Improvements to be made therein for the Benefit and Security of Navigation and Trade".[2] (Bligh suggested greatly lengthening the North Wall to as far as the Liffey Bar). In their letter, the Directors asked to have the chart back, and wrote very warmly of the speed and meticulous efficiency with which Bligh had done his work despite difficult weather conditions. (Bligh attributed the dismal record of loss of ships and life in Dublin Bay in part to the weather conditions met there, but in part to the inexperience of masters and crews in many merchant ships, and to the meanness of many ship owners who refused to pay for sufficient cable for their ships' anchors which, in stormy conditions, could not hold).

There was objection to copies being made of Bligh's chart at first for fear of a copy falling into the hands of the French, with whom Britain was at war. This was evidently overcome, as the Directors of Inland Navigation wrote again to the Lord Lieutenant on August 11th 1801. In all their correspondence the Directors stressed the urgent need to improve the safety of shipping visiting and leaving Dublin. In this letter (thirty six and a half pages long) they examined in detail all the proposals put before them for achieving this improvement, which they calculated would cost £2,385,702. 8s., if all was put into effect. They declared that "the Losses which are sustained by shipwrecks in Stormy Waters [in Dublin Bay] call forcibly for means of Prevension".

2 He was paid £682.10s. on February 5th 1801 for his effort.

The Directors then reiterated Bligh's claim that too many poor masters and crews and poorly provided ships came to Dublin, and went on to say that most ships visiting Dublin were of 300 tons, and that they expected the norm to be 200–300 tons for the foreseeable future. They then declared Dalkey Sound too narrow for square-rigged vessels to turn in with strong easterly winds. No vessel could in such ... "be brought to her anchor in sufficient time to prevent her being dashed to pieces by the surges against the Rocks of the Mainland". Bligh having condemned the anchorage in the Sound as bad, they deemed it "improvident to recommend execution of any work at Dalkey", though they saw a case for building a pier from Dalkey Island to Lamb Island to shelter small vessels "on the Inside of Dalkey Island under the old Church".

Page's great pier to be constructed in deep water off Sandycove and his conjoint suggestion of a short pier from the Codling Rock to the shore they considered "a noble idea", but thought the proposed shelter would be too little used except by smugglers and too expensive altogether (£1,204,305. 12s., they estimated).

Regarding the Ship Canal from Sandycove, they had serious doubts. It would be seven miles long and every ship using it would require towing, which would be very costly. A prolonged spell of strong wind from one direction would lead to congestion in one section of the canal, while others would be empty, and any serious accident would bring long delays. Moreover, the canal would have to be dug through "many gardens belonging to gentry", who would expect big compensation. Furthermore, there would be "an uncommon power of perpendicular pressure" on the lock gates, especially the lower ones, and a lengthy spell of frost would immobilise traffic. Altogether they predicted, if a canal were built, "a confusion, better to be conceived than described".

The Directors also rejected suggestions for a pier linking Howth with Ireland's Eye and saw no serious argument in favour of trying at great expense (£86,400 estimated) to make Howth Sound "an eligible Place of Resort for Ships of Great Burthen" and, anyway, various suggestions for Howth would "obstruct present daily use of the Sound by small vessels".

In all, therefore, the Lord Lieutenant was advised that the most sensible decision must be concentration on schemes to get the Liffey Bar scoured out (Page and Bligh agreed on this, but each had his own idea how to go about it), with the assistance of extra dredging. There is no way of telling if the Directors knew of the proposals in Bristol, before long to be put into practice, for building primitive steam dredgers, one of which was still in operation in Bridgewater in the 1950s. (It, or a sister vessel, is conserved at Bristol).

No doubt the interested public looked upon the attitude of the Directors of Inland Navigation as complacent and, meanwhile, as already recorded, wrecks continued to occur in Dublin Bay, where the newly established lifeboat service quickly found itself busy, and weather conditions in four successive years were particularly bad.

# 2
# THE CRUSADE

"What know they of harbours that toss not on the sea?"
NINETEENTH CENTURY SEA SONG

A generous Norwegian sea-captain, naturalised Irish and resident in what is now the County of Dun Laoghaire and Rathdown, horrified at the incessant death by shipwreck in Dublin Bay, took it on himself to get the people living around Dublin Bay to see the urgent necessity for a new harbour, and to demand that the authorities build one.

THEN ON NOVEMBER 18TH 1807 there occurred the most costly disaster in human life that Dublin Bay is known ever to have witnessed in peace time. Two ships, "Prince of Wales" and "Rochdale", had embarked large numbers of militiamen for foreign service, some with wives and families. The ships sailed out from the Pidgeon House as an easterly gale was springing up. The gale rose to storm force, with squalls of snow hampering visibility. It was impossible to anchor in Dublin Bay, but "Prince of Wales" managed to get an anchor down off Bray Head. However, the wind came round to south east and strengthened further, and the ship began to drag. She was driven right across Dublin Bay and cast ashore at Blackrock. The ship's master, the crew, two soldiers and a steward with his wife and child managed to get away in the ship's longboat, but the rest of those aboard, more than one hundred, perished as the wreck was battered to pieces on the shore.

"Rochdale's" case was even worse. She was seen on November 19th from Dalkey, showing blue lights and firing guns, but no boat could go out in the prevailing conditions. She tried to anchor, but several cables were seen to snap. She then drove past the pier of Old Dunleary under bare poles. People ashore heard shouts and saw men on board firing muskets to win attention. Some people ran along the coast to Salthill in the hope of being able to do something, but the fury of the storm and the bullets from the "Rochdale" forced them to take shelter. The ship drove ashore with extreme violence at the foot of the newly built Martello Tower at Seapoint. There were no survivors.

With some four hundred bodies to be buried in the graveyard at Merrion[3]

3 A headstone inscribed *Sacred to the Memory of His Majesty's 18th Regiment of Foot* is a feature of this neglected but recently tidied graveyard. It briefly records the catastrophe of November 1807.

(sometimes called Belle Vue Cemetery, silent and isolated still today behind a petrol-filling station and within earshot of roaring traffic on the Dublin–Dun Laoghaire road), shock echoed and re-echoed round Dublin Bay. The small band of enthusiasts who rejected the long-view optimism of Dublin Port Authority and the Directors General of Inland Navigation found itself suddenly reinforced by the most valuable of allies, awakened public opinion.

A single, improbable, somewhat enigmatic figure of idealistic determination and practical optimism was the embodiment of the storm of indignation for what was seen to have been neglect by authority, and this figure was the possessor of an indomitable will to use a quick and certain cure for the ever-growing list of deaths from shipwreck in Dublin Bay. This individual was a master mariner and minor shipowner from Norway, Richard Toutcher. Soon after "Rochdale's" end he began a campaign for construction of an Asylum Harbour with a protest meeting at Monkstown.

Toutcher was born in 1758 at Lund in Norway, and baptised there on April 18th of that year. His father, Daniel, a lawyer, and mother Anna, daughter of a judge, are known to have moved house several times before settling in the port of Stavanger in 1767. There Daniel eventually became controller of customs before finally filling the same position in the neighbouring port of Egersund. It is known that Daniel's daughter, Richard Toutcher's sister, Anna Regine, married a shipowner, Staalensen, who is known to have had a ship called "Elisabeth" as early as the year of Richard's birth, and another called "Anna Catherina" as late as 1796, by which time Richard had been for a long time resident in Dublin, acquiring citizenship in 1789. It is probable that Richard came to Ireland in ships of his brother-in-law exporting salted herring to Ireland in the period when the Irish fishing industry was about to experience a great revival with the rapid development of its own herring export trade.[4]

A seaman himself from one of Europe's most maritime inclined communities, Richard Toutcher was horrified by the continuous loss of life by shipwreck in the vicinity of the capital of the country of which, for reasons unclear, he had become a citizen. He seems to have begun his agitation for a drastic step to be taken to lessen the toll of shipwreck in Dublin Bay in the earliest years of the 19th century. He was a persistent opponent of the proposals put forward by Page (see above) and Thomas Rogers, Contractor to the Revenue Commissioners for Building and Repairing Lighthouses, for the construction at Howth of a large outport for Dublin. Nevertheless, after seven years of discussion and discreet pressure, the Parliament in London had, in 1807, passed an Act (45 Geo. III), appointing commissioners to oversee the construction of a new port at Howth.

By 1813 the new port was complete, and in 1818 it was designated the official mail packet station for Dublin. A steamship had visited Howth as early as 1816. In 1819 the steamship "Talbot" began carrying the mails, to be joined shortly by

4 J. de Courcy Ireland *Ireland's Sea Fisheries, A History*, Dublin 1981, p42

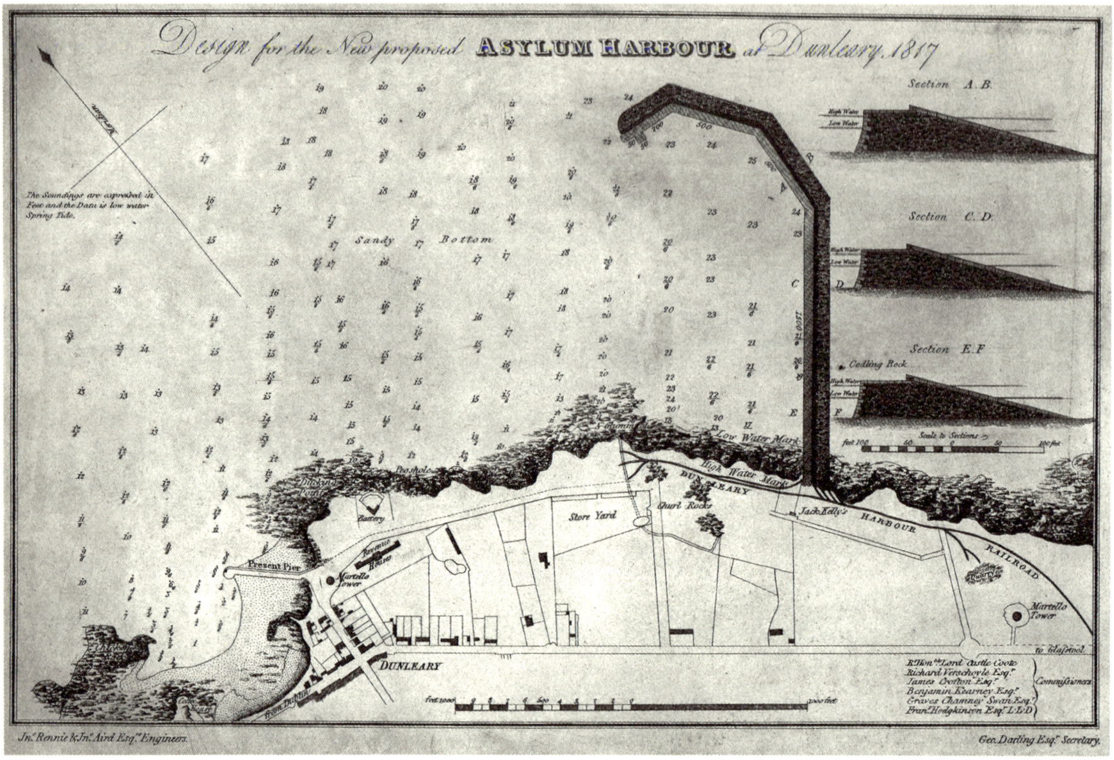


Asylum Harbour 1817

the steamers "Ivanhoe", "Meteor" and "Lightning". In August 1821 King George IV arrived from England in the "Lightning". But, as Harry Gilligan wrote in the official History of the Port of Dublin,[5] "... deficiencies anticipated by the parties opposed to the harbour became apparent soon after the arrival on the scene of the steam mail packets; complaints made of damage sustained by bumping or actually taking the ground at low water, due, it was alleged, to the high level of rock in the bed of the harbour. Situation at the entrance and in the berths was also a problem". When four new steamships were introduced by the Post Office for use by the mail service, they were found to be too big for Howth.

Toutcher, even before the decision to build the new port at Howth had been taken, had his eye on the little fishing harbour at Dunleary, the only hamlet of any size along the barren south shore of Dublin Bay between Dalkey and the small suburb of Dublin, growing fashionable, Blackrock.

Dunleary got its name from a prehistoric fort believed to have been built in 498 A.D. by a somewhat legendary 5th century local chief, Leary, for a time important well beyond the confines of present day Co. Dublin. It obviously came into existence and survived because of the only, if narrow and shallow, creek, that broke the inhospitable south coast of the Bay. The creek had, from time immemorial, housed a small fishing community and given timely shelter to small

5 Quotation from Norwegian Captain from Moi/Stavanger, Pioneer for Irish Harbour Performance, Captain Richard Toutcher (1758–1841). The Father of Dun Leary Asylum Harbour *Servant of Humanity and Champion of the Irish Merchant Navy* by S. Rygh in Clery Pearson Institute Yearbook, 1988, Stavanger.

Dublin Bay and Kingstown Harbour *c.* 1845

craft stricken by strong winds in the Bay. Unsheltered from surges driving in from the north, the community had managed to secure the construction between 1756 and 1767 of a short, round-ended pier, which gave valuable shelter to the small craft able to get in behind it. The creek dried out at low tide.

All through the 18th century there are records of Dunleary men going out to packets becalmed or waiting for the tide and taking off passengers for payment and seeing them off by road to the city after disembarkation. Celebrated travellers like Jonathan Swift, John Wesley and Arthur Young, came ashore at Dunleary. The last named enjoyed a stop at the Coffee House (noted, along with the New Quay, in the map made by the Huguenot refugee John Rocque in 1756) which was built on the cliff overlooking the creek, behind the present Purty Kitchen public house.

By now a shipbroker operating from Sir John Rogerson's Quay, Dublin, Toutcher became more and more convinced of the possibility of constructing an "asylum harbour" at Dunleary, where ships could shelter behind a long granite pier when strong easterlies sprang up, on their way to or from the port of Dublin. From November 1807 on he neglected his own business and started canvassing all and sundry to support his aim. He was a frequent writer of letters to any one of eminence whose backing would be valuable to his cause, employing a writer with an immaculate elegant sloping hand, rather than use his own strong but irregular writing. He declared: "I write not for fame, but for utility. It is my aim rather to be understood than admired. To elegance of composition I aspire not. But I have some nautical experience … [and] … the idea of an Asylum Port at Dunleary is ever first in my thoughts".[6]

Toutcher began his campaign with a public meeting in Monkstown, just inland from Dunleary, chaired by the local Church of Ireland Rector, Dr. Singleton Harpur, in March 1808. In due course, he recruited the support of the Dublin Chamber of Commerce, merchants throughout County Dublin, shipowners and masters of ships in Holyhead, Liverpool, Bristol and London, and above all the merchants, shipowners and ships' masters engaged in the then very lucrative trade in coal from ports in Cumberland. This is recalled in modern Dun Laoghaire by part of the main street coming in from Dublin being called Cumberland Street.

Toutcher not only paid out of his own pocket the printing and the (before the introduction of the Penny Post some twenty five years later) very expensive posting of one thousand letters to everybody in Dublin involved in the Cumberland coal trade. He then wrote:

> The Merchants, Ship Owners, and Ship-Masters of Whitehaven, Workington, Maryport, Harrington and Parton, are also preparing a petition to be presented to His Grace The Duke of Richmond, praying his aid and support for the erection of this much wanted pier at Dunleary. This I am not astonished at, when I reflect how many of their relatives have been lost on the coast of our Bay, the numbers of widows and fatherless children that are left to bemoan that this pier had not long since been built, which would have saved to them what was in this life most valuable.

Toutcher wrote in 1823 a memorial to the Commissioners of the Asylum harbour at Dunleary (recently renamed The Royal Harbour of Kingstown) now well on its way towards final construction, noting that in 1808 he had been convinced of the need for a pier at Dunleary. "… after four years of unwearied application …" he had succeeded in getting the interest of the Right Honourable Wellesley Pole, Secretary of State for Ireland, in 1812. He says he was granted an interview at which Aldermen Archer and Hardy and others were present, during which he was asked from where the material for such a huge building would come. He went on to explain how he had secured a lease of ten acres on the granite Hill of Dalkey, the granite from which he would provide free for the project, which he did, going into irreversible debt.

His Memorial continued: "Influenced by various publications circulated from time to time by your Memorialist among the Traders and Merchants of Dublin" (in which he clearly demonstrated the practicability and utility of the proposed Pier at Dunleary), "they became extremely anxious for its being proceeded upon. In consequence, it was decided that a levy on ships visiting Dublin would pay for

6 Letter discovered by Mr R.J. Mitchell of 2 Charlemont Avenue, Dun Laoghaire.

the work at Dunleary". (This is believed to have been his own idea).

Finally, he declared that his own financial position had become "much embarrassed", and asked for compensation for the sum he was having to find for the lease of the area of Dalkey Hill where the granite for the new harbour was being quarried. It was a principle of the British Constitution, he asserted, "that public good is not to arise out of private injury".

It is apparent so far as the present state of research goes among the voluminous (two thousand, two hundred and seventy two items) documents in the Irish National Archives referring to Dunleary (later Kingstown, now Dun Laoghaire) Harbour that the form in which the compensation requested by Toutcher was granted was employment as Second Assistant Engineer in the construction of the new harbour with, among other responsibilities, that of ensuring a supply of water (from what is now an unpostered pond close to the Irish National Maritime Museum in the former Mariners' Church, Dun Laoghaire) for all ships requiring it, a matter that caused a certain amount of somewhat acrimonious correspondence from the Admiralty in London to Kingstown Harbour Commissioners in the early stages of the harbour's construction.

Toutcher's salary as Second Engineer at the harbour works was £227 per annum. He died a bankrupt in 1841, evidently a glaring example of ingratitude in high places to a man who was probably the traditional thorn in their sides, but who clearly left vast numbers of fellow human beings in debt to him for his foresight and persistence.

Toutcher's campaign had reached its climax with a strongly worded Memorandum dated March 21st 1814 from 27 Merrion Square South, Dublin, from Richard Verschoyle, a prosperous merchant destined before long to become one of the Commissioners of the new port.

The Memorandum states:

> I am directed as Chairman of a meeting of the Merchants of Dublin to send you herewith a memorial of the Merchants of Dublin respecting the erection of a new harbour at the south side of the Bay, eastward of Dunleary, also two petitions to Parliament, one from the Merchants of Dublin, both of which you will please to lay before His Excellency the Lord Lieutenant. As this measure is called for by every feeling of Humanity as well as Policy, they look with confidence to you, Sir, to present said Petitions to Parliament, and afterwards that you will support a Bill which has been prepared by the Right Honourable the Attorney General, who knowing the great necessity of such a measure has consented to become one of the Commissioners for carrying it into effect and which has been submitted to the Right Honourable the Chancellor of the Exchequer.
>
> I have the Honour to be, Sir, Your Obedient and Honourable servant,
>
> RICHARD VERSCHOYLE[7]

7 Memorial in the archives of the Board of Works referring to the Royal Harbour of Kingstown in the National Archives of Ireland.

# 3
# DECISIONS

Who fares, on sea, may not command his way,
Nor wind and weather at his pleasure call:
The sea is wide, and easy for to stray,
The wind unstable and doth never stay.
But here a while you may in safety rest,
Till season serve new passage to assay;*
Better safe port, than be in seas distrest.

EDMUND SPENSER

The 16th century poet, who spent some time in this country, anticipated remarkably in this piece of verse what the new Asylum Harbour, or port of refuge, at Dun Laoghaire was, more than two centuries later, to provide for seamen hitherto at the mercy of Dublin Bay's notorious easterly gales.

VERSCHOYLE'S DOCUMENT WAS, very wisely, addressed to the rising star of British politics, Robert Peel, destined to be its dominant factor for many years. It demonstrates that the campaign initiated primarily by Toutcher had gathered momentum with the years and was now within sight of success. And indeed in 1815 an Act (55 Geo. III, Cap. 191) was duly passed by the Parliament in London making statutory provision for the appointment of commissioners (three at first) with powers to make surveys, plans and estimates for the erection of "... a harbour or place of refuge which would be of great advantage as well to the ships trading to the port of Dublin as to the ships and vessels of His Majesty's Navy which may be in the Irish Channel".

In 1816 an Act (56 Geo. III, Cap. 62) gave permission to proceed with the work, laying down that on completion the new harbour (which was clearly intended to be a harbour of refuge and not a port for landing or loading goods or passengers) would come under the jurisdiction (as was the little harbour of Dunleary) of the Corporation for Preserving and Improving the Port of Dublin.

But much thinking was already going into the best way to go about the construction of this new harbour off the barren wilderness between Dunleary and

*assay – to try

Bullock. Toutcher's original plan had been for a single pier, with a right angle turn westwards about two thirds of the way along it, a plan not dissimilar from, but far better considered than, Page's "noble" proposition fifteen years before. Now more ambitious, but also more methodical thinking, suggested that two piers should be built, considerably longer and embracing a substantial area of water (251 acres eventually). It was already being pointed out by John Rennie senior, soon to be made the project's chief engineer, that the wayward sandbanks west of Dunleary towards Blackrock, Merrion and the Pidgeon House, could, in the course of time, seriously affect the projected anchorage behind a single pier (originally two thousand, eight hundred feet long, eventually reaching three thousand, five hundred feet) running roughly north-east along the north-west edge of Scotch or Scotsman's Bay, by steadily drifting quantities of sand into it. So as early as August 30th 1816 it was agreed that a West Pier would have to be erected "starting from the Chickens' Rocks".

Then, even while the remarkable railway was being completed, whose wagons coming downhill from the Dalkey quarries full of granite were geared to balance uphill simultaneously the empty wagons discharged at the rail terminal on the original Dunleary creek, a third Act of Parliament was passed giving independence to a board of eighteen commissioners to construct a two pier harbour and get it into operation. John Rennie was their choice as their chief engineer, and they made a number of other wise appointments, including Aird, the site engineer, Richard Thomas Toutcher, as second assistant engineer (who succeeded Aird in 1832) and John Rennie Junior as overall "directing" engineer, appointed in 1826. They made another excellent appointment in their secretary, George Darling, who seems to have been conscientious and efficient.

The first stone of the new pier had been duly and ceremoniously laid by the Lord Lieutenant in the summer of 1817, with Rear Admiral Hallowell commanding from Cork British naval forces in Irish waters promising, in a letter from "H.M.S. Tonnant" written on May 19th, to release part of his squadron operating in the area of Dunleary to be present, though, owing to frequent demands on the South coast for warships to "chase smugglers", he could not have his whole squadron present.

It was in August 1821 that George IV paid the visit to the new port under construction which led to it being called Kingstown Harbour, and the town that grew out of it, from 1821 for nearly one hundred years, Kingstown. The town became Dun Laoghaire in 1920, but the harbour did not officially become the Port of Dun Laoghaire until 1924.

The monument that recalls the visit of George IV and enshrines the names of Kingstown's first Harbour Commissioners has from time to time been subject to vandalism. This was infantile, for the visit was an historic event that cannot be wiped out, and the Commissioners did a good job of starting the construction of the world's largest artificial harbour, the elegant appearance of which (at a spot which, people should not forget, had for centuries been a barren wilderness) has been praised by successive generations of locals and visitors in generous terms. Moreover, George IV, though no Adonis and no saint, with the rather common British royal trait of wife trouble, had the good taste to embellish his capital with Regent's Park and Regent Street, and to encourage the healthy habit of sea-bathing, in which he indulged in the insignificant Sussex village he discovered and made famous, Brighthelmstone, which later became Brighton. He was also the first English king to visit Ireland in peace, and the first monarch to dare to embark on a steamship, "Lightning", in which he visited Kingstown.

A few months after the King's visit the Commissioners of the infant Harbour, according to a letter sent by the Lord Lieutenant on December 10th, 1821, were optimistic enough to foretell one of mankind's periodic victories in its incessant struggle with the fathomless malice of the green and greedy seas, by predicting "... that the Royal Harbour, according to the present plans, will be more than sufficient for the Asylum of the Trade of Dublin, of the Channel trade that may wish to seek it, and at the same time of all Convoys and Ships belonging to His Majesty likely to resort to it".

Anyway, by 1822 work on the new harbour was in full swing and a town was beginning to grow behind it where there had previously been little but rocks and bushes, recently varied by the erection of a string of Martello Towers between Sandymount and Dalkey.

It was in this early stage of the harbour's construction that some fine buildings were erected, such as that which recently, after various vicissitudes, became, again, the Harbour Office, the one time first Presbyterian Church in the town (1828) later Kingstown School, a secondary school that produced a number of distinguished citizens[8] and the now Community Training Centre, and near what became "Commercial", "Packet" and "Victoria" Pier, and is now St. Michael's Wharf, the lovely Sailor's Rest, long a haven for shipwrecked mariners and later the first residence of the Irish National Maritime Museum, wantonly destroyed when the undistinguished and largely unsuccessful St. Michael's Pier was built thirty years ago.

Matthew Byrne, who died in 1994, one of the most intelligent and articulate citizens of the Dun Laoghaire of his generation, a stone mason of remarkable skill who knew every inch of this harbour as few can ever have done, wrote: "The magnitude of this 19th century engineering feat (the construction of the port) enclosing 250 acres of water [now 290] can best be imagined by combining the lengths of both piers at 1¾ miles built on a 300 foot wide foundation 24 feet below low tide mark, to realise the enormity of this unique granite structure".[9]

There is no end of documentary evidence of the transformation brought about

8 Eg. the artist, writer and environmentalist Peter Pearson, Captain Healy, former master of the training ship "Asgard" and the African scholar, Dr Sean Morrow.

9 In the chapter he contributed (pp149–55) to *The Book of Dun Laoghaire* published by the Blackrock Teacher's Centre in 1987 to mark the Year of the Environment.

The embarkation of George IV from Kingstown, 3 September 182

by this structure, a remarkable engineering feat which is also an architectural achievement of great beauty.

A comparison between Bligh's chart of 1800 and the British Admiralty chart representing the survey made by Commander J.H. Kerr in 1874, not greatly modified in the standard Admiralty Chart No. 1415, is a case in point. The thorough geographical examination published in Dublin in 1992, called "Dublin City and County from Prehistory to Present" in honour of Dr. J.H. Andrews, for years the leading geographer at Dublin University (Trinity College), is another.

Maps by William Petty in 1685 of County Dublin, based on information collected, by Burgh and Perry, of Dublin Bay in 1728, Rocque's map to which reference has already been made, Gibson's Dublin Bay of 1756 published as "a Chart", all emphasise the paucity of human habitation between the Ringsend and Irishtown area of Dublin city just South of the mouth of the Liffey and the medieval town of Dalkey, which had become little more than a large village at the southern entrance of Dublin Bay. A study on Markets and Fairs in Ireland, 1600–1800, published in the Journal of Historical Geography 11, 4 in 1985 by Dr. Patrick O'Flanagan of University College, Cork, confirms these impressions of the very poorly developed state of an area, changed beyond recognition by the building of Dun Laoghaire harbour into the seat of a thriving urban community, promoted in 1994 to the status of the County of Dun Laoghaire and Rathdown.

If much of the credit for the decision to build a harbour at Dunleary in 1815 goes to the former Norwegian seaman Richard Toutcher, much of the credit for the early success and subsequent development of what many must have considered an expensive gamble goes to another seaman, William Hutchison, born in 1793 in Dublin to a Co. Kildare family, who became the new port's first (and longest serving) Harbour Master.

# 4
# WILLIAM HUTCHISON

Today a rude, brief derivative ...
Of Sea Captain young or old, and the Mates – and of all intrepid sailors;
Of the few, very choice, taciturn, whom fate can never surprise nor death dismay,
Pick'd sparingly, without noise, by thee, old Ocean – chosen by thee,
Thou Sea, that pickest and cullest the race, in Time, and unitest Nations;
Suckled by thee, old husky Nurse – embodying thee,
Indomitable, untamed as thee.

WALT WHITMAN

In these lines from his "Song for All Seas, All Ships", considered by many the greatest sea poem in the English language, the North American Whitman pays tribute to the rare types of exceptional Master Mariners from which our port's Harbour Masters have been chosen, in the wake of William Hutchison, first and greatest of them, whose wisdom and courage turned the gamble, which many thought the building of Dun Laoghaire port to be, into the creation of one of our country's finest assets.

HUTCHISON HAD JOINED the British Navy as a youngster and had had a quite dramatic career in the Mediterranean and the Caribbean in the later years of Britain's long war against Napoleon, reaching the rank of Lieutenant.

When the war ended Hutchison, like scores of other naval officers, found himself on half pay. He applied to Dublin Port Authority in 1817 for the vacant position of Harbour Master of the original tiny port of Dunleary, controlled then by the authority, and Inspector of the Port Authority's quarries at Bullock. These quarries had been leased in 1804 from Lord Carysfort's large estate in the area to provide granite, carried in gabbards (the local flat bottom barge) across Dublin Bay for strengthening of Dublin port's South Wall and construction of the Bull Wall on the north side of the Liffey Bar.

In December 1817 Hutchison was appointed at a salary of £100 a year and given a comfortable free house close to Bullock Harbour. He was also given authority over the recently established lifeboat stations at Bullock, Sandycove and Dunleary.

Hutchison is one of the great figures in the history of the lifeboat service in

Ireland. He, for many years, acted personally as coxswain of the Bullock boat, and had already won great praise for his rescue in horrendous circumstances of the crew of the brig "Ellen" of Liverpool, aground on Sandycove Point in December 1821, before he became the new port's Harbour Master. In 1829 he was the first of only four Irish lifeboatmen to win the rarely awarded Gold Medal of the recently (1824) formed Lifeboat Institution.[10] He became the first Honorary Secretary (Director) of Dun Laoghaire Lifeboat Station, when it was taken over by the Royal National Lifeboat Institution in 1862.

It was on February 20th 1822 that the Commissioners of the new harbour wrote to Dublin Castle, seat of the British Government in Ireland, recording that on February 13th Lieutenant Hutchison had presented the Lord Lieutenant's warrant appointing him Harbour Master of the Royal Harbour of Kingstown. Their letter states that "... he desired in a very proper and respectful manner to receive our Commands". But they noted that he was not placed under their control by the warrant and requested, and eventually received, clarification of the exact functions of the new port's Harbour Master, who continued as long as British rule lasted in Ireland to be appointed by the Lord Lieutenant, and not by the Port Authority.

By Spring 1823 therefore, the new port, already busy with shipping, was, so far as its strictly maritime functions were concerned, in the charge of a young man not yet thirty, who was to remain Harbour Master till 1874, when he retired at the age of eighty.

During Hutchison's term of office the port of Dun Laoghaire, built essentially as an asylum harbour where shipping to and from Dublin could take refuge in stormy weather, became something totally different from what had been first envisaged. It quite soon began to build a reputation that it long maintained as the principal port in Ireland for servicing the ever-increasing exchange of mail between Ireland and Britain. Through its facilitation of the activities of the mail service, and because the vessels carrying mail quickly became also, and eventually primarily, passenger ships it became, and still is, the leading passenger port in Ireland. It quickly became a minor naval base for the British navy. It was already, by the middle of the nineteenth century, a flourishing yachting centre, which it still is, and a lucrative fishing port, which it is no longer. It became, in 1875, the depot and operative base of the Irish lighthouse service. It has attracted artists, inspired writers, been the scene of pioneering scientific experiments and become a recreation centre for the general public. Important centres of Irish marine activity have been drawn into its vicinity, such as Bord Iascaigh Mhara, the body responsible for the strategic policy of the Irish fishing industry, the National Maritime Museum, the Sea Scouts, who long had their base in a former lightship in the harbour, and the influential Irish Yachting Association. It once saw ships and boats built within its confines, and may do so again. The number of

10 The Gold Medal was obtained by Harry Gilligan, from a descendant of Hutchison resident in England and handed to the National Maritime Museum in Dun Laoghaire.

historically important individuals who have embarked or disembarked at Kingstown/Dun Laoghaire is legion.

As Hutchison began measuring up to the very considerable task he had undertaken as Master of a harbour already teeming with shipping, but a lot less than half built, he found that there were one hundred and twenty nine men at work employed directly by the Commissioners, and no fewer than six hundred and ninety by the contractor given the bulk of the work of bringing vast quantities of granite to Kingstown, shaping it once there and hauling it, often in very heavy pieces, to the sea's edge and the starting points of the piers from which, as these pushed out to sea, large chunks had to be lodged into the sea alongside the outside of the piers to strengthen them against the inevitable gales to come.

The pay for labourers was 1/8d. a day; for overseers 2/-. This was not generous, but others at the time were paid less.[11] Saturday was a working day. The year before Hutchison's appointment the Commissioners had lengthened the working day by insisting that work should continue to 7 p.m. instead of 6 p.m. A Memorial from the workers pointed out that this would prevent them having time to work their gardens, causing them economic hardship. A note at the bottom of their Memorial (March 13th, 1821) records that the Commissioners, in view of the workers' "submissive" attitude, directed that the order insisting on the extra hour should be revoked, but no "loaded wagons" were to be left lying on the pier at 6 p.m.

There is evidence that the Commissioners had some regard for the health of the workforce. The Commissioners withdrew their annual subscription to Cork Street Fever Hospital in Dublin because it refused to accept fever-stricken workers from the harbour works. Individual petitions for compensation for injured workers (frequent) seem to have been reasonably dealt with but when, early in 1823, snow and frost held up work for two weeks and the parish of Monkstown asked the Commissioners for a contribution as it had difficulty helping so many unemployed workers (when there was no work there was no pay), Aird, on behalf of the Commissioners, replied on January 29th, when work was being resumed, that the workers were well paid and had been in steady employment, so should have been able to survive without pay for two weeks!

But then there is the rather moving case of John Anderson whose thigh was fractured while he was working on the glacis of the East Pier in September 1829. A letter from him to the secretary of the Commissioners dated January 15th 1830 shows that he lost three week's pay through going absent following the accident, but had been since his return to work receiving 5/7 ½d. a week compensation, which had stopped with the end of 1829 and continuation of which he requested. On January 28th 1830 it was decided that the 5/7 ½d weekly should

11 For instance Wexford Harbour Authority paid ls 3d a day (see Minutes of Commissioners for the Improvement of the Town, Bar and Harbour of Wexford, January 15, 1827). By 1860 a labourer in Kingstown might, with luck, earn as much as 3/- per day (c/f Brian Scott, *Sealink and its Predecessors in Dublin*, Dublin, 1989), so in thirty years a labourers wage had gone up by some eighty per cent. But had the cost of living risen proportionately?

be continued to be paid till the first week in February.

During the period of this minor drama Engineer Aird was in communication with the Commissioners' secretary Darling about the Signal Tower on Dalkey Hill. He suggested a request to the Board of Ordnance for its demolition so as to give access to an area of very high quality granite. By now the Commissioners were drawing granite from beyond the original area of Toutcher's base. Darling in January 1830 was in correspondence with the contractor Smith, successor to the original G. Smith just deceased, insisting on an inspection of all stone delivered from the quarries (one thousand, one hundred and eighty four radiated ashlar blocks and two hundred and eighty square ones) which were "not … so correctly dredged as it is necessary they should."

Shortly after, Darling received Rennie's "specification of the mode of completing the East and West piers" a sixteen-page document in the most meticulously beautiful handwriting, including his, very urgent, specification of the "main sewer to prevent sewage from the Neighbouring Shores entering the Royal Harbour," all accompanied by a three page letter. In November 1830 Engineer Rennie Junior reminded the Commissioners that his father had stipulated an entry four hundred and thirty feet wide and said the existing gap was "far too large" and (bluntly) "made much of the harbour unserviceble". Six years later Francis Beaufort, recently appointed Hydrographer to the Admiralty, said that, owing to the wide entrance, part of the harbour was useless, and backed Rennie's plea for return to his father's proposal.

Secretary Darling then requested leave of absence to go London for "Mr Ahamadi the celebrated occulist to perform an urgently needed operation for cataract."

Contractor P. Smith on March 4 1830 wrote to the Commissioners to say that the quarrying activities on Dalkey Hill had now accumulated three thousand and seventy five waggon loads of shingle. He proposed to deliver all this along the beach between the East and West piers, and "being much in want of money" requested payment of his account for cut stone sent on January 4 (presumably the delivery that prompted Darling to demand inspection of each load of stone on delivery.)

On March 11 Aird agreed to supply twenty five additional "bang up waggons" for delivery of Smith's shingle which by May 20 was almost complete. One thousand wagon loads had been disposed of at the East Pier, five hundred "for filling the Beach adjoining the Boat Harbour," and the rest elsewhere.

In April a crane was acquired for the Boat Harbour, for the use of which Harbour Master Hutchison had just acquired a brand new barge and three boats "for his purposes".

At this stage Engineer Aird reckoned that two hundred and ten thousand square ft. of cut stone was still needed, exclusive of the stone required at the pier heads and the parapet.

On the whole this gigantic undertaking seems to have been carried out without serious labour trouble, though there are occasionally such references in the Commissioners' correspondence as one in 1835 recording "the overbearing attitude of Kingstown Harbour boatmen".

Incidentally, there does not seem to be much reference in the Commissioners' voluminous documentation to what we would now call technological aid to assist construction, though as early as 1817 the Commissioners made arrangements for obtaining a diving bell, and on August 6th that year a crane is recorded as being in operation at the quarries on Dalkey Hill and as having collapsed and killed James Weldon, a son of two residents there. The one great technological aid available to the harbour builders was undoubtedly the funicular railway that brought the granite from Dalkey Hill to Old Dunleary, the base of the East Pier and other destinations. Otherwise the work was done mainly by block and tackle, common sense and sheer brawn. Looking at the monumental solidity of the great piers still today, one can but marvel at the effectiveness of its achievement.

Hutchison, of course, had nothing to do with the day to day details of construction, but he very quickly showed a deep professional interest in the way in which Rennie's original plan was, and in certain important cases was not, carried out.

Back in September 1821 Captain Phillimore, R.N., who had brought George IV's royal yacht "William and Mary" to Kingstown when the King visited the burgeoning works, wrote to the Commissioners of the new Royal Harbour saying he intended to retain the yacht in the port for the winter, partly as "an encouragement to others to use the port", seeing it already as something more than simply an asylum harbour. On October 2nd he wrote again, reporting that the ship "Eliza" had been nearly wrecked in the harbour, but he wanted to assert that ships should not be discouraged from using Kingstown, "… being persuaded that with due care and proper attention it is perfectly safe, even in its present condition". He added that, even in the safest harbour in "tempestuous weather as was experienced yesterday", he always found it necessary to "get down lower yards", which "Eliza" had not done.

Not long after Phillimore was succeeded by Charles Malcolm, whose opinion of Dublin Bay has been quoted, and "William and Mary" was still at Kingstown where, on March 4th 1823 Malcolm reported to the Commissioners that the naval cutter "Tigre" had arrived and asked leave to lay the moorings with which she was provided between "William and Mary" and a ship called "Shamrock". This happened to be the day before Dublin Castle sent to the Commissioners a copy of the letter sent to their new Harbour Master, Hutchison, requesting him to "… put yourself in communication with the Commissioners of Dunleary Harbour [sic] and obey such instructions as Harbour Master … as they may think proper to communicate from time to time". The letter to the Commissioners suggested that "some or one of the Boats now under your directions" might be "advantageously employed by the Harbour Master".

Writing from Bullock on March 11th, Hutchison asked the Commissioners what he was to do about Malcolm's letter. On March 13th Commissioner Verschoyle replied that the Commissioners had only two boats so it would be necessary to purchase one for Hutchison, and that two of the seamen on their establishment had been appointed permanently as the Harbour Master's boatmen, and he would probably have "further light expenses".

Hutchison appears to have arranged for the moorings of the "Tigre", tender to "William and Mary", to be laid. But on March 27th Malcolm suggested that the port's temporary light should be removed as it was a danger "... for a ship that might strike the outer pier head [temporary too, incidentally] in an easterly gale". He also explained about difficulties and delays being experienced by watering trade and warships when a strong north-easter was blowing.

Hutchison wrote from Bullock to the Commissioners in April requesting them to stop "H.M.'s ships throwing their ashes into the Harbour", and waited until May 21st before dealing with Malcolm's letter to the Commissioners of March 27th "disputing the propriety" of his suggestion about the Lighthouse.

Here then was Hutchison, a few months after his appointment, showing the strength of mind and determination to defend his own opinion, no matter against whom, which were to characterise his long career.

The question of the new harbour's lighting was but one of Hutchison's problems. Like many of them, he got this one satisfactorily settled. Back in 1822 a temporary movable flashing light on a timber structure thirty four feet above high water was erected on the East Pier, warning mariners of its existence, and movable along it as the pier progressed in length. In due course Hutchison had a bell fixed in the temporary structure to be sounded in foggy weather. The Dublin Port Authority, still strongly in its original improving mood twenty six years after its institution, had, in 1812, one year after its daring establishment of a lightship for the first time on the Kish Bank,[12] endowed the creek haven at Old Dunleary with a fixed light on its pier. This was discontinued in 1831.

In the month of Hutchison's appointment, the "lanthorn" of the new temporary light on the East Pier had been smashed by high waves and been repaired next day when orders were given, presumably by the new Harbour Master, for "a few squares of glass" to be stored permanently at Kingstown to avoid having again to have glass fetched from Dublin.

Malcolm was still based at Kingstown in 1825 when, on May 19th, he wrote to the Commissioners urging them probably, one feels, in an oblique reference to differences with Hutchison, that "nautical men be consulted both from Dublin and Liverpool" over growing argumentation about the lengths of the piers and the breadth of the harbour's entrance.

Whatever about Malcolm, the temporary light on the East Pier was still in

12 The Ballast Office had, in 1735, imaginatively put a lightship with braziers at Poolbeg, near the Liffey mouth.

operation in 1830, though by then official indecision about how to continue the construction work had become critical. One of the problems was that, whereas money to pay for all the work had not ceased to come, it came very slowly, and anyway the levy on shipping using Dublin, believed to be Toutcher's idea, to meet the cost of building the asylum harbour, had proved to be insufficient (a shortfall of about twenty seven percent at one stage). The crisis was resolved for the time being when in 1831 the Lord Lieutenant's Commissioners were replaced (for the next one hundred and fifty eight years) by the Commissioners of the Office of Public Works (to the public, The Board of Works) as owners of the harbour and, consequently, with the responsibility of seeing its construction completed.[13]

One of the things that Hutchison, in the midst of all the controversy about the proper length for the East Pier and the width of the entry to the harbour, was evidently determined to see right was provision of proper light for the new harbour when completed. George Halpin, Dublin Port Authority's brilliant chief engineer, an authority on lighthouses, was called in. He designed the lighthouse needed for the far end of the East Pier. It was ready to function in 1842 and, with some modifications introduced by the engineer Jacob Owen, cost £937. The lighthouse building included dwelling space for lighthouse keepers. The light flashed white and red every half minute, forty one feet above high water, and had a strength of twelve thousand candle power. It came into permanent operation only in 1847, when the temporary light structure was finally demolished. In September 1852 a belfry was built beside the new lighthouse to house a bell to be rung as warning in fog.

Pressure had come in 1840 for a light also on the West Pier and, in September 1841, a small red light, fixed, was placed on a timber frame like the East Pier's temporary light, and moved down the pier as building works pushed it seaward. In 1850, Halpin designed the small but sturdy granite tower where the West Pier light shines every night to this day.

Halpin had proposed a cast iron lamp standard, but was overruled. On September 28th 1852 a storm damaged the temporary light structure while the light for the new stone light tower was still not ready, but Halpin and his team,

13 Duties for building Dunleary Harbour, under the Act of 56, George III, 1816

| | L. | s. | d. |
|---|---|---|---|
| Foreign Vessels entering the Port of Dublin per ton | 0 | 0 | 6 |
| Native ditto, except colliers, per ton | 0 | 0 | 4 |
| Colliers, per ton | 0 | 0 | 2 |
| Entry of goods per ton | 0 | 1 | 0 |
| Every invoice, docket etc. | 0 | 2 | 0 |
| Every coast and crosschannel permit | 0 | 2 | 0 |
| Every bond except master's and mate's | 0 | 7 | 6 |
| Every certificate of registry | 0 | 7 | 6 |
| Anchorage, slippage, and city dues, each vessel | 0 | 7 | 6 |
| Every bill of view, etc. | 0 | 2 | 6 |
| Every license to navigate | | 10 | 0 |
| Every transire certificate | 0 | 10 | 0 |

by great effort, managed to get the new light operational the very night after the storm. There were no further changes to Kingstown Harbour pier lights in Hutchison's time, though a lighthouse keeper's dwelling was erected on the West Pier and on the East Pier the fog bell was replaced by a gong, and from 1861 onwards, when the City of Dublin Steam Packet Company's mail steamer was due in fog, a gun was fired twice in quick succession every fifteen minutes till an answering gun from the mail steamer was heard. (This gun, manufactured for the British Navy in 1852 was, at the moment of writing, still beside the East Pier lighthouse, alongside the Army's battery used to salute visiting foreign warships but has since been taken for a general inspection and polish up for eventual museum presentation).

But between the last quarter of 1816, when the port had started doing business behind its single, still short, pier, and the third quarter of 1817, one thousand and sixty four ships had come in, all sailing ships and nearly all sheltering (a typical exception being the "Sally" which arrived on April 30th 1817 with railway equipment from Chepstow worth £1,342. 10s. 2d.). In 1842, between one thousand and forty five sailing ships of one hundred and one thousand, one hundred and sixty eight tons came in to shelter, also one hundred and twenty nine of eleven thousand and twenty one tons to load or discharge cargo, plus one hundred and sixty six steamships of forty two thousand, two hundred and two tons. This was excluding H.M. mail steamers which were not recorded in the Port Dues Book of the year and twenty "men of war and cruisers", so it can be seen that the business of the port had altered drastically. It was in this year that one of Hutchison's many far-sighted proposals for the port was adopted with the decision to build a new wharf parallel with, but longer and more robust than, the original Dunleary Pier of 1767 (the "Day Pier"). This was the Traders' Wharf, still used, the construction of which created a sheltered basin in the west end of the harbour where not only coasters, fishing craft and small steamships, but also medium-sized sailing ships from as far off as the Caribbean, the European continent and even, occasionally, South America,[14] could and did load and discharge cargoes. Innumerable ship masters were thus given good reason for gratitude to Hutchison for facilitating their activities.

Up to the decision to build Traders' Wharf, and with the Commissioners satisfied that now the port was as good as finished, the cost had been £690,717, against an original estimate of £801,059[15] and the Commissioners must have been patting themselves on the back. The "final" cost appears to have been £830,000, in gold Victorian sovereigns indeed, but even so it seems remarkably cheap.

Quite early in his term of office Hutchison found himself dealing with steamships. As these became faster, larger and more reliable, they began to oust

14 Eduardo Coglan's 963 page history *Los Irlandeses en la Argentina* 1987, records emigrants from Ireland to Argentina in the mid 19th century having embarked at Kingstown.

15 J.H. Isherwood, writing in the Liverpool *Sea Breezes*, July 1975.

the sailing ship from the short sea trades, a process that took more or less a whole century to complete. For the carriage of passengers and mail over short distances, sailing vessels were very quickly displaced. This completely altered the destiny of the Asylum Harbour, conceived as a refuge for sailing vessels in trouble in Dublin Bay, or anywhere in the western part of the Irish Sea.

The original Kingstown Harbour Commissioners had received a letter from "the proprietors of the Steam Packets between Dublin and Holyhead stating their intention of resorting hereafter to the new Harbour of Dunleary if convenience for landing and embarking passengers is prepared for there". This proposition was forwarded to the Lord Lieutenant in a letter of March 6th 1821.

On April 14th 1821 the Lord Lieutenant had replied, stating his opposition to the project. This was partly because a temporary landing stage would, in his opinion, cost too much, also partly because there was no guarantee that the steamer owners would stick to Holyhead as the terminal to use in Britain, and partly because the travelling public might prefer "the Government Steam Vessels", which were committed to the use of Howth.

Events however soon demolished opposition to using Kingstown as a regular terminal port for steamships. By 1834 the go-ahead City of Dublin Steam Packet Company had put into service ships too big for Howth to deal with. Even more important, Admiral Parry, the Welsh Arctic explorer who became Hydrographer to the Admiralty and who had gone around the appropriate coasts of Britain and Ireland to select the most satisfactory ports for dealing with the passage of mail, had very decisively selected Kingstown as the ideal port in Ireland for handling "the Government Steam Vessels" that were then, and for another fourteen years, entrusted with the carriage of mail between the two islands.

Kingstown consequently became not only the mail port on the Irish Sea, but by far the most important port for the carriage of passengers, whether in "Government Steam Vessels" or those of the private proprietors of the growing fleet of passenger steamers plying the Irish Sea. This opened a whole new perspective before the management of the still uncompleted new port, and it was largely the up-to-date thinking, energy and patience of Hutchison that won conclusively for Kingstown, nowadays Dun Laoghaire, the reputation as the major passenger port in Ireland on the Irish Sea, which it still holds.

There were, however, many problems still to be overcome before 1848, in which year the construction of the basic features of the port could be defined as complete, including a landing stage for passengers along a stretch of land purchased from the Board of Ordnance in 1835, starting nearer to the base of the East Pier than that of the West Pier, which came to be known as Victoria Wharf when that monarch disembarked there. It is now St. Michael's Wharf, where the greatest innovation in the port since Hutchison's day reached completion in 1995, the new, long needed, "airport style" passenger terminal, largely the idea of the first secretary of the newly established Department of the Marine, Fionán

Ó Muircheartaigh.

The two most serious of the many problems facing the management of the port in the years immediately following its passing into the ownership of the Board of Works in 1831 were, as already stated, the questions of the length of the piers and of the width of the entrance of the harbour.

In 1833 the contractor, apparently with the consent of the Board of Works, was prepared to push the East Pier a further three hundred and sixty feet out into the sea, beyond the three thousand and four hundred feet or so which had already been built. Hutchison strongly objected, for reasons stated in a letter he sent to the Admiralty in London. Hutchison won his case, after only one hundred feet of the three hundred and sixty feet projected had been built, leaving the East Pier three thousand and five hundred feet long.

Over the question of the size and shape of the entry Hutchison lost the argument, and the harbour has been suffering as a result ever since. Rennie Senior had proposed an entry of not much more than four hundred feet wide, with each pier ending in a stretch turning back inwards towards the interior of the harbour at an angle of about eighty degrees. The object of these inward turns was to break the swell liable to surge into the harbour with winds between north-east and north-west, as it does to this day. The Admiralty thought the entry was far too narrow for large frigates tacking inward in certain wind conditions, and would have been quite content to leave matters as they were when the pier-ends were as far apart as one thousand and sixty six feet. This was eventually narrowed down to the seven hundred and sixty feet that it remains. The inward turning pier-ends were discarded on account primarily of cost, a short-sighted decision which led to proposals first mooted in 1858 and revived periodically thereafter, the last time by the Harbour Master from 1951 to 1956, Captain Reginald Kearon (for which he was reprimanded by the Board of Works), to construct a mole some distance out to sea from the entry, parallel with and covering it.

# 5
# OPINIONS

There you merchant traders, and worthy sailors,
Who steer your course through each boisterous wave,
Our worthy master, from on high assisted,
Will save some thousands from a watery grave.
He is preparing a delightful harbour,
Which will be completed in some few years;
May the Lord defend still our grand employer,
Our stewards, labourers, and bright engineers.

A VERSE FROM THE 1821 DUBLIN STREET BALLAD,
*The Praises of Kingstown Harbour.*

Evidently composed by one of the workforce involved in the construction of the new Asylum Harbour, this ballad captures something of the excitement and bustle of the years while the harbour was under construction. "Our worthy master", named in the ballad, was one of the entrepreneurs engaged in the business of building the harbour, Smith, recalled in the name given to part of the seafront looking on to Scotsman's Bay, the area of Dublin Bay between the harbour's East Pier and Sandycove – NEWTOWNSMITH.

THE FOLLOWING LETTERS give an idea of both of the arguments put forward about how to proceed with the work begun in 1816. They are by Rennie Junior, Hutchison and two naval experts called in to give advice, and they disclose some of the day-to-day problems that the ever more busy port was continually having to contend with. The original letters are all in the archives of the Office of Public Works.

1

MR. RENNIE, JUNIOR
ON THE BEST MODE OF COMPLETING KINGSTOWN HARBOUR
LONDON, 16TH JUNE, 1826

GENTLEMEN,

In consequence of your having confided to my charge the chief management of the works now carrying on for the construction of the Royal Harbour of George the Fourth at Dunleary, I proceeded thither in the beginning of April last, and minutely inspected the whole of the operations. These have hitherto been conducted according to the original plan laid down by the late Mr. Rennie, and the East Pier has now advanced to the termination of the third kant, and the West Pier to about 370 feet beyond the termination of the second kant. Thus far this important harbour has been conducted well, and considerable benefit has been derived from the piers, even in their present unfinished state, both to the ships belonging to His Majesty's service as well as to all classes of trading vessels frequenting the Port of Dublin and the Irish Channel. The grand object now seems to be, what plan shall be adopted for its completion? This certainly is a subject of the greatest importance, and demands the most serious consideration; for upon a correct decision depends the success or otherwise of this great undertaking. I have, therefore, in compliance with your instructions, taken every pains to investigate the subject fully, in all its bearings, and have perused with great attention the different reports and documents which have been made in favour of the various alterations proposed, and beg leave to offer my opinion as follows:-

The general principle and utility of this harbour have been approved of by all parties, and the alterations suggested are chiefly confined to the following points: namely, the position, the dimensions, and the form of the entrance.

With regard to the first, it has been objected to the entrance, as laid down in the plan designed by the late Mr. Rennie, that it is too far to the eastward and, in consequence, if executed according to that direction, the harbour, during easterly gales, would be so exposed and disturbed within, that the protection would be considerably diminished, and that vessels, unless provided with more than ordinary ground tackling, would be unable to ride in safety. To this it may be replied that the present harbour is intended as an asylum during easterly gales for all classes of vessels, but more particularly for those frequenting the Port of Dublin, and as such it should present the greatest possible facility for entrance and departure; and by referring to the plan, it will be seen that this important object has not been neglected; but this would not be obtained, provided the entrance was to be placed further westward, because vessels in that case, during gales of wind (when they are most unmanageable), would in all probability be driven too far to the leeward, and would find it extremely difficult, if not impracticable, to work far enough to windward so as to enter the harbour, and would consequently be liable to be driven ashore and wrecked upon the South Bull, which could not take place with the entrance as originally designed, because it would be directly under their lee, and they would enter with a leading wind without difficulty. Moreover, as the prevailing winds are westerly these, with a more westerly entrance, would blow directly into the mouth of the harbour, and would consequently prevent vessels from sailing when most advantageous to make their passage; so that, in fact, the harbour by the alteration, would become most difficult of access and departure, at the very times when most desirable that it should be otherwise. It may be argued that in consequence of the perfection of navigation by steam this objection would daily diminish, but it must be remembered that the same advantages and disadvantages apply to steam vessels, although not in so great a degree as to sailing vessels. Arguments similar to the above have been so clearly stated by the Commissioners in their letter to the Treasury, of the 5th of May last, that it is useless to argue them further. Moreover, such an entrance, as being exposed to the set of the various currents, which more or less agitate the sands in the bay, would be liable to receive them, and consequently to produce an accumulation of sand within the harbour, which in process of time might prove very injurious. The free flux and influx of the tide, into and out of the entrance, would also be checked by the opposing counter currents, which would tend still further to increase the deposit within, and to affect the preservation of the harbour. It has been argued that the water in this part of the Bay of Dublin is constantly clear, both upon the flood and the ebb. This, however, is merely comparative; and from the actual decrease of depth, or shoaling, in the upper end of the bay, there is every reason to believe that it is not so, and every tendency of this nature should be most carefully avoided. Lastly, as the depth decreases to the westward by altering the entrance more in that direction, a depth of three feet of low water would be lost, which certainly is a matter of the greatest importance.

The apprehension that the harbour, if constructed with an entrance as designed, would be unquiet within, appears groundless; because the entrance being four hundred and thirty feet wide at the narrowest part, any waves that might pass within would be so broken, and have such an extended space to disperse themselves over, that the undulation would be comparatively imperceptible, and certainly not of that nature to affect vessels provided with the ordinary anchors and cables. Independently of the space occupied by the entrance, there would be ample protection under the piers for more than the number of vessels that would be required. It is true, at times there are hurricanes which would drive vessels from their anchors even in a close dock. This, however, is a contingency not likely to occur; and if it did, this would take place under any circumstances. In this respect, therefore, the position of the entrance would make little or no difference. The accidents which occurred during the late gales have been adduced as an argument in favour of altering the entrance to the westward; this, however, will not apply; because, from the statement of Mr. Aird, it appears that they arose principally from mismanagement; and the opening between the present terminations of the piers is above one thousand, four hundred feet wide and consequently, little protection is comparatively derived against this quarter at present; but in proportion as the piers advance towards each other this will diminish, so that no correct conclusions can be derived from the harbour until it be further advanced.

With regard to the second and third, it has been objected to the dimensions and form of the entrance as designed by the late Mr. Rennie, that it is too narrow, and that the agitation that would be produced between the pier heads by the waves being reflected from one angle to the other would be so great as to endanger vessels whilst entering and departing from the harbour, and render them liable to be wrecked on the pier. To this it may be replied, that the narrowest part of the entrance is four hundred and thirty feet, but that the width between the extreme angles – which in point of fact must be considered as the entrance – is one thousand, one hundred and fifty feet, and this consistently with the object of giving due protection within the harbour, forms a considerable opening, although this can be regulated by experience, and be extended hereafter to about five hundred feet wide at the narrowest part, if during the progress of the work it shall be deemed advisable: and as to any agitation of the sea that may be produced between the piers, it may be observed, that the waves, by recoiling from one angle to the other, will be checked in their progress and reduced in violence, so that the centre for which vessels will naturally steer, will be comparatively tranquil; moreover, the recoil of the waves will prevent vessels from striking against either pier, so that they will be inevitably kept in the centre between the piers, and must enter the harbour without difficulty, whereas, without some precaution of this kind, there would be a heavy sea in the entrance during gales, and vessels would find considerable difficulty in steering clear of the piers; moreover, the run of the sea into the harbour would be considerably augmented.

The principle of an inclined entrance has been tried upon the hod harbour at Whitehaven, and although executed very inefficiently, vessels during the most violent gales have never been known to strike against the pier; and as to any difficulty in departing from the harbour, there could be comparatively none, because the prevailing winds generally blow out from the harbour; and even supposing the winds should be adverse, they could lie out upon either tack, or might readily be warped out if the weather should be moderate enough to enable them to keep the sea when out of the harbour. Upon the whole, therefore, viewing this important subject impartially in all its bearings, it appears that every circumstance connected with it has been duly examined and considered previous to the determination of the present design, and although in the formation of harbours it is extremely difficult to avoid every objection, nevertheless, in the present instance I am of the opinion that as much has been done as the nature of the situation will admit, and if executed accordingly will be most likely to effect the different objects originally contemplated, namely, the formation of a complete Asylum harbour. Upon these grounds I cannot recommend any material deviation from the plan already laid down, although during the progress of the work I shall not fail to avail myself of the circumstances as they arise, and report to you my opinion accordingly.

The principal object however, at present, should be directed towards advancing the western pier as fast as possible, in order to give protection to the interior of the harbour, and the last arm or kant of the eastern pier might be for the present deferred, which would give time for further consideration; but the necessity and advantage resulting from continuing it as originally laid down will, I have no doubt, become daily more apparent.

With regard to that part of your instructions which relates to the formation of the sea slope or face of the eastern pier, I have to observe that, provided the rubble has become sufficiently consolidated (and judging from the time that has passed since it was deposited, I should conceive that a considerable portion of that part of the pier towards the shore must by this time have in it a great measure acquired its ultimate slope), I should recommend it to be formed in a more regular manner, in order to prevent occasional repairs in restoring the surface, which otherwise will probably from time to time be ripped up and pulled out by the violence of the waves. In commencing this operation, the greatest difficulty will be found in securing the base or toe of the slope, for when once this has been effected, the remainder becomes comparatively easy; to secure the toe of the slope, therefore, I should recommend that a beaching of foreshore, varying in width according to circumstances, should be left in front of the slope; this foreshore will act as a barrier against the most violent waves, and prevent them from breaking upon the base of the slope, and will, moreover, enable the workmen to secure it more effectually; from thence upwards the slope should be carried on according to the general inclination already determined by the sea, which appears to be about five feet horizontal to every foot perpendicular: the stones for this operation should be composed of the largest slope, header and stretcher alternately, and well bedded into the rubble below. Upon this subject I had frequent discussions with Mr. Aird, when in London lately; as he now understands the principle upon which this operation should be carried on, I should recommend that a portion of about one hundred or two hundred yards should be commenced upon that part of the eastern pier which is best adapted for the purpose, and in proportion as this proceeds the effect of the sea upon it will be seen, and the further progress of this work can be regulated according as circumstances shall render it most advisable.

I cannot close this report without offering my apologies that it has not been sent earlier, but I unfortunately have been prevented by indisposition; at the same time I am extremely happy that no inconvenience has arisen to the works in consequence.

I have, etc.,
JOHN RENNIE
TO THE COMMISSIONERS OF KINGSTOWN HARBOUR.

## 2

MR. RENNIE
ON THE BEST SITE FOR A LANDING PIER IN KINGSTOWN HARBOUR
LONDON, 29TH JUNE, 1829

GENTLEMEN,

I have to acknowledge your letter of the 9th of April last, accompanied by two Memorials to the Lord Lieutenant of Ireland, praying for the erection of a Landing Pier for passengers, within the Royal Harbour of George the Fourth, together with Mr. Aird's report thereon; and you inform me that the Commissioners desire to have my opinion, together with a Plan and Estimate in Duplicate for completing the work. I have accordingly taken the subject into consideration, and beg leave to make the following observations:-

That some additional landing place, as prayed for by the memorialists, is necessary to accommodate the numerous passengers embarking and disembarking to and from the steamboats which now carry on the extensive and continually increasing communication between Dublin, Liverpool, and various other parts of England, there can be no doubt, as this has been long wanted, and the principal reason hitherto why the attainment of this very desirable object has been deferred is the unfinished state of the harbour, which has prevented the possibility of determining with accuracy the most advisable situation, as well as the precise kind of accommodation that would be required. It was in consequence of this reason alone that the Post Office, in the month of June, 1826, determined to erect only a temporary wooden landing jetty on the east pier, until the finished state of the harbour would admit of the adoption of some more permanent plan, which, for work of this description, has, I understand, answered very well. The next question to be considered is, first, whether the harbour has not arrived at that state to admit of a proper decision for a permanent station; and if so, which is the most advisable place, and kind of construction for the purpose intended.

With regard to the first – the outer piers have certainly not yet been carried to their full extent, and it might be inferred with some reason, that until that event has taken place, no correct opinion can be formed of the ultimate effect; sufficient, however, has been done to enable this point to be decided with tolerable accuracy, namely, that if the present plan be carried into effect to its fullest extent, the original object of making this harbour an effectual asylum for all classes of vessels detained by contrary winds, or taking shelter on account of stress of weather, will be completely obtained; but as the embarkation and disembarkation of passengers require accommodation of a different kind, namely, greater convenience and more tranquility, the cost of which was never included in the original estimate, some additional work is necessary to obtain that desirable object.

With regard to the second – there are three places where the required accommodation for steam packets may be obtained, either on the east or west pier, or towards the centre of the harbour, to the eastward of the present boat basin.

The east pier is rather too far out of the way from Dublin, and would interfere with the present Post Office station, although by widening the upper end, and running out an arm from it, a convenient landing-place might be made at a moderate expense, as the pier would form so much of the work. The west pier, unless the extremity, when finished, be adopted, would be rather exposed to the entrance, and has less depth of water, although it would interfere less with the general form of the harbour, and its great proximity to Dublin would render it advantageous in some respects.

The middle of the harbour to the eastward of the present boat basin would be equally convenient, and there being sufficient depth of water near the shore, a pier of moderate dimensions would suffice, the roads and approaches being already made, and consequent saving to that extent would arise. It would be easily accessible to and from the sea during the prevailing winds; and it would be well protected by the eastern pier from the dangerous quarter, and the range of the sea during storms would be more limited. Under all these circumstances, the situation marked A, or thereabout, upon the accompanying plan, appears advisable for the general purpose of a landing-place.

The next point to be considered is, what kind of construction would be most likely to obtain the desired object? From the great depth and extent of water contained in the outer harbour being nearly two hundred and forty acres, [i.e. the whole new harbour as added on to the original diminutive harbour of Old Dunleary as created in the 1760s] and from the frequent and violent storms which occur, there is reason to believe that without some work more enclosed than a bare quay wall there would scarcely be that tranquility and security for the embarkation and disembarkation of passengers and carriages that is so desirable, and almost indispensable, for a Packet Station; for this reason I would recommend that the pier should have a returning arm, in order to prevent the inrun of the sea; it should also be provided with landing-slips and stairs, for carriages and horses on both sides, and every requisite for extensive accommodation.

The expense of this work will amount to the sum of £35,360. If the landing place was to be made on the east pier, it would only cost £24,140, but then the accommodation would not be so good.

With regard to the propriety of uniting the Station for the Post Office packets with those of the public, it may be observed, that the services are of such a dissimilar nature, that I think they would be better by being kept separate, and when the outer piers are finished, a very convenient station might be found for the former within the jetties and pier heads, where a certain portion of both heads will require retaining walls of masonry, at all events; and as the Post Office are already provided with temporary accommodation for their packets, so far as they are concerned, it may be deferred until the harbour is finished; if however, it should be found preferable to have the packets nearer to the shore, a small jetty might be run out from the east pier for their accommodation.

I have, &c.,
JOHN RENNIE
THE COMMISSIONERS OF THE ROYAL HARBOUR OF GEORGE THE FOURTH
&C. &C. &C.

3
CAPT. WARREN'S REPORT ON THE STATE OF THE WORKS
AT KINGSTOWN HARBOUR.
DUBLIN 19TH JULY, 1831

The east pier head having suffered much from the gales in the winter, in consequence of the coping not having reached that length, I consider the first object would be to repair it without loss of time, and before the bad weather sets in.

The next object I would recommend is a wharf, to be constructed of stone, on the south side, as shown on the plan, which would have twenty feet at it at low water, for the use of steam packets, there being at present but one built of wood, by order of the Post Office Department, and which is in a very dilapidated state. There is already a quantity of stone prepared for this purpose, and if it was made to extend to four hundred feet, merchant vessels could take out their cargoes at it, which would be an inducement to forward the proposed railroad between the harbour and Dublin and be a great saving to the trade, as vessels that draw too much water for the Dublin bar are in the habit of having their cargoes taken out and carried round at a great expense, and when lightened sufficiently, pay a considerable sum to be towed there by steam vessels; this measure will be likely to create a revenue for future improvements. [This was the first serious proposal for extending the railway beyond the recently completed station to the eastern part of the new harbour. Eventually after Carlisle Pier had been completed, the railway, now extended onward into Co. Wexford, had a spur built from it on the passenger landing stage on Carlisle Pier. The short spur accommodating it can still be seen from any DART train about to enter or leave Dun Laoghaire Station. The wharf proposed by Captain Warren became Victoria, later St. Michael's Wharf.]

There are various opinions as to the plan that would most likely prevent the swell which sets into the harbour with an easterly wind. I consider that anything carried across the set of the tide would cause an eddy, and be likely to form a bar at the entrance. The most effectual plan would be an outer breakwater, placed at the distance of about two cables'* length from the pier heads in the direction of the tides, but this could only be done at a very considerable expense. [Proposals to build an outer breakwater outside the harbour entrance to lessen the surge coming into the port in certain conditions were resurrected from time to time, most recently by Harbour Master Captain Kearon in the early 1950s.] If the east pier head was carried on for half a cable's length, a little inclining to the west as shown on the plan, I think it would have, in a great measure, the desired effect, but would cost, according to the estimate of the engineer, not less than £50,000, including a permanent finish of cut stone.

Whether the pier head is projected in the way I have mentioned, or remains as it is, vessels making for the harbour with a wind that prevents their fetching in to an anchorage, can anchor a little short of it, so that when they bring up they would have the harbour open. If a buoy were placed just within the lighthouse, as shown in the plan, a hawser run to this would swing them in without difficulty. It would be desirable to have a buoy placed in a similar situation at the west head pier.

SAM WARREN, CAPTAIN R.N.

N.B. The southern corner of the harbour appears well adapted for Morton's patent railway slip for heaving up vessels for repairs.

*1200 feet: one cable is 100 fathoms

LETTER FROM SIR JAMES GRAHAM REGARDING COSTS
ADMIRALTY, 26TH JULY, 1831

Acquaint the Treasury, that in transmitting this report of Captain Warren, with certain other documents relative to the works in progress at Kingstown Harbour, their Lordships recommend the completion of the sewer, the casing of the piers with masonry, the immediate repairs of the extremity of the eastern pier, so as before winter to protect it against further damage, and the building of the wharf at the point marked out on the plan enclosed, adopting the advice of Captain Warren, that it shall be four hundred feet in length, and extended outwards into twenty feet depth at low water.

Their Lordships cannot recommend the extension of the eastern pier at an outlay of £50,000. The eastern side of the harbour is now completely sheltered without this extension, and affords ample accommodation for the present trade frequenting it; at any future time this addition may be made, if considered prudent and found necessary; but the advantage of greater protection within the harbour must always be weighed against the certain evil of narrowing the entrance, and increasing the difficulties of ships in distress fetching into the anchorage.

J.G. (Sir James Graham, one of the Lords of the Admiralty)

4

LIEUT. HUTCHISON'S OBJECTIONS TO WORKS IN PROGRESS AT HARBOUR
LONDON, MAY, 1833

MY LORD,

I most respectfully beg to address you on a subject, which I consider of the first importance to the mercantile and shipping interest of Dublin, and the trade in general of the Irish Channel.

From my holding the appointment of Harbour Master to the Asylum Harbour, at Kingstown, since January 1823, an opportunity has been afforded me from continual observation and experience, of forming a pretty accurate opinion as to the manner in which the entrance of that harbour should be finished; it is, therefore, with infinite regret I understand, that a projection of three hundred and sixty feet on the south pier, in a parallel line to the west pier, has been determined on and commenced, and to which I now humbly beg leave to state my objections. In the first instance, it will make it extremely difficult for large vessels to enter the harbour during S.W. gales; secondly, for wind bound vessels to put to sea with north and N.E. winds; and, thirdly, a decrease of near two feet depth of water at the point of the south pier; and ultimately, the contraction of the mouth to a totally inadequate space, by the positive necessity of a turn on the west pier; as by the proposed extension the easterly sea will be inevitably directed even more than at present into the N.W. side of the harbour.

In my opinion, there is but one way to form the entrance, which will not be liable to objection, and I would most urgently advise that the eastern pier should cease at its present extent, forming a circular abutment of cut stone to erect a light-house; the west pier to receive a turn of three hundred, four hundred feet in a S. by E. direction, which is essentially necessary to exclude the sea or swell, which rushes along the inside of the north pier, and causes such uneasiness to the shipping in the old harbour during easterly gales, and prevents wind bound vessels anchoring at the north side, their proper berth, and from which they could proceed on change of wind with much greater facility than at present, and that difficulty will be increased if the present intention in progress be carried into effect. Trusting these observations, which I have deemed it my duty as a naval officer to suggest ere it be too late for your Lordships' consideration, I am emboldened to hope the importance of the subject will be sufficient apology for this intrusion.

I remain, &c.,
WM. HUTCHISON, LIEUT. R.N.
HARBOUR MASTER.

(Note that Hutchison sent his comments, over the heads of the Board of Works Commissioners managing the harbour, direct to the Admiralty in London, the ultimate arbiter of all maritime problems in the United Kingdom as then constituted).

TO SIR JAMES GRAHAM, BART, &C. &C.,

N.B. – In consequence of this representation, I was ordered to attend at the Admiralty, before Sir James Graham, Sir Thomas Hardy, Sir John Burgoyne, Sir John Rennie, Admiral Warren, and Captain Beaufort [later Admiral]; and having stated my opinion, I believe to the satisfaction of these gentlemen, the Commissioners of Kingstown Harbour were directed to stop the advance of the east pier, having then carried it out about eighty feet of the intended three hundred and sixty. (Note that Warren had become an Admiral. Navan-born Beaufort was perhaps the greatest of all hydrographers and is known also for his Wind Scale).

5

REPORT ON THE ROYAL HARBOUR OF GEO. IV., AT KINGSTOWN, DUBLIN
BY W. CUBITT, C.E.

16, PARLIAMENT STREET, LONDON, 21ST MARCH, 1835

SIR,

In pursuance of instructions with which I was favoured on the 20th ult., I proceeded to Kingstown immediately after the 2nd instant, for the purpose of inspecting the Royal Harbour of Geo. IV., at that place, with a view to forming a plan for its final completion.

In making my investigations and inquiries, I received every facility for the purpose from the Commissioners of the Harbour, and every assistance that could be rendered by Mr. Thomas, the resident engineer, and Lieut. Hutchison, R.N., the harbour master, for which, together with free access to all papers and plans on the subject, in the office of the Board of Works in Dublin, and Harbour Office in Kingstown, my acknowledgements are due to Colonel Burgoyne, his coadjutors, and officers respectively.

Having made the requisite inspection of the harbour, I returned to London again on the fifteenth, since which time I have engaged in the investigation of the subject, and forming plans and estimates for the final completion of this great undertaking, and have now the honour of submitting to your notice, for the information of the Lords Commissioners of the Admiralty, the following report on the subject, together with the accompanying plans therein referred to, which I trust will prove satisfactory, and of which I shall be most happy to hand any further explanation.

I have, &c.,
W. CUBITT

TO THE RIGHT HON. G.R. DAWSON

This harbour, the general form and situation of which will be seen on referring to a chart of Dublin Bay, is formed by means of two extensive piers of breakwaters of rough stone, projected into the sea so as to enclose between them about two hundred and forty acres of water, varying in depth from fifteen to twenty six feet at low water of spring tides.

The piers being now brought to a distance of less than one thousand feet of each other, it became a matter of the very first importance to determine in what manner the entrance of the harbour shall be completed, so as to combine the grand requisites of a safe and quiet harbour with those of the greatest possible facilities of ingress and egress for vessels under all circumstances of winds and tides.

Many and various are the plans which have been proposed for this entrance, both by naval gentlemen and engineers, but they almost all resolve themselves into the single principle of contracting the entrance by an addition, in some particular direction, to the end of one or both piers.

Now there is no doubt but, by contracting the entrance, the harbour may be rendered more quiet in almost any wind; but in proportion as the entrance is narrowed, so will the difficulty of entering it be increased in adverse gales of wind, when the harbour, as an asylum, is most needed; or the difficulties of departure increased, when the wind shall become fair for vessels sailing: and it is my decided opinion, that if the entrance be made much narrower than it is at present, it will be too narrow to be entered, with facility or safety, under difficult cases of adverse gales of wind; but, if left of its present width, without something being done to keep out the heavy range of the sea, which rolls in with the wind anywhere to the southward of Howth Head, more than half the harbour will be so much exposed as to render it unsafe riding at anchor within it, and impossible to lie in at a wharf at any part in gales of wind, from the N.E. to the S.S.E. inclusive.

*Under these circumstances, I am led to the conclusion that nothing will meet all the difficulties of the case so well as covering or protecting the present entrance by means of a detached pier or breakwater, and finishing the harbour piers with good bold circular cut stone-heads, 300 feet in diameter, and 800 feet apart, as shown on the general plan.*[This proposal of Cubitt's was not adopted. Many, including one time Harbour Master Kearon, have lamented that it was not]

Covered in this manner, the harbour would be rendered (in my judgement) safe and quiet in all winds, particularly in those to which it is now the most exposed; and, at the same time, the means of ingress and egress would remain just as free and easy as at present, or even more so, with the advantage of covered anchorage at the back of the breakwater, in strong gales from the W. and W.S.W., in a good situation to make sail from on a change of wind or tide, to enter either of the harbours of Dublin or Kingstown.

This breakwater would be one thousand, two hundred feet long, twenty feet above high water, and with a paved slope or glacis of five horizontal to one perpendicular on the sea face, with a low distinguishing light at its eastern end.

Adverting again to my instructions in which I am desired to examine into the "the whole question, and to report as to the best mode of completing this great undertaking", I take it for granted that not only the completion of the entrances, but also what may be termed the "necessary appendages" to the harbour, when so completed, should also come under my consideration.

With this view of the case, I have examined into the subject, not as an asylum harbour merely, where vessels could enter in stress of weather, and remain in safety, but also as a naval and packet station, and, in some degree, also, as applicable to the mercantile marine; for, by the aid of the new wharf, and the Dublin and Kingstown Railway, foreign vessels, and East or West Indiamen, might be enabled to discharge their cargoes, instead of waiting too long a time for wind or water to get into the River Liffey.

I, therefore, deemed it essential in this harbour that there should be, first, a graving dock, capable of receiving and refitting one of His Majesty's largest class steamers or frigates. Second, a patent slip, ready for hauling up, examining, and repairing all the smaller class of vessels under 300 tons, that may come into the harbour, with damage, or want of repairs, on the instant. Third, Wharfs, viz., one good wharf at least on each of the piers, and one at the upper end of the harbour, as shown on the plan.

Now, the first of these objects (the graving dock) has not been lost sight of by Mr. Thomas, the present able resident engineer, who had proposed a plan for that purpose, which I have inserted in the plan accompanying this report; and a wharf at the upper end of the harbour has been for some time in progress, under the directions of the present commissioners, to the extent of four hundred feet in length, one hundred and thirty feet of which is up and ready for use, and the remainder will probably be completed this summer. [This before long, following Queen Victoria's visit to Ireland via Kingstown/Dun Laoghaire in 1849, became Victoria (now Saint Michael's) Wharf.] Mr. Thomas's plan is to extend and combine this wharf with a graving dock as shown in the plan, which, if means can be found in course of time to effect it, will render the harbour very complete for naval purposes. An excellent situation for a patent slip exists at the southern end of the harbour. The wharfs I would recommend on the piers are, a stone wharf three hundred feet long, parallel to the eastern pier, in the place of the present Post-office wooden wharf, at which three packets or vessels could lie alongside; and a pier, projecting at right angles from the western pier, two hundred and fifty feet long, and one hundred feet wide, at which two vessels could lie alongside, and one at the end. This pier would not only possess, at all times, the advantages of a lee side for vessels to lie at, but, at the same time, serve as a protection to the old harbour of Dunleary, and the merchant-vessels lying within it.

In carrying these works into effect, I would suggest that the works in hand (viz., the four hundred feet wharf, and the finishing up the roads, slopes, &c., to piers) be completed forthwith; and that preparations be made, at the same time, for completing the entrance of which the eastern pier head should be the first work set about, and then the wharf in the place of the present Post Office wooden wharf. [Some years later, on Hutchison's insistence, Carlisle Pier was built and opened in 1859, fulfilling largely Cubitt's suggestion].

The works above enumerated constitute all that I think requisite (over and above what is at present in hand) for the completion of Kingstown Harbour, and are all tinged red on the plan to distinguish them as new works; and the probable expense of all, which would not, in my estimation, after the most careful inquiry and examination on the spot, exceed the sum of £265,000, of which I estimate.

| | £ |
|---|---|
| The completion of the pier heads at | 100,000 |
| The external breakwater at | 75,000 |
| The graving dock, wharf, patent slip, &c., at | 50,000 |
| The new east and west wharfs at | 30,000 |
| The completion of the present wharf, rough coping, and finishing off piers, &c., and finishing off piers, &c., and finishing works in hand, at | 10,000 |
| | 265,000 |

reckoning all the present stock of stone in hand to stand against extraordinary contingencies, over and above the contingencies included in the above estimates.

In carrying these works into effect, I would suggest that the works in hand (viz., the four hundred feet wharf, and the finishing up the roads, slopes, &c., to piers) to be completed forthwith; and the preparations to be made, at the same time, for completing the entrance of which the eastern pier head should be the first work set about, and then the western, after the breakwater should be commenced; or should it be thought desirable to give the harbour a few seasons' trial with the finished heads, the interior appendages of the harbour could be proceeded with in the interim; because, if used, either with or without a breakwater, I deem the pierheads, as proposed on the plan, the most suitable for the purposes.

I would also urge, most respectfully, that much will be saved by coming to an early determination on this important subject, whatever and whatsoever plan for the purpose may be chosen to carry into effect, inasmuch as a great deal of capital lies waste in material and apparatus, and an establishment necessarily kept up for doing but little, which could effect a great deal, if arrangements were made accordingly, and means provided to set them to work.

To complete the works now in hand, and make preparations for, and get fairly entered upon, the foundations of the east pier-head would occupy the present year; in doing which, a sum of from £25,000 to £30,000, or even more, might be disposed of advantageously; and when the works are brought into full and steady operation, it would require from £40,000 to £50,000 per annum to carry them on to completion, with the greatest degree of economy, and take about six years from this time to complete finally, at that rate of proceeding.

W. CUBITT

NOTE: The pier-heads recommended in the foregoing report are proposed to be circular heads or towers, with walls of solid masonry at least twelve feet in thickness, brought up from the bottom by means of the diving-bell.

The diameter of the heads will be three hundred feet, which will not only afford a good return pier to protect the inside of the main piers from the range of oblique seas entering the harbour, but afford ample space in the circular platforms within the parapets for the purposes of stone-houses, boat-houses, pilots' dwellings, or even batteries, for the means of defence, if necessary, and for which they are, from size and form, well adapted. A plain plan and section of one pier head, with the dimensions written in, is shown on the following page.

W.C.

Careful perusal of Captain Cubitt's letter gives a fascinating picture of progress of the port's construction at the date when it was written, of what the next steps should have been according to an intelligent contemporary, and of most of what was and was not done in the later stages of the original construction work.

Though Cubitt's advice about the final length of the West Pier was preferred to that of Hutchison who evidently saw more clearly than Cubitt that the day of the sailing ship was slowly passing. A wide enough port entrance to facilitate the entry of large sailing ships was of less importance than restricting the amount of surge entering the harbour. The final shape of the harbour was largely the consequence of the harbour master's opinions formed after ten years of careful observation of the effects of the first stages of building the great new port and how to complete the job.

The construction of Victoria, now St. Michael's Wharf, was basically due to Hutchison, whose foresight led, before two more decades had passed, to the imaginative addition of the Carlisle Pier, and his leaving to his successors for nearly a whole century, a harbour fully adequate for the tasks so different from those at first envisaged – a port primarily landing passengers but also concerned with fishing, some importing and exporting of goods, a naval presence, and provision of facilities for a lighthouse service.

# 6
# EVERYDAY PROBLEMS

You'd be filled with wonder to hear claps like thunder
And rocks burst asunder in the atmosphere,
With brave stone-belvers, and jolly miners,
From different nations you'll find them there;
The loyal lovers here you may discover,
Down by the banks of the enamelled ground,
With sweet romancing down by wild meanders,
While the scaly ramblers do sport all round.

ANOTHER VERSE FROM *The Praises of Kingstown Harbour*

This verse recalls some of the technical problems facing the engineers and the workforce involved in the gigantic and unprecedented task of shaping hundreds of tons of granite blasted out of Dalkey Hill and transported by a pioneer funicular railway system to a seashore desolate from time immemorial, and marshalling them into the great piers within which the new port would come to life. The arrival of miners and other craftsmen from far and wide to work on this enterprise clearly impressed the balladeer.

SOME MORE LETTERS give an idea of some of the problems that had to be met in the years when the harbour was still being completed. Another problem for the new harbour's authorities had been the decision of the government in London to station convict ships at Kingstown.

One of these was a famous North American frigate, "Essex", captured by the British in South American waters in the British–U.S. war of 1812–14. Some of the inmates of these vessels, but only a small minority, were political prisoners. Most of them had been convicted of what would not today be considered serious crimes. They were kept in the ships at Kingstown prior to being transferred to Cork for shipment to convict settlements in far off Australia and Tasmania, or even to plantations in Bermuda.

Some correspondence concerning convict ships follows. "Essex" was in a poor state when she left Plymouth for Kingstown and much worse when she arrived. She stayed in Kingstown from 1824 to 1836. Her consort was the "Surprise". Similar hulks lay in Cork harbour.

C/O WILLIAM GREGORY ESQ.
HIS MAJESTY'S SHIP "ESSEX",
ROYAL HARBOUR,
KINGSTOWN.
FEBRUARY 23RD 1824

SIR,

Having since my arrival here employed part of my time in looking over the Harbour for a proper place to Moor the Ship, "Essex", I am of opinion that the most proper place will be outside His Majesty's Yacht, under your command, but a vessel being sunk near the spot, it will not be in my power so to do without she is removed; and I have further to add, that if it is not shortly done, it will soon become impracticable, for, from the constant ground swell in this Port, and having her mast standing, she will sink down into the sands so much, that it will be impossible to save her.

CHARLES MALCOLM ESQUIRE
CAPTAIN OF HIS MAJESTY'S YACHT "WILLIAM AND MARY",
ROYAL HARBOUR,
KINGSTOWN.

ON HIS MAJESTY'S SERVICE

LETTER FROM:
CHARLES MALCOLM ESQUIRE,
CAPTAIN OF HIS MAJESTY'S YACHT "WILLIAM AND MARY,"
ROYAL HARBOUR,
KINGSTOWN,
FEBRUARY 25TH 1824

SIR,

I beg to enclose you a letter which I received yesterday from Mr. Baren who is sent over from Plymouth Dock yard in Charge of the "Essex" Convict Hulk, and to have to request you would be pleased to give direction to the Commissioners of the Royal Harbour to have the snow* "Hackey" removed without delay, which I believe can be easier effected at this time than any other. As Mr. Baren can.

*A small two masted sailing ship of light construction with a square mainsail below a square top gallant sail

MONKSTOWN GLEBE HOUSE,
NEAR DUBLIN

MY DEAR SIR,

A Convict ship is in a short time to be established in Kingstown Harbour, to which a Gentleman, for whom I entertain a very sincere regard and esteem on account of his good qualities, is very anxious to be appointed Physician. He already lives in this neighbourhood, being our Dispensing Physician, in which capacity he conducts himself with the greatest *humanity*, zeal, and prudence. As to his Professional qualifications he can produce the most satisfactory certificates and testimonials. He now comes forward under the patronage and recommendation of Dr. Rennie, which I consider to be much in his favour. But it is a point of principal importance to him that somebody should speak in his behalf to Mr. Gregory, whose approbation would, as I understand, secure to him the object of his wishes. I can scarcely venture to expect that Mr. Gregory would pay any attention to my opinion, and wishes, on this subject, for in truth, for a very considerable time past, he has declined any acquaintance or intercourse with me. But as I do feel much anxiety on this subject I should really be much obliged to you if you would state to Mr. Gregory what you have heard about this Gentleman from me, and also beg his attention to his peculiar merits. His name is *Dr. Plant.* He lives in Montpelier Place near Blackrock. He is a man of excellent moral character, and as attentive to the public duties of one Religion as the nature of his avocations will permit. In all respects I do assure you that I think him a man particularly adapted and calculated for this station, *I pray go to Mr. Gregory without loss of time*, and believe me.

Yours very truly,
CHARLES LINDSAY

TO THE COMMISSIONERS' SECRETARY (DATE UNCLEAR)

SIR

Ship Carpenters were brought from Cork to be employed on Board the Hulk Essex at Dunleary.

The agreement made with the men so brought from Cork was that their wages would be 4/4d. per day, that two days would be allowed for the journey, their wages to commence from the day they proceeded on their journey, and some gratuity would be allowed on account of additional travelling expenses, and accordingly £1.10 was paid to each which, with the accommodation and fuel they received, I consider liberal payment.

PAUL TREVOR

TO HIS EXCELLENCY THE MOST NOBLE THE MARQUIS WELLSELEY
LORD LIEUTENANT GENERAL AND GENERAL GOVERNOR OF IRELAND

THE HUMBLE MEMORIAL OF THE SHIP-WRIGHTS AND JOINERS
OF THE PORT OF CORK, EMPLOYED ON THE REPAIR OF HIS MAJESTY'S
HULK OR SHIP ESSEX NOW LYING IN KINGSTOWN ROYAL HARBOUR
NEAR DUBLIN –

PASSAGE WEST
30TH OCTOBER 1824

SHEWETH,

That about June last, Lt. Hodge the acting Master Carpenter of said Vessel did in the Port of Cork employ Memorialists (Seventeen in number) to go to Kingstown to repair the above vessel, on the stipulated wages of Four British Shillings* per man per day, with other luffing accommodations on Board of said vessel, their wages to commence the day of their departure from Cork Harbour to Kingstown and to continue until their arrival back in return, together with defraying their expenses in going and coming (all of which items being the long affixed custom of the Port of Cork)

Memorialists most respectfully beg leave to submit that in proceeding from Cork Harbour to Kingstown some went by land & some by Sea, those by land had to pay £1. 2. 6 for the outside of a coach each from Cork to Dublin, together with their expences from Cove to Cork, then expences from Dublin to Kingstown, the whole thereof with finding subsistence in said interim amounts on the most reduced calculation to more than Thirty Shillings which was all they received each for conveyance thereto.

The men who proceeded by Sea lost from the change of weather a longer time.

Some of these Memorialists being lately discharged from said work for want of employment had to send their several chests of tools by water home about five weeks since, which did not as yet arrive from the inclemency of the weather – And from Memorialists, as being incumbered with heavy young families to support them they were obligated to send home what they could spare of their wages weekly which left Memorialists

*Valued at £4.4 shillings Irish

in a very distrest state to return to their families together with the loss of their working tools still. And as Memorialists received no pay or wages but while they were at work on the Vessel and no compensation to bring them home or their tools all of which violation of agreement have utterly ruined & beggared some of their families particularly from the non arrival of their tools.

Memorialists therefore beg leave to solicit His Excellency's gracious and humane attention in condescending to comment on their grievance and disappointment, in greatest hopes as his being the fountain of Justice & consideration that he will allow Memorialists the amount of their agreement or what compensation his Great wisdom may be pleased to grant for their above losses. His gracious design directed to John Sarsfield Barry Ship Wright Passage West will be ever gratefully prayed for by him & the rest of his above fellow workmen – who have the honour to be His Excellency's most faithful & distrest, humble Servants:-

JOHN SARSFIELD BARRY
WM. HEGARTY
THOMAS STEPHENSON
JAMES BANE

30TH NOV. 1824. PORT COMMISSIONER'S DECISION

Shipwrights & Joiners of Pt. of Cork employed in repairing the "Essex" Hulk lying in Kingstown Harbour – May be compensated for losses sustained by them. Refer to Mr. Laneburn.

So at the end of a month the Memorialists were at last compensated. The exact terms of the compensation were not discovered. The episode throws light on the difficulties faced by even skilled members of the working class in Ireland (and no doubt also in Britain) in the early years of the 19th century, when trade unions were still illegal.

Captain William John Williams, an English Inspector of Prisons, wrote, probably at about the time that "Essex" was decomissioned (and sold for a few pounds to a Mr. Galsworthy after a squabble between the government in Ireland and its superior counterpart in London about which of them owned her).

"The Hulks at Kingstown and Cork are similarly fitted, and are nearly of the same size: they are arranged upon the very worst form of prison discipline although not the worst for security:- the upper deck is part fitted as a hospital, and before the mainmast as a mess or dining room: the lower deck as a sleeping room: the plan strikes one as precisely that which would be adopted for securing and lodging wild beasts; upon the upper deck they pass the day, lounging in idleness or basking in the sunshine, or when it rains in taking shelter under the awnings which project over the sides and wall of their airing yard: and at close of day they are mustered and passed into their sleeping room through a confined aperture, admitting the entrance one at a time with difficulty, and thus rendering a rush outwards next to impossible – in this place they are locked up for the night. A glimmer of light is furnished to their department by a lamp placed behind an illuminator in both the fore and after bulkheads, and should disturbance take place during the night, these lights are instantly extinguished: but no one dares to enter into the prison.

"There is no means of finding employment on board, none of inciting the prisoners to habits of industry by uniform or routine occupation: none even of fatiguing the body, so as to diminish the activity of vicious minds by inducing sleep: no means of classification in separation, the youngest boy associating with the most hardened felon or murderer – there is an attempt at a school on board each ship, but it would appear that by far the greater part of a convict's time is passed in recounting his adventures in vice and infamy to his less wicked companions …"

Williams however remarks how healthy the inmates were and how low the ships' hospital expenses. His report has frequently been copied from the original in the British Public Record Office.

The presence of any hulk must have been most irritating to Hutchison both on moral and aesthetic grounds and because it would permanently be in a berth that could have been more profitably used in a port growing steadily busier. Convict hulks were a security risk too, in more ways than one, and, as some of the correspondence reveals, the cause of place-hunting intrigues and incipient labour troubles. Dr. Trevor, mentioned in this correspondence, who fell out with carpenters who had been imported from Cork because the local ones had "combination", or what we would now call trade union sympathies, seems to have been an official in the Irish prison service.

Further complications for the activities of the first harbour master of the Royal Asylum Harbour brought about by the ways of the British penal system of those days have been revealed in a comprehensive thesis for the degree of M.Litt. written by Rena Lohan of the National Archives, entitled "The Treatment of Women Sentenced to Transportation and Penal Servitude 1790–1898".

Convicts sentenced to transportation were sailed out of Cork. But this was in the years before or at the very start of railway construction here, and the problem was how to get them to Cork. In Chapter 2–3, p. 32, of her thesis, "Removal from Dublin to Cork for Embarkation", Rena Lohan notes "It was the usual practice to bring convicts to Cork in sloops or brigs". Their passage was paid till 1818 by the Government, but an Act of Parliament then directed that henceforth local Grand Juries should meet the expense. At first the female convicts, having been collected at the female convicts' depot at Grangegorman (incidentally, the first prison purely for females opened in these islands), and kept there for an average of three months for "training and instruction", had to be literally "carted" down to Dublin docks, a disorderly and undignified process. Once embarked there they had to wait as long, occasionally, as six weeks aboard these small vessels in strong easterly weather, before the ships' masters could venture out.

The eventual consequence was an official decision in 1842 that the female convicts would henceforth sail for Cork in small craft hired, no longer from Dublin but from the new Asylum Harbour of Kingstown. The "carting" from Grangegorman to Kingstown was then, of course, in quite a large part through unbuilt-on country, which spared the carted the scenes their predecessors had suffered going through narrow and insalubrious streets to the Liffey quays. Equally important for these unfortunate women, the ships bringing them to Cork could get out of the new harbour in conditions that would not have been possible sailing from up the Liffey, and quicker. Nevertheless, Rena Lohan discovered that the journey from Grangegorman to Kingstown was not without its own problems. "It was necessary to provide a large military escort to guard the cars carrying the convicts because of the rowdiness and frequent drunkenness on the journey", she found. She mentions that in April 1843 sixteen "cars" had been necessary to bring sixty-four convicts from Grangegorman to Kingstown. The result was a decision to cart the convicts from Grangegorman to the North Wall and there embark them (about two hundred at a time) in "a barge with a roof and sides" that was then towed by a steam tug across Dublin Bay to the new harbour. [Before 1842 the convicts had had to embark from the quays in open barges]. It was found that the final solution to the problem saved the authorities £60 a year, largely as only a very small guard was needed on board the towed covered barge.

The troubles of the unfortunate convicts, the majority of whom had been convicted for crimes considered not only today but even only a few years after conviction quite minor, were not over by a long way when their sloops or brigs set sail from Kingstown. It was officially reckoned that their passage from there to Cork would take about two days, but it was often nearer a week and they were then very frequently kept waiting in sordid accommodation along the quays in Cork before at last embarking for the Antipodes. Rena Lohan quotes Inspector General of Prisons in Ireland, Foster Archer, stating that the period spent in harbour was more distressing than a twelve month voyage, and the convicts "underwent more suffering and sickness on the passage to Cork than on that from Cork to Botany Bay".

Incidentally, it is not surprising that the number of transportees went up sharply between an inspection in 1846 at Grangegorman when there were only twelve and 1853, when transportation ceased, hundreds of women having been brought to that prison from among the multitudes of victims of the Famine wandering around the interior of the country and forced into petty crime by sheer want.

However, a rare ray of light reflected from those grim days is the story Rena Lohan discovered of the success of the "training and instruction" introduced at Grangegorman well in advance of the general custom of treatment of prisoners in that period. Many "depraved" women are reported to have become so "reformed" (so like their natural selves?) that many were not only appointed "matrons" to look after their fellow prisoners on their voyages from Kingstown to Cork and Cork to Australia, but, in considerably larger numbers, able to obtain paid employment immediately on disembarking in the Antipodes. During the years of the involvement of Kingstown in the transportation process it is noteworthy that the reformers at Grangegorman had become aware that the clothing in which these hapless women were being sent across two oceans was "lamentably defective", and for the final years of the transportation system they were dressed in suitable clothing made by themselves with material supplied by the prison.

Strollers along Dun Laoghaire harbour's piers will have had their imaginations stirred by tales of the funicular railway bringing the granite that made the piers down from Dalkey Hill, of British royalty coming into the harbour accompanied by grim men-of-war, of the latest and most reliable mail and passenger ships of their time coming in with exemplary punctuality day after day under threat of a fine of 3/4d. for each minute late beyond the time scheduled, of some of the world's greatest yachts leaving the harbour for races the results of which were awaited half way round the world, of young Irishmen saying their last good-bye to their native land on the way to the hell of the Western Front in the 1914 war, of the forlorn emigrants from the farthest corners of Ireland stumbling aboard the "mail boat" in the 1950s in the hope of finding gold in English streets: but we should remember those ill-fated Irishwomen leaving for Cork in their "brigs and sloops", with their newly-made garments upon them and a voyage before them that would take months longer and pass through worse perils than a trip to the moon in the 20th century.

But of course there were plenty of other problems besides convicts, storm damage in the new harbour, arguments about the final width of the harbour mouth and about the most suitable type of moorings for the harbour to provide for visiting vessels to test the ingenuity of the tireless William Hutchison and the Board of Works Commissioners of the harbour, who seem to have worked out a reasonable method of sharing control in it despite the very different source of the authority of each. Of these many other problems space forbids a full catalogue, but a few typical specimens follow.

The finances of the harbour proved to be a difficult question from early on. It was built much more cheaply than had been estimated, though various additions such as the Carlisle Pier were quick enough to add considerable sums to the original bill, and the early method of meeting the day-to-day expenses of running the port brought in only twelve seventeenths of the sum expected. How to make up the difference without making nonsense of the reputation that Kingstown harbour quite casually acquired as a "free" because an "asylum" harbour was no easy matter. The difficulty was complicated by the demands from Whitehall, where the accounts of the whole British Empire were cast up. It was intolerable for a port over which the all-powerful British Admiralty had no precise authority but very real influence not to have its accounts in the order that the bureaucrats of Whitehall deemed proper.

One of the consequences of all this was a letter of 25th September 1831 from the City of Dublin Steam Packet Company, already building itself a reputation for safety, efficiency and punctuality, objecting, in measured terms, to the Lords of the Treasury threatening proceedings to obtain dues demanded by Kingstown Harbour from the company's mail steamships "Saint Columba" and "Llewellyn". A further letter from the said Lords, signed by the well known Charles Trevelyan, whose financial policy during the Famine in the next decade was and still is the cause of much controversy, ordered the O.P.W.'s Commissioners to proceed with the proceedings. But the City of Dublin Company proved obstinate, and based its case on the assumption that "Saint Columba" and "Llewellyn" (which had indeed belonged to the British Admiralty, which was shortly to relinquish the duty of carrying H.M. mails across the Irish Sea), were technically the property of Her Majesty, so not liable to pay harbour dues.

This contention went on for years, and must have taken up a good deal of Hutchison's time. Before it was settled at last twenty years later in 1851 two complicating decisions had been made, at Kingstown and in London. At Kingstown on 21 September 1836 the Harbour Commissioners announced that it was "but reasonable" that a charge of five shillings should be made on every vessel discharging or taking on passengers in the new port – but they exempted H.M. Mail Packets from such charges. Regular passenger ships visiting might ultimately compound for a regular rate. Hutchison was requested to record the name of every visiting passenger ship and of the company owning it.

Then not long after the accession of Queen Victoria in England (1837) a lengthy questionnaire was sent by "Victoria by the Grace of God of the United Kingdom of Britain and Ireland Queen", etc., to three individuals, one of them a senior naval officer, to enquire extensively and in exact detail about the charges demanded from shipping in every port in the British Isles, as well as the Channel Islands and in other imperial possessions.

There seem to have been very considerable differences between the Queen's Commissioners and the Asylum Harbour of Kingstown, and perusal of a series of coldly polite letters leaves the impression that the Shipping Dues Commission Office, 15 Parliament Street, London, by no means always got the better of the Commissioners of the Royal Asylum Harbour here.

Meanwhile, on 6th April 1851 a letter of the Commissioners' secretary to Trevelyan about the apparently interminable problem of the City of Dublin

Company's refusal to pay dues on its mail steamers complained that a full report on the subject sent months before had not been answered. In this letter counsel had assured Kingstown Commissioners that the now ageing "Saint Columba" and "Llewellyn" were still the property of H.M. (that is the Admiralty). Trevelyan seems to have acted quickly this time and in favour of the Kingstown Commissioners, for on 20th April 1851 the City of Dublin Company wrote to them saying that they would pay dues to them if told how much. The sum due was £194. 10s. and on 11 October 1851 the Commissioners demanded £21. 15s. at once on account, and this was the beginning of the end of this particular difference between the port and the most famous company using it. The City of Dublin Company let its debt go up to £216. 15s. before a definitive opinion of the Law Officers of the Crown of England was finally accepted by it, laying it down that the "Saint Columba" could not be regarded as H.M.'s property and therefore free of dues.

In 1853 London demanded to know the gross amount levied on shipping at Kingstown the previous year under the headings Tonnage Dues, Quay Wall Dues, Duty on Timber and Duty on Heavy Goods, and there followed a long correspondence on the differential duties applied to foreign shipping, under what Acts certain charges had been made, and so on. If the Kingstown Commissioners answered the direct question asked there is no copy of their answer in the relevant O.P.W. file in the National Archives, but perhaps it is evidence that the difference between Kingstown and London had at least been toned down that a letter from London dated 7th March 1855 requesting the figures for aggregate dues levied at Kingstown Harbour in 1854 was answered on the 12th of the same month, tonnage, ballast, quayage dues and all others in detail. The total came to £1189. 13s. 10d.*

An interesting sequel to the Asylum Harbour's battle between the 1830s and the 1850s over dues it could charge was the imposition (unchallenged) of a charge of 1/- from 1861 on tugs landing passengers from Dublin at Kingstown, a practice that had recently become and long remained common, as will be shown in a later section.

MR. BARRY GIBBONS ON THE DAMAGE CAUSED BY THE E.S.E. GALE
OF THE 1ST AND 2ND NOV., 1844
KINGSTOWN HARBOUR, 4TH NOV., 1844

SIR,

I beg leave to submit to the Commissioners the following statement of the effects on the works here of the late storms, which, for extreme violence

*In contrast in 1998 the port's income was from ships entries £1.5 milion, cargo dues £4.6 million, yacht moorings £1.01 million, total £6.2 million (which excludes income from rents and properties).

and duration, have rarely, if ever, been equalled since the harbour was commenced.

I am happy to say that the piling and timber framing, and all the stone work connected therewith, at the West pier-head, have effectually stood this severe trial, although the sea broke most tremendously over it. There has been little or no injury done, and there will be no interruption to the progress of the work as soon as the weather moderates. A large portion of the rubble slope north of the framing has, however, been drawn down, and, in order to secure the temporary light-house, and prevent any further extension of this travelling, it will be necessary to face it with a rubble wall for its protection till the work of the circular head has progressed sufficiently to enable us to commence the sea-pavement.

At the east pier-head the rough dressed pavement immediately adjoining the circular head has not been in the least disturbed, except at the raking of the work, where the last two courses, as may be expected, have been displaced; but I regret to say, that the whole of the rough pavement which we have been setting during the last three months has been carried away. This has been chiefly occasioned by its not being connected with the other parts, which there was not time to effect; and when a mass of rubble which protected this was swept away, the rake of the work became exposed. The amount of the damage done is about 140*l.*, besides the loss to the contractors of their two cranes. Along the eastern pier, the rough mound of rubble placed there to strengthen the toe of the slope, has, in a few places, been carried out and down to the plane of the sea-pavement, and directly opposite where this occurs the temporary rough parapet is thrown down, and a small breach made; the tramway on the top of the level has been disturbed in several places, and the footpath along the pier turned up by the fall of the sea, and the small rubble scattered over the surface. I expect to have these damages put to rights again at no very material expense. There has been no additional breach of any importance made in the sea-pavement along the pier, as far as I could examine, with the rough sea and neap tides now.

I have, &c.,
BARRY D. GIBBONS
TO HENRY R. PAINE, ESQ., &C., &C.

8TH NOVEMBER, 1844
SIR J. DOMBRAIN,
COAST GUARD OFFICE

SIR,

I have the honour to send herewith a requisition from the Commander of H.M. Cruizer Kite, for payment of sums appended to their names to the officers and men who were engaged in assisting the Barque "Kingston" and the Brigs "William and Isabella" and "Capricorn", during the gale of second November (1844) instant, in Kingstown Harbour. The board request your opinion on these charges, as they will be made against the vessels.

The Harbour Master reports that the "Kite's" officers and men rendered him valuable assistance and the comments are quite of the opinion that they should receive some compensation.

I am, &c.,
HENRY R. PAINE,
HARBOUR SECRETARY

FROM WILLIAM HUTCHISON,
HARBOUR MASTER
KINGSTOWN, 14TH NOVEMBER, 1844

SIR,

I beg leave to answer the interrogatories of the Commissioners in as explicit a manner as is in my power:-

First – The number and class of vessels in the harbour when the gale came on: There was in the harbour on the morning of the first inst., before the gale assumed the violence it did that evening, and on the second inst., the following vessels:– the "Stromboli", war steamer, "Lucifer", surveying steamer, "Shamrock", "Kite", and "Racer", revenue cruisers, two brigs, twenty seven schooners, twelve sloops, and a number of trawlers.

Second – The order in which the vessels that subsequently arrived came in, and what happened to each?

On the 1st inst. p.m., put in by stress of weather, one full-rigged sailing ship, one barque, one brig, five schooners, and two sloops. On the 2nd inst., one ship, six brigs, and one schooner, of which one barque and two brigs parted their chains, and drove against the west pier, and were lifted by the sea and carried along until they took the ground in the entrance of the old harbour.

Third – Of the vessels which went ashore or were injured, whether the accident in each case was inevitable, arising from certain disadvantages of the harbour, or intirely or partly from want of proper anchors and cables, or mismanagement, or want of, sufficient crew or means on board, considering these not with reference to the equipment of a man-of-war, but what is usually to be expected in a merchantman of this class.

The barque "Kingston", of two hundred and eighty two tons, from Liverpool to Africa, with cargo of salt and casks, drawing thirteen feet water, parted before daylight on the 2nd inst., had top-gallant masts up, the master states he had seventy five fathoms of chain on one anchor; and fifty on the other; she was anchored too far to leeward, and not in shelter of the east pier; her sails were clewed up as she came round the pier head, she could not therefore reach a weatherly berth; this vessel was well found and manned.

The brig "William and Isabella", from Archangel to Gloucester, with cargo of deals, drawing twelve feet, parted early on the morning of the 2nd inst., and drifted in and across the bows of the barque; her top gallant yards were aloft; had a very inactive master and crew; was well found.

The brig "Capricorn", of two hundred and forty tons, from St. Domingo to Liverpool, with cargo of mahogany, drawing fifteen feet, arrived from sea at two p.m. on the 2nd inst., in the worst of the gale, and clewed up her sails too soon; I hastened to her assistance, and also a boat from the "Shamrock"; she brought up with two anchors, but shortly after drove, in consequence of the stock of one of them having broke; she then again held on, and about four p.m. parted her chain. I had directed the mate of the "Shamrock" to strike her yards and masts, and then hastened to other duty. She drove on shore with top-gallant masts up; her crew were one-half disabled from fever and fatigue on the home voyage.

The schooner "Hercules", of eighty four tons, coal laden, parted chains and run in and bilged against the west quay at six p.m.

The schooner "Commerce", of fifty tons, coal laden, parted chains and run in, grounded and bilged at about eight p.m.

Several small schooners and sloops either slipped or parted, and run in the morning for the shelter of the old quay; from their light draft of water they succeeded in securing to the quay, but the swell caused all the colliers and them to receive much injury from beating on the ground and against each other; one sloop laden with oats sunk.

The origin of these wrecks is to be ascribed to several causes – the unsheltered anchorage of one half of this harbour, open to easterly winds and swell, the liability of chain cables to snap in a rough sea or swell, if not manufactured of the very best iron, as they were by the patentees in the first instance; they are now a general manufacture, and no dependence can be placed in them, for many are not much better than cast iron; the same applies to anchors, which repeatedly break in this harbour in gales of wind; and, lastly, to the utter indifference and aversion masters and crews of merchant-vessels have to strike masts and yards, the vessel being insured; nothing, I do believe, but fear of loss of life, will make them reduce top weight, or cut away the masts, when either one or the other course would preserve hundreds of vessels from a lee-shore by easing the strain on their ground tacklings.

Fourth – Whether any loss of life occured, or what injuries were sustained by the men on board, or those giving aid?

No loss of life occurred during the gale; the mate of "Kingston" had his hand crushed by the falling of "Capricorn's" mast.

Fifth – Which of the vessels have been entirely lost, or must be broken up? and which is likely may be repaired, and generally what cargoes are lost or damaged?

The "Kingston", having taken fire on the night she was stranded, is the most injured – almost a total wreck; she will be sold as she now lies for the benefit of the underwriters; her cargo salt and casks, the former destroyed. [It was on helping aboard "Kingston" that Hutchison was injured].

The brigs "William and Isabella" and "Capricorn" were dismasted, and much battered; the first has been, and the other will be, floated to Dublin for repair.

The schooners "Commerce" and "Hercules", on the removal of cargoes, will be repaired; they are not insured.

Sixth – How Mr. Hutchison and his men were engaged? and what means of hawsers or stores were employed? and what has been the consumption of them?

During the 1st inst., myself and boat's crew were employed berthing the vessels as they arrived, and directing them to make their vessels secure. At daylight on the 2nd I was called to the Old Harbour to the wrecks; I immediately procured drays, and was backwards and forwards hastening my men to load the hawsers; as they arrived they were run out by the yawls I had hired; my boat, if brought down, would have swamped. A six-inch was run to the sloop "Busy", of forty seven tons, laden with grain, and beating against the west quay: she was preserved from sinking, and got over to the coal quay. A seven-inch was run out to the brig "William and Isabella", on board which vessel I went myself with my men; she was across the bows of a barque, grinding and surging with every sea; she was hove clear; but being a-ground, could not be got (until the tide should rise) over the Old Pier; her masts went by the board, her bowsprit having been carried away against the wall; by this time the "Kite's" men had come; with their assistance the large nine-inch hawser was got on board the barque from Pier Head, and her side hove clear of wall, and secured with another hawser. At the time all this was effected it was one o'clock, when myself and crew went to breakfast, and put on dry clothes. At two p.m. I went out in my boat to assist the brig "Capricorn", the sea and wind then raging in the harbour, could barely be stemmed, and on our return to the shore the water was over our ankles; I then again went to Old Harbour, it being high water, and found that the hawser to "William and Isabella" had broke, and she had drifted towards the west quay, and the end of same had also broke from the schooner "Commerce", the rope was a good one, but when vessels are on the ground, the rolling motion caused by swells stretches the rope, and if she does not draw ahead it will burst. I had no other hawsers to run to these vessels. At this time the "Kingston" was comparatively safe, when the brig "Capricorn", between three and four, drifted in and on board her. I hailed the brig to cut away her masts to arrest her drifting along the wall, but there was no person at all active on board; and when they were cut away, she had come in collision with the "Kingston", rendering all further efforts to save either fruitless. When informed of fire on board the barque, eleven p.m., I attended with fire-buckets, and those of my men I could get; but the report of gunpowder being on board prevented any exertion, and the police would not allow any man to go on board.

All hawsers used are much injured, and rendered useless for harbour purposes.

Seventh – What boats and men he engaged extra, and on what terms? I had two yawls and crews to get the hawsers on board, the crews of the vessels gave but little assistance when wrecked; and as a few active seamen are of great value at such a time, I requested the mate of the "Kite", cutter, to come down to carry into effect my directions.

The terms demanded were half-a-guinea per man, and I agreed with them for seven-and-sixpence each.

I have, &c.,
WM. HUTCHISON,
HARBOUR MASTER, LIEUT. R.N.

TO HENRY R. PAINE, ESQ., &C., &C.

The above letter gives a dramatic idea of the skills required and the perils faced by the harbour master of a busy port in gale force conditions in the days of sail. On another occasion when a ship caught fire in bad weather in the Coal Harbour, Hutchison lost an eye while leading the fire-fighting. Commerce with St. Domingo was fairly common in the Kingstown of the 1840s and only fairly recently Dun Laoghaire Lifeboat Station was in correspondence with that

DESTRUCTION OF THE KINGSTON BY FIRE.

At eleven o'clock on Saturday night an alarm of fire was was given on board the Kingston, and immediately Lieut. Hutchinson, R.N., harbour master, and some members of the coast guard, police, &c., were on the spot. An opinion generally prevailed that there was a great quantity of gunpowder on board, and this naturally had the effect of preventing the necessary exertions to extinguish the fire. The consequence was, that the devouring element got head. it burned during the entire night, and yesterday the vessel appeared completely consumed to the water's edge. The Capricorn, which lay near, had the side next the fire considerably injured—the burning mast and rigging of the Kingsston fell across her deck, set fire to every thing with which they came in contact, and were it not for the timely assistance afforded, she would, no doubt, have shared the fate of the other. Opinion is contradictory as regards the origin of the fire; however, the prevailing supposition is that some persons contrived to get on board with dishonest intentions, and that having made rather too free with rum, of which there was a large quantity in the vessel, the fire took place by accident. This idea is strengthened by the fact that a boy, in a deep state of inebriation, was found concealed between the rocks where the brig lay. The Kingston was the property of Hossfell and Co., of Liverpool, but we have not been able to ascertain if the vessel or cargo were insured.

Exerpt from the *Freeman's Journal*, November 4, 1844
regarding fire on board the "Kingston"

country's embassy in London concerning a legal case over there arising from an incident to a ship from there in Dun Laoghaire nearly a century and a half ago. Hutchison's report shows what a busy commercial port Kingstown was in the 1840s and what a variety of vessels it served.

LIEUT. HUTCHISON, R.N., ON THE NECESSITY OF
ADDITIONAL MEANS OF SHELTER FOR SHIPPING
KINGSTOWN, 14TH NOVEMBER, 1844

SIR,

In reply to the second part of the Commissioners' letter of the 6th inst., as to any additional means that could be provided that might tend to lessen the injuries which occur to shipping in the harbour during occasional gales from the east, excluding for the present any proposition for additional jetties or breakwaters:-

First – Whether the harbour boats are in number and quantity sufficient, assuming that Mr. Hutchison has authority to hire in cases of emergency whatever he may require?

The most important prevention to wrecks during gales from the east, when driven by stress of weather to bear up for Kingstown, in my opinion, is the invaluable assistance of a sensible pilot, to keep sail on the vessel to bring her to an inside and sheltered berth. The pilot cutters do remain out in the bay at times when there is imminent risk in boarding, and if a proper encouragement were given, would be more on the alert during easterly gales; but, as they are only entitled to the smallest rate (1s. per foot only) for boarding vessels in the bay, in fine weather as in a storm, it is not surprising they come in when they are most required. I would, therefore, beg to suggest that the most active of these men should be hired at pilots' wages, 5s. per day, to assist me to meet the vessels at Pier Head as they round it, and assist to clew up sails and bring them to an anchor in proper situations, and to veer the requisite scope of cable. Another six-oared boat would be required for this special purpose. [Hutchinson's proposals were largely found to cost too much.]

Second – Whether any moorings could be laid down usefully on the west side of the harbour, or in front of the entrance of Old Harbour, which vessels driving, or having parted, would have a possibility of catching, and which at the time would present no inconvenience to the anchorage or entrance at other times?

In the instance of the late convict hulk "Essex", formerly moored in the angle of the east pier, by one hundred and forty fathoms of heavy long-linked chain, I have known many vessels, driving with their anchors, to have been preserved from going against the pier by the anchor hooking the chain. On the same principle a chain stretched across from north to south, at a proper distance from the entrance of Old Harbour, would, if the vessel's cables had not parted, give her a fair chance of preservation from going ashore; but then it is to be considered, that if the vessel is of large draught of water, she would strike with heavy swell at low water, and become leaky. Her sinking in such a situation, and removal to the very beach she would have drifted on, would cause a great outlay, as well as the destruction of her cargo. If moorings were placed further out in the harbour, vessels would hook them continually. Of the two, I should prefer the extended chain, as it would present no inconvenience.

Third – Whether any additional anchors, cables, hawsers, or other disposable stores would be desirable, or capsterns, mooring posts, &c.?

From the frequency of large vessels being stranded, and smaller vessels driven in during easterly gales, at the Old Harbour, there is a demand for the use of hawsers, chains, and fenders, and a capstern on Pier Head. I consider a store should be built on the same spot for those articles, in which store four hawsers, sixty fathoms long; six pieces of chain, thirty fathoms long, of different sizes, to secure vessels, and twelve elm fenders and capstern bars would be kept; also three or four stout posts on the West Pier, with pieces of chain, to arrest a vessel until hawsers and anchors could be brought to heave them from the wall, would, on occasions, be found most useful. These articles would last many years with care, and safe from depredation.

Fourth – Whether good boats and men are always to be hired on such occasions without delay?

The fishing skiff or yawl answers the purpose very well of laying out a line to which the end of a hawser is attached and hauled on board; but in hiring the aid of the crews of these boats, you cannot select a crew, but must take the usual fishing crew attached to the boat, and they rate their services at half-a-guinea to a guinea a man, which, in some cases, where real good service is rendered, is not unreasonable; but, on other occasions, exorbitant. Their demand before launching boat is, "What are we to get?" and should their effort be fruitless, the sum is still rigidly exacted. These men are not seamen, and the extent of their assistance is running out a hawser and assisting to heave at the windlass. To furl sails, strike yards and masts, they are quite incompetent: and when real active exertion is necessary, one able seaman is worth a score of them. During the late gale these boatmen exacted great value for their exertions, as every small vessel which run in required a rope to be run to the pier. To my knowledge one yawl's crew made 2 1/2d. a man on the 2nd inst. There were many employed in the same way.

Fifth – Whether the charges for hawsers and assistance are unreasonable or unusual, or indeed, more than the actual cost for wear and tear?

The printed regulation of charges for use of hawsers, anchors, and assistance, are very moderate, and not more than sufficient to defray the wear and tear of same. No owner or master of a ship could expect the use of those things gratis, without they paid port charges; but I think a distinction should be made where they do, to Kingstown Harbour.

I take this opportunity of calling the attention of the Commissioners to the urgent necessity of accommodation for my boat's crew. Living, as I do, at the harbour, I am frequently called up at night to send assistance to vessels adrift or driving; before I can get a boat's crew together, the vessel might sink or be burned. The price per week of dirty cabins or lodgings, if to be obtained near the harbour, is exorbitant. It would require as many messengers to assemble six men in any reasonable time.

I am, &c.,
WM. HUTCHISON.

HARBOUR MASTER, LIEUT. R.N.
HENRY R. PAINE, ESQ., &C. &C.

[The risk run by the "hobblers," self-appointed "pilots" in Scotsman's Bay – a few of whose cottages still survive at Bullock Harbour – and their miserable pay are legendary still in the Sandycove, Glasthule and Bullock areas.]

Correspondence relative to the necessity of Screw Moorings in Kingstown Harbour.

TO THE COMMISSIONERS OF PUBLIC WORKS,
DUBLIN,
22ND NOVEMBER, 1844

GENTLEMEN,

Much inconvenience and loss having occurred at various times to vessels frequenting Kingstown Harbour, occasioned by their anchors hooking the moorings which are at present laid down there, of which numerous instances can be adduced, in most cases attended with loss of anchors, we the undersigned, respectfully beg leave to suggest that these should be removed, and the patent screw moorings substituted, the efficacy of which has been already full tested in other ports.

Under judicious arrangements, there are few places where such could be made more serviceable than in Kingstown Harbour: the number of which ships anchoring there have greatly broken the ground, and rendered it not so good for holding as formerly, which the recent disasters there fully proves, some of which might possibly have been averted had buoys with this description of mooring been within the vessels' reach.

We are, &c.,
HENRY H. MILLS, Duke of Cornwall
J. HIRSTE, Jupiter Steamer
MICHAEL MCKINNON, Vanguard Steam Ship
WILLIAM STOKES, Eagle Steam Packet
JOHN HYDE, Shamrock Steam Packet
JOHN JONES, Duke of Kent Steam Packet
ISAAC DAVIES, Ballinasloe Steamer
JAMES R. CHRISTIE, Commander of the Birmingham
ROBERT KEMPSTER, Shannon Steam Ship
W. SWAINSON, Royal William
A. CHURCH, Queen Victoria
WILLIAM WILLIAMS, Master of the Duke of Cambridge
W. MCGRALTO, Master of the Brittannia Steamer

ROBERT WILLIAMS, Master of the Nottingham
WILLIAM LANE HOOKER, Master of the Ship Indian Queen
ARTHUR H. KEMP, Master of the Brigantine Emma

"JUPITER" STEAM SHIP,
DUBLIN,
9TH JANUARY, 1845

SIR,

I beg to enclose a Memorial to the Commissioners of Public Works, signed by the masters of steam vessels trading to this port, and which they trust you will lay before the Commissioners at your earliest convenience.

May I also take the liberty of remarking, that the steam company and ship owners generally agree on the subject of the Memorial, and will, if necessary, call the attention of the Commissioners to the unsafe state of Kingstown Harbour.

I am, &c.,
J. HIRSTE

KINGSTOWN, 17TH JANUARY, 1845

SIR,

I beg to report on the statement of the commanders of the Dublin Steamers and other vessels, and although I respect the opinions of such experienced seamen, I regret to differ, and cannot coincide in all they recommend.

First – The inconvenience of the present moorings in hooking anchors is very often the case, but I have never known an anchor to be lost, as stated; on application they are always recovered, the parties paying the regulated price for clearing same.

That those moorings occupy part of the best anchorage of the harbour is the fact; and if the outer line, or revenue moorings, were placed from the southernmost packet buoy, in a line to the east pier head, they might be found useful to merchant vessels in gales of wind; anchors would hook the chains, but that I consider an advantage, and the buoys might be occasionally struck by steamers in dark nights. The Frigates' Moorings, which is a large chain extending one hundred and forty fathoms, might be laid down in a north-eastern and south-western line to intercept vessels driving with east and south-east gales, towards the old harbour, and three large buoys should be secured by a large chain at thirty fathoms apart to secure a driving vessel at.

Second – Mitchell's Patent Screw Mooring has been tested in this harbour, and one of two has broken, by very moderate strain, at the shank, leaving the screw in the bottom; and even supposing them to stand a jerking strain, and a number of them laid down, I do think it would be no easy matter to secure ships to them, when adrift, in such a disturbed sea as is presented in this harbour, in two-thirds of its space, with a violent easterly gale; but I do not say, they would not be useful on solitary occasions.

Third – The free anchorage afforded at Kingstown brings more vessels into it than need enter; vessels from Belfast, Glasgow, and Liverpool, that put in wind-bound, should pay a small charge to keep up two good boats and crews to assist them in and out; and half the vessels that anchor here to wait tide a few hours, should also pay, for they could on most occasions anchor or lay to in the bay. The bottom will be injured by the unnecessary influx of vessels. At present, the holding ground is good, and vessels more frequently part their chains than drive with their anchors.

I am, &c.,
WILLIAM HUTCHISON, HARBOUR MASTER, R.N.
HENRY R. PAINE, ESQ.,
&C., &C.

OFFICE OF PUBLIC WORKS
21ST JANUARY, 1845

SIR,

The Commissioners have received your letter of the 9th instant, which transmitted a memorial from many commanders of steam-vessels, trading to the port of Dublin, and which suggests the substitution of patent screw moorings for those now used in Kingstown Harbour; and have directed me to inform you, that their representation was immediately referred to the Harbour-master, who, while he declares his respect for the opinion of so many experienced seamen, cannot coincide with them in many of their propositions.

SECRETARY,
THE COMMISSIONERS OF PUBLIC WORKS, DUBLIN

While all these letters and memorials were going to and fro the harbour was becoming very busy – busy enough to warrant the building of another pier.

# 7
# CARLISLE PIER

How I'd dance like a fairy
To see ould Dunleary
And think twice ere I'd leave it to be a dragoon.

CHARLES LEVER

Dubliner Charles Lever studied at Dublin University, (Trinity College) and became a doctor in Belgium, but gave up medicine for writing and wrote a series of novels, such as *Tom Burke of "Ours"* and *Charles O'Malley*, about Irishmen who in order to earn a meagre living left home generation after generation to serve in the armies of France, Britain and other states. These books made a great impression on successive generations of young people here, not least the author of this book. Lever went to Trieste, where he died in 1872 always homesick for Ireland. There by sheer chance, in December 1972, I found myself at the dedication of a monument to his memory by the local Historical Society, the president of which was an officer in the Italian merchant navy. Lever had watched the early stages of the construction of our harbour, and had left Ireland from it. He spent many years in handsome Trieste – as British Consul – forerunner of a more celebrated writer, James Joyce, and was extremely popular.

THE COMPLETION OF THE PIERS, landing-stage, lighthouses and Traders' Wharf left Kingstown ready for a busy and in many ways really "epoch making" decade of activities. It was in 1848 that the railway link between London and Holyhead was completed, leading to the introduction on the line of the world's first named train, the famous "Irish Mail", out of Euston Station at 8.45p.m. each night.

And it was in 1848 that the already celebrated City of Dublin Steam Packet Company, which had been operating out of Kingstown for fourteen years, decided to use Holyhead instead of Liverpool for its British terminal. On July 31st 1848 three new steamers arrived at Holyhead, the "Banshee" and "Llewellyn" belonging to the Admiralty which had in the previous decade taken over from the Post Office the carriage of mail across the Irish Sea, and the "Cambria" belonging to the Chester and Holyhead Railway Company. "Banshee" was a six hundred and seventy two ton steamer built at Rotherhithe, London, the year before, "Llewellyn" of six hundred and seventy one tons had been built at Blackwall, also in London, and "Cambria", a little larger, had been built at Birkenhead, also in

1847. The first and last named had iron hulls, "Llewellyn" was wooden. The famous "Lightning" which had brought George IV to Dunleary only twenty-seven years before had been a wooden ship of only two hundred and five tons. She was one hundred and two feet long compared with "Llewellyn's" two hundred and forty feet and she was also much slower. The two Admiralty ships had been known on occasion to reach sixteen knots, while "Lightning" barely made twelve knots. All these vessels were paddle-wheelers.

The three arrivals on July 31st 1848 had come to take passengers off the London train and their arrival opened a hectic period of nearly two years during which the Admiralty and the Post Office, knowing that the state owned ships had won themselves a poor reputation with the public, decided to put out the carriage of mail on contract to private firms. The Chester and Holyhead Railway Company expected to win the mail contract, but was undercut by the City of Dublin Company, which obtained from the Admiralty "Llewellyn" and "Banshee" and had built a new six hundred and fifty three ton iron steamer "Eblana", which came into service in 1849.

The arrival of many more passengers from various parts of Britain now that it was possible to reach Holyhead by rail, and the improved service offered by the City of Dublin Company, which was to continue to hold the coveted mail contract for seventy years in spite of fierce and well backed railway company competition (for a time railway owned steamers continued to use Kingstown, then switched to Dublin's North Wall, but reverted to Kingstown in 1908) meant that the Royal Asylum Harbour of Kingstown, built as a refuge for sailing ships in rough weather, was finding itself more and more operating primarily as a port for passengers and mail in some of the fastest steamers of the time.

The growing importance of the "mail boats" (as the Kingstown–Holyhead passengers ferries came soon to be, and today, inaccurately, still are called) became clearer still when at the end of the next decade the City of Dublin Company prepared to introduce four new far larger and faster ships into their service, which would bring a great many more people, some more freight and a series of new problems to Kingstown.

Hutchison, who had been presiding over a situation not only rapidly changing from the point of view of increasing passenger traffic but also one where the earlier development of overseas sailing ship traffic was tailing off but being more than compensated by increasing short-sea traffic, was now able to put a very strong case to the Board of Works Commissioners for the construction of a far more satisfactory area for dealing with incoming and outgoing passengers than Victoria, now St. Michael's, Wharf had proved to be. Indeed when the British monarch had come to Kingstown in 1849 the disadvantages of the Wharf had been highlighted. As Hutchison, Rennie and other clear headed professionals had continuously pointed out, the harbour entrance seven hundred and sixty feet wide, without the turned in pier ends planned by Rennie Senior, or Cubitt's outside mole, would always allow a serious swell to surge into the new harbour when strong winds blew between north and north-east.

The consequence of the poor reputation of Victoria Wharf, with passengers and horses discommoded embarking and disembarking to and from a vesssel unsteadied by the incoming swell, and of the prospect of the arrival of larger ships with more passengers, was the decision to build a new pier, soon to be called Carlisle Pier after the dignitary who inaugurated it, parallel to and in the vicinity of the inner length of the East Pier. Here for the next one hundred and thirty six years the great majority of passengers using the port would join or leave their ship.

Back in 1834 Ireland's first railway had come into operation, from Westland Row station in Dublin to Old Dunleary; it was not continued to where the present very impressive Dun Laoghaire railway station was eventually opened until 1837, owing to the need to haggle with the owner of the intervening territory over compensation for its use.

The railway was built across the neck of the creek at Old Dunleary, seriously diminishing the size of the inner basin near the base of the West Pier. Presumably it was considered cheaper to lay it that way, and Dargan, the engineer who designed the Dublin to Kingstown railway, later extended to Bray and of course beyond, was one of the greatest of Europe's pioneer railway engineers. The diminution of the harbour in that area behind the "Dry Pier" was nevertheless a pity.

The opening of the railway (which was opposed by a number of local businessmen who thought a new main road and increased traffic across the Bay would be sufficient link between the emerging new town and the capital) brought many people from Dublin to see the new harbour under construction. There is a fascinating letter in the French national library in the huge collection of documents belonging to and concerning Admiral Armand de Mackau describing a railway journey to Kingstown in 1837. This fine seaman, who was educated at the famous Irish College in Paris, a McCoy from Co. Galway by origin, was shortly to become France's Minister of Marine, and in the opinion of leading maritime historians like Professor Mollat du Jourdin of the Sorbonne, the best such Minister that France had in the 19th century. In his letter to his wife about his journey he mentions (without comment) that the ticket cost him 8/-, which seems very dear, nearly five times what one of the workers building the harbour would have earned that day. He spoke excellent English so he could well have argued the point at the ticket office and one wonders if one of the Lord Lieutenant's officials assigned to look after the Admiral was on the make.

In due course after the completion of Carlisle Pier a short branch from the railway was built to it, so, as older travellers from Holyhead making for Dublin will remember, however unpleasant the sea-crossing may have been the disembarking passenger had at least the comfort of being able to walk straight from the ship to the train alongside. This ship to rail link has been restored, now the new passenger terminal is in operation, though the walking distance is now considerably greater.

Throughout the period when Hutchison was Harbour Master the town of Dun Laoghaire was rapidly growing out of the insignificant hamlet it had been. A number of well-built houses and shops on quite pleasant streets, a few attractive buildings, just a few really elegant ones, and a fine sea front looking across the once death-dealing but now partially reformed Dublin Bay, this, with its one big hotel and a couple of smaller ones and numerous boarding houses was the Kingstown that the grandparents of my generation knew and where many of them came, one, occasionally, by way of its eye-catching station or off "trip" steamers like the "Dodder", to enjoy themselves. The Kingstown climate was supposed to promote long life and the proportion of the population over the age of forty-five rose steadily. All this was a direct consequence of the construction of the beautiful asylum harbour and the trade and employment that it generated. If in Hutchison's day the sightly Pavilion, recently boorishly demolished had not yet been built and the new town lacked certain amenities that others had, those splendid granite piers reaching out towards Howth, the activities always going on between them, the excitement on the arrival and departure of the regular "mail boats" and sometimes the visit of an unusual looking merchant ship, a warship or a stately yacht made up for anything lacking and gave the town a unique attraction that it must never be allowed to lose.

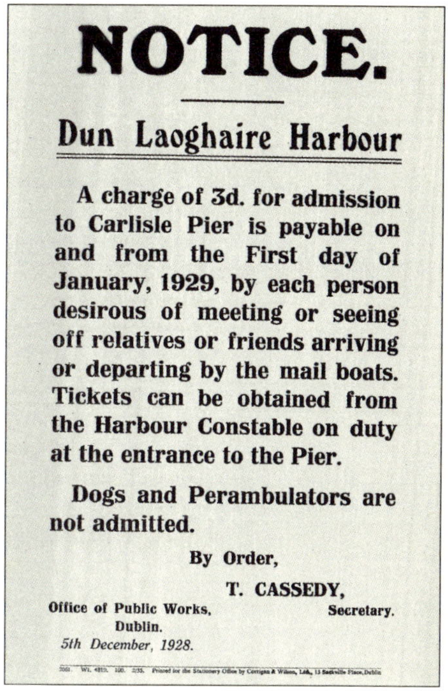
NOTICE.

Dun Laoghaire Harbour

A charge of 3d. for admission to Carlisle Pier is payable on and from the First day of January, 1929, by each person desirous of meeting or seeing off relatives or friends arriving or departing by the mail boats. Tickets can be obtained from the Harbour Constable on duty at the entrance to the Pier.

Dogs and Perambulators are not admitted.

By Order,
T. CASSEDY,
Secretary.

Office of Public Works,
Dublin.
*5th December, 1928.*

There was of course a less agreeable side to the very speedy growth of a new town where before all had been wilderness which should not be disregarded. Mary Daly in her valuable book *Dublin: the Deposed Capital* brings it out well, writing "The building of the harbour was regarded by one local developer, John McEvoy, as 'not an unmixed blessing' because it attracted many unskilled labourers to the area. Squalid cramped houses emerged convenient to the harbour while the building of the railway attracted labourers. The employment by both port and railway was inadequate for the labouring population". This passage refers chiefly to the 1870s and 1880s, but even today more than a century later Dun Laoghaire has not eliminated unemployment or bad housing – one of many reasons why the continuous development of the harbour is imperative to ensure a satisfactory life for the town's inhabitants.

# 8
# DEVELOPMENT OF THE PASSENGER PORT

"Know that we fools, now with the foolish dead,
Died not for the flag, nor King, nor Emperor –
But for a dream, born in a herdsman's shed,
And for the secret scripture of the poor".

TOM KETTLE

Inevitably, thinking of the hundreds of thousands of passengers who have left Dun Laoghaire to cross the Irish Sea – and, the vast majority of them, safely arrived on the other side, the mind turns to the dauntingly large numbers of them who were destined never to return, taking with them as a last memory of home the harbour of Dun Laoghaire, the Hill of Howth and Dalkey Island. Sad, and often dismal as was the fate of the swarms of emigrants who left our harbour to seek a livelihood that their own country could not give them, bitterer still must be the memory of the thousands of Irishmen who sailed off to meet death in some foreign field in one of Britain's numerous wars. There is much verse, some of it very fine, about the desolation of emigration, but I have chosen Tom Kettle's famous lines because they have immortalised the utter futility of the waste of so many lives full of stirring promise, destroyed in the butcheries engineered by the so-called statesmen of the "great" powers. Tom Kettle would surely have had a notably constructive influence in the Ireland of the 1920s and 1930s had he lived. He had already achieved much; and sadly, his sacrifice, for all his idealism, did nothing to help promote the rightful aims of the poor.

THERE WAS NO MAJOR EXTENSION OF FACILITIES for passenger ships coming into Dun Laoghaire (as it became) until 1965. Then British Rail (distant successor to the Chester and Holyhead railway) had two ships in regular service, "Cambria" and "Hibernia", traditional names on the route, which had limited facilities for carriage of cars, the proliferation of which in these islands was now in full swing. The cars were discharged by crane.

Car owners were not content with the craning of their vehicles and British Rail, foreseeing a big increase in the number of passengers wishing to bring their cars, ordered the building of the first Holyhead–Dun Laoghaire car ferry. This was given the clumsy name "Holyhead Ferry 1", which was not yet ready when the service was scheduled to start in July, so the British Rail English Channel car ferry

"Normandia" substituted briefly for her.

Advised that a car-ferry service was coming, the Board of Works erected a temporary car-ferry terminal near the base of the East Pier. This unlovely structure was extremely unpopular, and the Board of Works eventually had to listen to public opinion. A new pier was constructed out from Saint Michael's Wharf when a second car ferry came into regular service, which meant the demolition of the attractive Sailors' Rest, housing Ireland's new National Maritime Museum since 1959, and a group of pleasant harbour constables' houses. In 1974 construction was undertaken of a new ramp to cater for the wider third generation ferries being built, on the west side of Carlisle Pier, linked to a vehicle marshalling area between the recently built and never very satisfactory Saint Michael's Pier and the fine building of the Royal Irish Yacht Club. A new lorry, car and foot-passenger multipurpose ferry "St. Columba" was introduced in 1977; the last of the foot-passenger only "mailboats", the one-time craner of disembarking cars, was phased out in the autumn of 1976.

"St. Columba", the first of the multipurpose ferries, soon joined by "Stena Cambria", ex-"St. Anselm", displaced the earlier car ferries. The "St. Columba" was a vessel of seven thousand, eight hundred and thirty six gross tons, one hundred and twenty nine point two metres long, and capable of a speed of nineteen point five knots. "Stena Cambria", originally "St. Anselm", was slightly smaller – seven thousand, four hundred and five tons, carrying a maximum of one thousand, four hundred passengers. Both vessels were superceded by the large, H.S.S. "Stena Explorer" catamaran in 1996; this catamaran having a service speed of forty knots which enabled it to complete five round trips per day as opposed to two trips a day for each of the other two vessels.

The decision of Stena Sealink, [from 1996 Stena Line – part of the multi-million Swedish all-North European waters short-sea passenger carrier] which had succeeded railway owned Sealink, to introduce high-speed catamarans to supplement and no doubt eventually take over the Dun Laoghaire–Holyhead passenger and vehicle ferry service, made it evident that the Carlisle Pier passenger terminal had had its day.

The Department of the Marine, with its dynamic first secretary, already mentioned, Fionán Ó Muircheartaigh, which took over the port from the OPW in 1989, established an Interim Harbour Board. This Board, after a series of public conferences and discussions, advised the Department to undertake a complete modernisation of the port's facilities. The major part of the first stage of this huge reconstruction, which one would like to think would be approved and encouraged by the shades of those doughty champions of the original construction work on the Asylum Harbour of Dunleary/Kingstown, Captains Toutcher and Hutchison, the two Rennies and Engineer Aird, is the new passenger terminal. The first stage is estimated to have cost about £23 million, funded jointly by Dun Laoghaire Harbour and (forty percent) by the European Union, more than twenty six times the cost of the original harbour though, of course, the great decrease in the value of the pound since Victorian days, has to be taken into account.

The Dun Laoghaire Chamber of Commerce reckoned in 1992 that the commercial shipping using the port, mainly car, lorry and passenger ferries, provided the local community with eight hundred and fifty jobs and a total income of £14 million. It was estimated that passenger numbers should double in the next ten years, bringing a huge boost to the local economy.

It is probably correct to ascribe largely to Hutchison's pioneering efforts the steady growth of the passenger traffic in and out of Dun Laoghaire since the time of the "Banshee", "Llewellyn" and "Cambria". Credit has also to be given to the City of Dublin Steam Packet Company which, once it had obtained the mail contract, succeeded in running between 1860 and 1920 what can only be called a model mail and passenger service for the epoch.

It is true that the wages paid by the City of Dublin Company were, in common with those paid to seamen almost everywhere, shabby until the great seamens' strike of 1911, but they were a little bit above the average, and the celebrated trade union leader, Larkin, succeeded with a movement to raise pay by nearly thirty percent not long before the Great War broke out. It is true also that wages paid to dock workers by the Company meant that a long day had to be worked to get as much as 27/-d., but there is no doubt that the Company provided steady employment in conditions somewhat above the average for the time. It is true as well that if the passage for third class passengers in the Company's ships, even in its last most successful sixty years, was never truly comfortable, it was safer than in other short-sea passenger vessels, and the City of Dublin Company was able to command a fair amount of loyalty during most of this time, both from its employees and especially its passengers.

The "Ulster", "Munster", "Leinster" and "Connaught" of 1860 were ships of a new type altogether, "vastly superior [to their predecessors] ... in fact in many ways the most remarkable cross-channel vessels ever built", according to one expert.[16] These ships had a gross tonnage of one thousand four hundred and eighty eight and were three hundred and thirty eight feet in length, thirty five feet two inches beam and eighteen feet eight inches depth. They were iron paddle steamers, with two-cylinder oscillating engines. ("Llewellyn" was two hundred and forty feet long with a beam of twenty seven feet). The "Leinster" was built in London, the other three at Birkenhead at the famous Laird – later Cammell Laird – shipyard. They had four funnels, reduced to two on refit in 1886. "Connaught", on trials, was the first ship known to have steamed at over eighteen knots. On one of her first crossings from Holyhead she arrived in three hours fourteen minutes, quicker than many a crossing made by post-1945 ships

16 She was also reported at that time "the fastest merchant ship afloat" and "the fastest and largest cross channel paddle-streamer to date" (*Sea Breezes*, October 1952 and July 1961). Her third crossing of the Irish Sea took her from Holyhead to Kingstown, (breakwater to breakwater) in only two hours, forty seven minutes.

on the route. The average crossing of the four ships during their years of service took just over four hours, which includes delays by fog, storm and accidents.

These ships and their successors, the two thousand, four hundred ton steel paddle-steamer "Ireland" of 1885 "claimed as the finest cross-channel steamer ever built",[17] and the second group of "Four Provinces" of 1896–97 carried the time (in the form of a specially checked chronometer from Greenwich Observatory) every day to Kingstown, having been carefully guarded on the way by the guard of the Irish Mail train, and the master of the mail steamer to whom it was confided at Holyhead. At Kingstown the chronometer was checked again by a harbour official in a miniature observatory behind the water reservoir near the Mariners' Church, then sent by train to Westland Row, where it was received by a Dublin Port Authority official who saw that the famous metal ball at the Ballast Office near O'Connell Bridge, visible from the street, dropped precisely at midday signalling "urbi et orbi", giving the exact time to a community without radio, television or telephone to tell it how right or wrong its clocks and watches were. The "midday" time was actually twenty-five minutes later than Greenwich time until a law was passed at Westminster in 1916. These twenty-five minutes are the longitudinal difference it takes the sun to be at its maximum height in Dublin after being at its maximum height at noon in Greenwich.

A clause in the City of Dublin Company's contract with the British Post Office stipulated that if the whole trip by land and sea at any time exceeded one hundred and ten hours the company had to pay a fine of £80, and if any mail steamer arrived later than the time scheduled she must pay a fine of £1. 14s. for each minute late.

The second group of "Four Provinces" was built to meet a Post Office stipulation that the ships tendering for the next contract must have a speed "not inferior to the 'Ireland'." The ships were designed for a speed of twenty three point five knots. They again were "far in advance in size, speed and accommodation of anything in that [cross-channel steamer] class". They were all two-funnelled steel twin screw-driven vessels which, in their first year in service, made the crossing in an average of two hours fifty six minutes, a gain of forty one minutes on the recent average of their predecessors. All were built by Laird's yard, with tonnage of two thousand, six hundred and forty one and length of three hundred and seventy two feet.

These ships carried on the mail service for nearly eighteen years with a regularity characterised as phenomenal. Their only serious mishap was in 1902 when in dense fog "Leinster" rammed and sank the Kish lightship "Albatross", but there was no loss of life.

When the Great War began "Connaught" was requisitioned by the British government as a troop carrier. The other ships carried on service, steaming at night without lights, without much incident until 1917. In that year German submarines became very active in the Irish Sea.

17 *Sea Breezes*, July 1961, p.41

The company requested an escort, but one was provided only when the Lord Lieutenant or troops from the United States were on board and, briefly after "Leinster" was missed by only a few yards by a torpedo on December 27th, 1917. In March and April 1918 "Ulster" was narrowly missed by torpedoes and in April both "Munster" and "Leinster", and "Leinster" again in August, spotted the periscopes of submarines but avoided attack. Meanwhile, "Connaught" had been sunk by torpedoes in the English Channel.

Then on October 10th, 1918, just thirty two days before the war ended, "UB123,", commanded by Ober-Leutnant Ramm, succeeded in hitting "Leinster" on her way to Holyhead and already beyond the Kish lightship, with two torpedoes. She had six hundred and eighty seven passengers, including the thirty post office mail sorters working on board each trip on these ships, and a crew of seventy. Of these five hundred and one, including the ship's master Captain Birch, perished. Two destroyers, "Lively" and "Mallard", operating like other British warships such as the Dublin-built gunboat "Helga" (later Irish Marine Service "Muirchu") out of Kingstown, now a busy wartime naval base, together with other non-naval ships, picked up survivors.

This was the greatest sea disaster Dublin Bay has known, surpassing that in which "Rochdale" and "Prince of Wales" were lost in 1807. One of "Leinster's" anchors was many years later recovered by the Dublin diver and marine expert Desmond Branigan and in December 1995 was appropriately located, and unveiled by Eamon Gilmore, Junior Minister for the Marine, within the harbour close to the King George monument built to commemorate the start of work on the construction of the Harbour. "Leinster's" anchor remains thus a permanent monument to the Irish shipping company that contributed so much to the early success of Dun Laoghaire as a passenger port.

It is now known that a second U-boat was in Dublin Bay with "UB123". They were experimenting with an elementary system of underwater communication.[18] "UB123" never got home to base. Her consort did, and was taken over by the British after the war. She parted her tow line off the Seven Sisters (Sussex) when being towed to a British base and grounded, remaining there for over twenty years as a prominent sea-mark.

With only two vessels left and without a solid body of Irish M.P.s at Westminster to lobby for it when the Post Office contract came up again, following the decision of most Irish members elected in the 1918 General Election not to attend a British parliament, the City of Dublin Company made little effort to retain its valuable contract. This fell at last to its old competitor, the London and North Western Railway, successor to the Chester and Holyhead Railway, soon to become part of the London, Midland and Scottish Railway. The L.N.W.R. had changed from Kingstown to Dublin's North Wall as terminal in

18 Information received at the National Maritime Museum, Dun Laoghaire, by the author in front of the Museum's model of "Leinster" (acquired by one of the survivors of the disaster and on permanent loan from his heirs) from Dr R.B. Grant of Chicago University, author of *U-Boats Destroyed*, London, 1964 and other authoritative works on submarine warfare in both World Wars.

Ireland for its passenger steamers in 1864, but resumed sailing its ships to Kingstown in 1908.

The L.N.W.R. had, in 1900, introduced into its passenger service four three hundred and twenty nine feet long twin-screw passenger steamers, known as "The Kingdoms" – "Anglia", "Cambria", "Hibernia" and "Scotia", which were replaced in 1920–21 by four ships of the same names, three hundred and eighty one feet long, driven by steam turbine engines. These now became the regular "mail boats" serving Dun Laoghaire in the new Irish state.

After announcing the return of its service to Kingstown in 1908 the L.N.W.R. had been taken to court by the City of Dublin Company, endeavouring to prove that the railway company was trespassing on its territory, but the judge held that the fact that the Chester and Holyhead Railway had operated its service out of Kingstown unopposed in the last century gave them the right to return and do so again.

There are many documents in the Office of Public Works archives about this acrimonious dispute, including instructions from the Harbour Master, then Captain, shortly to be Rear Admiral, then Vice Admiral Tudor to the Assistant Harbour Master, Commander Drury. Drury had to draw up an elaborate timetable to ensure that the railway steamers would be able to maintain their schedule without interfering in any way with the paramount activities of the all important mail service. He accompanied his timetable with a fascinating diagram showing the times and directions of the ships' movements of the two companies round Carlisle Pier from waiting berth to loading/discharging berth. On the rare occasions when Dublin Bay produced one of its notorious dense fogs patience was notably strained. The mail contract, having passed to the railway company was, nearly fifty years later, acquired by the B. & I. Line, legal heir to the City of Dublin's titles. But by now, for many years, with nearly all mail going by air, it is perhaps difficult for those alive in this epoch to imagine the extraordinary mystique surrounding the twice daily arrival and departure of the post across the Irish Sea in the famous Dublin Company's express steamers, each with its large attendance of postal sorting staff on every passage. The acrimony developed by the dispute between the City of Dublin Company and the railway company can be gauged by the tone of the following letter:

COPY NOTICE TO THE MASTER OF THE SS "MUNSTER"
2ND APRIL 1908
KINGSTOWN HARBOUR

NOTICE
TO THE MASTER OF THE SS "MUNSTER",

I order you to forthwith and immediately remove your vessel from her present moorings to the East side of the Carlisle Pier so as to leave the

West side clear for the incoming day mail boat and in case of your refusal or neglect to forthwith obey this order I will at once have you proceeded against for the full penalty of £10 imposed by the 22nd Sec of the 6 & 7 Wm. IV cap, 117.

OSWALD P. TUDOR,
HARBOUR MASTER,
HARBOUR OFFICE. KINGSTOWN, 2ND DAY OF APRIL 1908

(Tudor of course was warning "Munster" to make way for a sister ship to avoid a clash with the next arriving railway steamer).

When the Great War began the British government at once requisitioned the four railway steamers, one thousand eight hundred and forty two ton ships with triple expansion engines, as "armed boarding steamers", painted grey and armed with three Hotchkiss six pounder guns. "Anglia" was converted into a hospital ship in April 1915. She brought the British King George V home after he had had an accident while visiting troops in France, but on November 17th she struck a mine laid by submarine "UC5", going down in a quarter of an hour and taking eighty wounded and hospital staff with her. "Hibernia", renamed H.M.S. "Tara",

One of the City of Dublin's Steam Packet Company's Four Provinces

as the British navy had a battleship called "Hibernia", had various adventures off the Scottish coast and in the Mediterranean. Approaching the North African port of Sollum where Britain's ally, Italy, had a garrison, she was torpedoed by "U35" and sank in eight minutes, though most of her crew got away in boats, which were courteously towed by "U35" to the port of Bardia, where they were handed over to the local commandant, a Turk. Turkey was allied with Germany. They were later rescued by a fleet of armoured cars.

Under the contract received in 1920, the L.N.W.R. "Kingdoms" were to reach Dun Laoghaire on each trip, and Holyhead on each return, in two hours fifty five minutes from or to Holyhead inner harbour. Transfer of mail from train to ship was not to take above twenty five minutes by day and thirty by night at Holyhead, but only ten and fifteen at Dun Laoghaire. A fine of £20 would be imposed for every full hour's delay in sailing after arrival of the mail train. These ships were licensed to carry one thousand, five hundred and five passengers – nine hundred and thirty six first class, five hundred and sixty nine third class. They were built at Denny's shipyard at Dumbarton, Scotland.

It was on November 27th 1920 that City of Dublin's "Munster" carried the mail to Dun Laoghaire for the last time for that Company. At 3.50 on the morning of the next day the new "Anglia" sailed from Holyhead with two hundred and fifty passengers and arrived at Dun Laoghaire carrying the mail for the first time for the railway company.

At first the railway company kept all four ships on the service, with twice daily sailings, one ship sailing by day, another by night, and a third standing by with fires banked at Holyhead, the fourth undergoing overhaul.

After the L.N.W.R. became part of the new L.M.S. system, the company ran the service with "Cambria", "Hibernia" and "Scotia" only, bringing in one of the

R.M.S. 'Hibernia,' 'Cambria' and 'Scotia.'

ships normally serving the Heysham–Belfast route for holiday rush times. In 1932 the three ships were modernised, and a number of comforts added.

The "Scotia" was withdrawn from the service in summer 1940 to help evacuate British and French troops isolated at Dunkirk after the German invasion of France. She was bombed and sunk on June 1st with two thousand French troops on board. The other two ships maintained the service to Dun Laoghaire throughout the rest of the war. "Cambria" drove off a German aircraft that attacked near the Kish light vessel in December 1941, "Hibernia" escaped attack. Through constant use with little chance of anything but elementary maintenance they got into poor state, one of them suffering the loss of thirty feet of plating falling from her hull. From Dalkey and Killiney, Co. Dublin, in the last years of the 1939–45 war, a vast cloud of dirty smoke on the eastern horizon preceded the first sight of "mail boat".

Almost as soon as the war was over the L.M.S. placed an order with Harland and Wolff's great Belfast shipyard for two five thousand, two hundred ton motorships, "Hibernia" and "Cambria", the vessels we have already met discharging tourists' motors by crane. They entered service in 1949. Meanwhile the "Princess Maud", built in 1934 for the Larne-Stranraer service, was brought on to the Dun Laoghaire route as a relief ship. She was a two thousand, nine hundred and seventeen ton ship, changed from coal to oil-firing to drive her turbines, before coming to this route. She had had remarkable war service. Badly damaged off Dunkirk, she was repaired and finished hostilities having carried one million, three hundred and sixty thousand, eight hundred and seventy troops to various destinations and having taken a risky part in the Allied landing in Normandy in June 1944.

When Britain suffered a stringent shortage of coal in 1947, resulting in temporary laying up of "Cambria" and "Hibernia", oil-fired "Princess Maud" carried on the service alone. She was not popular in Dun Laoghaire though she was a fine seaboat, conditions being considered cramped on board. When she was withdrawn in 1965 following the arrival of the already mentioned "Holyhead Ferry 1" on the route, she was sold to Lefkosia Cia Nav. S.A., Cyprus, renamed "Venus", and entered upon a new and, for quite a long time, successful career. The author was on her last voyage from Dun Laoghaire to Holyhead, and obtained a number of souvenirs of her for the National Maritime Museum.

Probably the sharpest memory of the Harland and Wolff "Cambria" and "Hibernia" in Dun Laoghaire is the streams of emigrants, many from the West of Ireland, embarking often in poor condition to seek work in (then) fully employed Britain, reconstructing after the war. The Red Cross personnel from Dun Laoghaire who patiently and tirelessly looked after these unfortunate people were on several occasions carried off to Holyhead when attending to particularly exhausted or sick emigrants whom they had not been able to leave when the gangways had been raised and the ferry got under way.

Besides the "Holyhead Ferry 1", a few other of the numerous ships (so sharply in contrast with the long-service, inevitably better known and on the whole better liked City of Dublin Company's two groups of "Four Provinces" and L.N.W.R./L.M.S.'s two groups of "Kingdoms") that served the Dun Laoghaire–Holyhead route between 1965 and the portentous "Sea Lynx's" appearance thirty years later do, perhaps, deserve mention. "Holyhead Ferry 1" has already been mentioned. She served on our route for a comparatively short spell and was then shifted by Sealink to other routes that enterprise ran on the seas around Britain. She had, as noted, been briefly preceeded, owing to the prevalent disease for many years on the Holyhead-Dun Laoghaire route of "late delivery", by the British Rail Company's pioneer car-ferry, which began life in 1952 in Dumbarton, where she was built, as the three hundred and nine feet long "S.S. Normandia".

"Holyhead Ferry 1" proved to be a glutton for fuel and was discarded by her owners after a relatively brief career. She was accommodated, to the general disgust of the Dun Laoghaire public, at the "temporary" terminal at the base of the East Pier, the unpopularity of which led to the port authority constructing a permanent terminal west of Carlisle Pier. In the latter part of her sixteen year spell of service the ship served, first between Rosslare and Fishguard (1971–3) and afterwards on the English Channel.

Another early car-ferry for a time on the Dun Laoghaire route was a twin-screw steamer built on Tyneside in 1965, three hundred and sixty nine feet long. Like many vessels of the post-"Kingdoms" age she suffered a change of name, becoming "Earl Siward" after a refit in 1976 and, in that guise, turning up again briefly here.

Ships that became familiar in Dun Laoghaire in the 1980s include the cargo ferry "Stena Sailer", normally visible at St. Michael's Pier and renamed "St. Cybi", the 1981 built "St. David", which was switched off the Dun Laoghaire–Holyhead route (to which she had been somewhat of an ornament) to Dover in 1985, and later to Larne, and the M.V. "Hibernia", originally "St. Columba", Danish built in 1977, and re-greeted at Dun Laoghaire under her new name as something of a phenomenon, and the M.V. "Stena Cambria" (back to a traditional name) built at the celebrated Harland and Wolff yard at Belfast in 1980.

What does it signify, and what would William Watson, the formidable managing director of the City of Dublin Steam Packet Company in Harbour Master Hutchison's time have said, that the passengers on the Dun Laoghaire–Holyhead ferry route are nowadays referred to in advertising as "guests"?

# 9
# OTHER ACTIVITIES

"Ships … they go", said Murphy,
"Like a spent pay roll …
They're sunk in the deep water
Or they're wrecked in the shoal;
Burnt or scrapped in the long run,
The big ships an' small;
An' the ships a man remembers,
They're the best ships of all".

FOX SMITH

C. Fox Smith was born in Liverpool in 1874 and grew up in what was then one of the world's greatest ports. She was fascinated above all by the big sailing cargo ships in the sunset years of the age-old epoch of sail, and the large numbers of Irish seamen to be found manning them. By the time she died in 1947 she was being hailed as one of the finest sea-poets in the English language. She was far too well-informed to romanticise the allegedly "good old days" of the nitrate laden Cape Horners and the ships and barques on the Australian wheat-run round the Cape of Good Hope, and she achieved a notable insight into the thinking of the seamen who made up the crews of those celebrated, hard-driven vessels

## THE LIFEBOAT SERVICE

The so-called Royal Asylum Harbour of Kingstown evolved quite quickly, as noted, from being essentially the harbour of refuge for sailing ships in danger in Dublin Bay or further off into, primarily, the major port in Ireland for dealing with the carriage of mail and passengers. But other activities also became quickly associated with the port, and added to its growing reputation.

Of these activities it is proper to mention first those of the lifeboat service. This, as already mentioned, dates back to the period well before the decision had been taken to build the asylum harbour, when the Corporation for Preserving and Improving the Port of Dublin (Dublin Port Authority), as part of the frantic campaign already underway to try to diminish the loss of life by shipwreck in Dublin Bay, set up Europe's first co-ordinated lifeboat service round the bay. Three of the original lifeboat stations were along the coastline included now in the County of Dun Laoghaire and Rathdown, at Old Dunleary, Sandycove and Bullock. The first of the three stations to receive its boat was that at Sandycove. It cost £75, a sturdy twelve-oared rowing boat, arriving in 1803. Bullock got its boat, also built by Clements of Ringsend, for £105, in 1808, and Old Dunleary its, costing £100 in 1817.

Unfortunately, a full record of the achievement of these early lifeboats has not survived, but there is enough detailed evidence to suggest that several dozen lives were saved from the sea by them. The most spectacular rescues were some carried out by the Bullock boat with Hutchison, as first Harbour Master of Old Dunleary and Inspector at Bullock, then Harbour Master at Kingstown. His Gold Medal was won when the Maryport owned brig "Duke", built in Wales in 1748, was wrecked on Sandycove Point in appalling conditions before dawn on August 14th, 1829. Four men, a boy, three women and three children were plucked from the wreck of the collier brig.

The Dublin Port Authority stations seem to have operated as well as their comparatively primitive boats permitted until about the middle of the century. By then Bullock station seems to have been suppressed, and the chief responsibility for life saving in the southern half of Dublin Bay fell on the boat stationed at Kingstown Harbour. On several occasions Hutchison complained of the condition of the lifeboats, declaring in July 1840 that the Sandycove boat was "rotten with age". The Port Authority sought the advice of Trinity House, the London pilotage body, which referred it to the Lifeboat Institution, which does not seem at that stage to have been interested. Eventually, following Hutchison's advice, in 1852 the Port Authority ordered two new lifeboats, but they were stationed at Howth and Poolbeg.

In 1854 Hutchison submitted plans for a proper lifeboat house at Poolbeg, but reported that the boathouse at Sandycove was adequate. In 1855 a new boat was at last provided for Sandycove, but it proved too big for the boathouse there and Hutchison had it transferred to Kingstown Harbour. Not long after the Sandycove station was closed.

In 1860 the Port Authority sent a new boat to Kingstown which Hutchison, after trials, reported to be "cumbersome and ill-formed", with numerous other faults, and so heavy that it took thirty men to launch her. He was convinced that it would be impossible to row her to windward in a gale. Dublin Port Authority was asked by Hutchison to request the London builder of this boat to take her back and provide a suitable substitute. He refused.

Then on February 10th 1861 catastrophe came. Already on the 9th the schooner "Clyde", with a cargo of salt for Cork from Runcorn, which had been sheltering at Kingstown, was caught by a powerful north-easterly gust while sailing out of the harbour and was piled up on the rocks at the back of the East Pier lighthouse. Boats from H.M.S. "Ajax", the British Navy's guard ship in the port, saved "Clyde's" crew.

Captain John McNeill Boyd

By February 10th the intermittent north-easterly had increased to hurricane force, "one of the most disastrous storms that has occurred for many years in these latitudes", as the *Freeman's Journal* described it. Twenty two vessels were destroyed between Bray Head and the Baily lighthouse. The mail steamer "Leinster" sustained £500 worth of damage (£500 was a huge sum then) and had, exceptionally, to return to port. The railway steamer "Anglia" did not venture out of Kingstown at all.

Two colliers were lost on the outside of the East Pier. In the endeavour to rescue them Captain John McNeill Boyd, the Donegal-born commander of "Ajax", and five of his men, were drowned, sucked off the pier by the backwash of a monstrous wave which had knocked them down. The Lifeboat Institution gave Boyd, posthumously, its rare Silver Medal. Boyd was buried at St. Patrick's Cathedral, Dublin, where there is a monument to him. He had been an exceptionally brilliant naval officer, author of the last official navy handbook for training on board sailing warships. His five seamen lost, Porcell, Murphy, Johnston, Curry and Forsyth, were buried in Carrickbrennan Cemetery, Dun Laoghaire,

Duncan's View of Kingstown from Anderson's English Landscapes and Views 18
"The most dangerous port in the worl

'Dunleary II'

and their graves were extensively refurbished in 1985.

Hutchison, as he wrote in a strongly worded letter to the *Irish Times*, published on February 13th, explaining why the new lifeboat was not launched, had judged that to take the unsatisfactory lifeboat out in the conditions "would have been the most rash act of my life". Instead, he had organised a shore party to deal with vessels suffering storm damage in the harbour, and another, which he led, to help Boyd trying to save the crews of the colliers "Neptune" and "Industry", driven against the outside of the East Pier. He and two of his party, a man called Anderson and Lloyd's agent Walsh, both of whom suffered painful injuries, were also struck by the gigantic sea that killed Boyd and his men, but managed to survive. The party ended by saving all the crew of "Industry" save her master, who was drowned trying to help members of his crew, but only one man from "Neptune". Hutchison, now sixty eight years old, was also awarded the Lifeboat Institution's Silver Medal.

The consequence of these events was the transfer the following year of responsibility for the lifeboat service in Dublin Bay from Dublin Port Authority to the Royal National Lifeboat Institution, with which it still rests.

The Kingstown lifeboats (there were, for a number of years at the end of the 19th and start of the 20th century, two operative at the station) were active year after year, and have continued to be so (forty five sorties in 1994, for instance) since they became the Dun Laoghaire lifeboats. Dun Laoghaire lifeboat has for most years in the past decade been the most called out lifeboat in Ireland. Rowing lifeboats were replaced while Hutchison was still in charge, as first R.N.L.I. Honorary Secretary of the station, by sailing and rowing boats. These were improved with time and experience. Then came "Dunleary", (1919) costing

£6,074, was a handsome craft driven by a petrol engine and launched from the station's recently built and gaily painted boathouse down a long slipway into the waters of the harbour. Petrol driven "Dunleary" was succeeded in 1938 by diesel-powered twin-screw "Dunleary II", R.N.L.I. official number eight hundred and fourteen, which cost £8,258 and saved one hundred and thirty nine lives in a long and distinguished career. She gave way in 1967 to the first steel-hulled lifeboat commissioned by the R.N.L.I., and the first equipped with radar, "John F. Kennedy". This one cost £45,000, and saved one hundred and twenty nine lives. She was succeeded by the "Lady of Lancashire" of the same class, replaced in her turn in 1995 by the first of the new twenty five knot Trent class ultra-sophisticated lifeboats, costing just over £1 million, "Anna Livia". For more than five years now the station has been served by the "Anna Livia". The station has also been reinforced by the provision of an Inshore Rescue Boat, housed in the elegant Old Life Boat House, dating from Hutchison's time, from which the "Civil Service No. 7" left on Christmas Eve 1895 to rescue the crew of a grounded Finnish barque. She had been capsized by freak seas, losing all fifteen of her crew, an event to be noted in the next section of this work.

In 1901 a very handsome new boathouse was opened for the lifeboat station approximately where the present long overdue lifeboat station was opened on May 6, 2000. The 1901 boathouse was one of the town's architectural gems, badly missed when demolished in 1963 to permit widening of the road leading to Carlisle Pier. It cost £2,350. The new properly equipped station was at last built to replace the miserable premises under the road to Carlisle Pier "temporarily" provided thirty-seven years ago.

Kingstown/Dun Laoghaire lifeboats have, it can be estimated with some accuracy, saved over six hundred people from death at sea, and given comfort and succour to many more in trouble but not in danger of death, as well as escorting or towing to safety craft of many types and sizes, which lifeboats are under no obligation to do, their remit being confined simply to lifesaving.

The volunteer crews of these boats have greatly embellished the reputation of the port to which they have been attached.

## SEA FISHING

Old Dunleary was for many generations a little port dependent on inshore fishing. When the new asylum harbour grew up around it, it quite quickly attracted owners of fishing vessels more sophisticated than those used by the fishermen of Old Dunleary. There was, in particular, an influx of fisher-folk from Devon and Cornwall, who were responsible for building a Methodist Church in the new town. Whereas in the few known illustrations of Old Dunleary there are rarely more than one or two small fishing wherries to be seen, records show that in the early 1830s there were twenty fishing yawls registered in Kingstown, and the port was already acquiring a reputation as a flourishing fishing port.

was recorded as one of the leading
Herring and mackerel were the main
Dublin Bay prawns and lobsters. The
nt pleas for a revival of the Irish fishing
of the 19th century, for example by
gure in the R.D.S. at the time, in a paper
the Society in February 1866.
ys since its early days interested in fishery
century, particularly after the establish-
nd Technical Instruction 1898, a new

"Harlequin", operated by the R.D.S.
well equipped fishery research ships
II" (1906) – later the Marine Service's
reers operating out of Kingstown.
enty ton beam trawlers were owned in
er the Great War the local fishing fleet
to provide local employment. When
headquarters in Dun Laoghaire in
e potential for a real, and this time
ustry. It was responsible for the Dun
etting a big debate on the industry
tion's Annual Congress at Kilkee in
issuing a widely read pamphlet on
ry.
ficial body set up by the govern-
ng industry, had its scope and
nd came under the control of a
He was largely responsible for
l in 1971 for the first time in

very modern fishing vessels
equipped German fisheries
the then new St. Michael's
essels, with an unlimited
for 10s. a head! It was
period from 1962 to

ghaire, which still in
f the thirty or so chief
h and twentieth place.
ive main fishing ports,

including Howth, which followed the 1973 oil crisis, led to the virtual extinction of the fishing industry in Dun Laoghaire. The port is, however, still occasionally used as a temporary base, as has happened since well back in the 19th century, for fishing vessels from Arklow at Trader's Wharf. Smaller, local, half decker boats have changed to pot fishing, and the Ice Plant on Trader's Wharf, so welcomed when built some thirty years before, was decommissioned.

The year of the great Biennial World Fishing Exhibition in Dun Laoghaire (1971) before the government decision to concentrate the Irish sea fishing industry at Howth seemed to be presaging a rapid development of the industry here. The latest figures for the local annual catch (for 1969) showed a highly respectable figure of £122,788 (pre-oil inflation pounds) and the number of vessels regularly fishing out of Dun Laoghaire had recently grown from four to fourteen. The fish caught was discharged at Trader's Wharf and run by road to the Dublin Fish Market, but plans were under way for the construction not only of the ice plant that did materialise but also a filleting plant on a plot of land that was part of the Coast Guard grounds. The Corporation had moreover, stopped switching off the lights at the Coal Harbour at midnight, which had necessitated the bringing of cars to the quay and stationing them so that their headlights could facilitate the discharge of fish. The quay and approach to the Coal Harbour had been resurfaced and other improvements were under discussion.

Much of this activity, a credit to the last Dun Laoghaire generation of regular professional fishermen, was inspired by the Dublin Bay Fishermen's Co-operative, and some considerable personalities had helped to organise what looked like a coming Dun Laoghaire fishing boom, such as Mick Kavanagh, owner of a successful modern trawler, the "Brazil", foretold.

## SEA ANGLING

As far back as living memory goes, line fishermen have been trying their luck from the asylum harbour, more particularly from the end of the West Pier. The arrangement to go out in a boat from Kingstown to fish in the sea with a friend or a party of friends was already quite common by the end of the 19th century. It became more common in the 1930s, and resumed fairly soon after the end of the Second World War. In the 1950s the habit prospered, and in the 1960s and 1970s Dun Laoghaire had quite a reputation in Ireland, and even some repute abroad, as a sea-angling centre. One or two quite sophisticated craft were brought in, and there were at least two well-known local sea-angling clubs, with one or two celebrated members, such as the famous air pilot Captain Kelly Rogers.

The sport seems to be in decline for a number of years. This is no doubt partly as the result of a growing scarcity of fish to be caught, consequent upon the extent to which Dublin Bay had become polluted by industrial waste and sewage. Fairly stringent official efforts to deter industrial concerns from using the rivers entering Dublin Bay as waste removers, and an improvement in sewage disposal, though no final solution to the problem, both in the capital and in Dun Laoghaire, have brought about an amelioration of which public opinion may not be yet fully aware. There is also a continuing though to date unproven suspicion that the sea in Dublin Bay may be polluted by outflows from the British Nuclear Fuel centre at Sellafield/Thorpe in Cumberland, and the transport of nuclear waste through the Irish Sea to feed the process there is looked upon as a menace.

## THE COMMISSIONERS OF IRISH LIGHTS

The disastrous wreck in 1853 near the Baily of the City of Dublin Steam Packet Company's "Queen Victoria" on the way to Dublin from Liverpool resulted in an enquiry that was very critical of Dublin Port Authority as the country's lighthouse authority at the time. In due course a new body, the Commissioners of Irish Lights, was established to take over this responsibility. In 1874 it acquired from the Board of Works space along the harbour edge west of the Royal Irish Yacht Club to set up a depot and workshop. They are still there, busier than ever.

Kingstown/Dun Laoghaire harbour has seen a succession of elegant Irish Lights tenders; "Tearaght", that saved the crew of the Finnish ship to which Kingstown lifeboat had put out, only to be overwhelmed by exceptional seas on December 24th 1895; "Alexandra", the most beautifully proportioned and finely shaped of them all; "Isolda", sunk by a German aircraft near the Tuskar Rock on December 19th 1940 with six of her crew killed and seven wounded, in spite of having Lighthouse Service marked on her hull in letters five feet high; "Granuaile", the present tender; and many more. All have spent spells at the asylum harbour, taking in stores from their depot and preparing to tow to its station off the coast one of the lightships of which Irish Lights once had a sizeable fleet (now only two in actual service), or one of the giant buoys that gradually replaced the lightships on stations like the Barrells off the Wexford coast, even before the recently completed automation of coast lighting began. It is still an intriguing sight to see one of the lightships towed out to sea or back to Dun Laoghaire for refit. But what for many years was quite a common treat has now become a rarity.

Giant buoys and smaller ones are made and repaired at the Dun Laoghaire workshop of Irish Lights (which services the coast of Northern Ireland as well as that of the Republic), one of the many ways in which the activities at the harbour create employment for the town.

At Dun Laoghaire port too Irish Lights achieved, between 1963 and 1965, what must be the most ambitious of all the undertakings which have given it a world-wide reputation for the excellence of its lighting and buoyage of our coasts. Irish Lights is a body celebrated for the many innovations it has introduced elsewhere, but of all its pioneering ventures, none has been so daring as, and none more successful, than the construction in Dun Laoghaire of a great light tower to replace the last of the lightships that for more than a century and a half had marked the perilous wreck-strewn Kish Bank, to be towed out and fixed permanently out there. Some details of this epic project follow in a later part of the present work.

## THE COAST GUARD STATION

An imposing building west of the Irish Lights depot and still east of the road going down to Traders' Wharf is the old Coast Guard building. A Coast Guard service was established in Ireland in the 1830s. It had several functions: to watch the sea off the stretch of coast under its jurisdiction so as to become aware of vessels in distress; to man its own vessel or vessels if there was no local lifeboat service to go in aid to any distressed vessel seen in its sector; to watch its sector of sea for sight and details of any suspicious vessel out there; to prevent smuggling; and to help the civil power in times of emergency.

The Coast Guard was normally manned by former naval men and worked under semi-military discipline. Its officers were usually ex-naval men. Though not wholly trusted by the local population, who would be inclined to sympathize with smugglers and with opponents of the civil power as then constituted, it cannot be denied that the British Coast Guard Service in Ireland has a remarkable record for the successful work it did saving lives from wrecks in areas where there was no lifeboat. The Coast Guard also provided a constant coast watch, so that any lifeboat within its area could be assured of ample warning if wreck or other danger at sea seemed likely. The lifeboat service sorely missed this help when the first government of the Irish Free State abolished the existing Coast Guard and gave scant approval to efforts by Tom Casement to create a new National Coast Guard. The creation of a Coast Watch by the Garda Siochana at a very large and enthusiastic meeting in Dun Laoghaire Motor Yacht Club in 1996 has started a movement to fill the void for Dublin Bay, and early in 1998 Minister of the Marine Dr. Woods announced the forthcoming establishment at last of an Irish National Coastguard as so often down the years demanded by Dun Laoghaire. An idea of some of the activities of the local Coastguard in the last century can be gathered from a perusal of some of the correspondence recorded above in part of this work when the Coast Guard head here was Sir J. Dombrain. The old Coast Guard station the primary function of which till 1922 was to keep a watch for mysterious activities at sea and to help rescue and salvage services has not altogether lost its original maritime vocation, as An Slua Muiri, the Naval Service's reserve force, trains there.

## FROM "DODDER" TO "INGOT"

It has often been noted with surprise, by visitors to Dun Laoghaire harbour, and even by residents in Dun Laoghaire town, that from its position on a fine scenic bay, with another one adjoining beyond Dalkey Island, there is no regular cruise service round one or other or both of the two scenic bays.

However, there have been periods when this splendid amenity for visitors and locals has been available, as a similar amenity certainly is available from so many European ports, from Lübeck or Stockholm in the Baltic to Marseille or Venice in the Mediterranean Basin.

Some time between 1857, when one hundred and sixty seven sailing vessels and two hundred and ninety seven steamers visited Kingstown harbour (warships not included) and 1867, when seven hundred and forty one vessels visited Kingstown (excluding regular mail steamers and warships), some such service did get going. In 1857 certain steamers which visited Kingstown twice in a day are recorded in the register of ships paying harbour dues. Unfortunately there is no indication whether these were tugs, dredgers or despatch vessels of some kind, or special pleasure steamers.

By 1867 it is quite clear that a steamer called the "Dodder" which is classified as a "passenger steamer", called during the year, between the months of March and September, no fewer than eighteen times for the purpose of "trips", or in July, "trips from and to Dublin". In the same month "Dodder" was joined on four occasions each by "trip" steamers called "Anna Liffey" and "Kingstown".

"Anna Liffey" came also in September, making, like "Dodder", three visits during the month, in which the busy little steamers made between them no fewer than thirty, sixteen and nineteen "trips". On "Dodder's" first September visit, on the sixteenth, she made seven "trips", and on the twenty third fourteen. Later in that century and in the first years of the 20th century the pleasure steamers visiting seem to have been larger, though the then particularly popular cruises via Dublin and Killiney Bays round Tuskar Rock to Land's End and Falmouth and back (return fare 22/6d first class, 17/6d second) were run by the B&I Line from Dublin.

In 1909 local cruises were restarted by a Clyde built steamer, "Duke of Abercorn", one hundred and fourteen tons, which distinguished itself by running aground on Dalkey Island in fog on one cruise. She was got off with little damage and no hurt to crew or passengers. She seems to have continued to operate till 1914.

The "Dodder" had been built by the London and North Western Railway Company in Dublin, which saw in the 1860s one of several periodical revivals rarely long-lasting in the nineteenth and twentieth centuries, of its ancient art of shipbuilding. It was not for love of ships that the L.N.W.R. undertook this venture. The still young Dublin and Wicklow Railways was going through a bad spell, with constant complaints of uncomfortable and unpunctual trains. The L.N.W.R. visualised the operation of a permanent service by sea from the capital to Wicklow, but shortened the "Dodder's" voyages to cross simply between Dublin and Kingstown, as the Dublin and Wicklow Railway improved its performance. Eventually, now simply a pleasure steamer, she spent her last years in this capacity in Carlingford Lough. She was a paddle steamer, iron hulled, one hundred and forty seven feet long, of which photos or other illustrations are rare. "Anna Liffey" was also a paddle steamer, built in Dublin as well, in the 1860s, while the paddle steamer, "Kingstown", one hundred and fifty one feet long, was built in Whiteinch, and was equipped like the others with a single-expansion steam-engine. They may have had only fairly limited careers but were the first steamers built to show tourists the beauties of the coasts of Counties Dublin and Wicklow after embarkation at Kingstown, they were pioneers, the example of which has been too little followed. Return tickets for the run between Kingstown and Dublin in these steamers cost 9d. for saloon passengers, 6d. for deck passengers. Packets of one hundred tickets could be bought at twenty five percent discount.

Attempts were made to revive pleasure cruising round Dublin Bay between the World Wars, in every decade since the end of the 1939-45 war an effort has been made to inaugurate pleasure cruising again from Dun Laoghaire. In most cases the venture made a prosperous start but then had an abrupt end.

The "Duke of Abercorn", mentioned above, was a twin screw steamer built at Grangemouth, one hundred and twenty tons, first called "Britannia" and operating in Scotland. She came to Dublin Bay to run pleasure trips in 1909 but went to join the celebrated West of Scotland MacBrayne fleet just before the Great War. The same owner, the Duke Shipping Company, employed a one hundred and eighty ton single-screw steamer "Storm" built at Goole in 1875 to run a pleasure ship in and out of Dun Laoghaire not long after the Great War, and off and on between the wars the Dun Laoghaire mail steamers gave pleasure trips on a larger scale. The "Duke of Abercorn" was succeeded by the South Shields built paddle steamer "Cynthia", one hundred and fifty three feet long, in 1932 and that June she was a tender, along with the Mersey tender "Royal Iris", famous for her part in the 1918 Battle of Zeebrugge, for the fleet of passenger ships bringing visitors to the Eucharistic Congress in Dublin. Laid up in Dun Laoghaire Harbour for the winter she was driven from her moorings by a severe gale in February 1933 and became a total wreck. On various occasions over a long period in the late 19th and early 20th century Dublin tugs were hired to bring trippers to watch the big regattas originating at Kingstown, and to have a look at British navy units visiting Kingstown which, it must be recalled, was a British naval base, if a minor one.

The "John Joyce" (built 1910) later "Shandon", was a one hundred and fifty two foot long tender brought to Dublin in the winter of 1936–7 to act as tender to the Anchor Line passenger ships, regular visitors, which did one season of cruises before being transferred to Cork.

The Office of Public Works Archives show that in the period 1938–40, small cruise ships were still charged the original 1d. for each call to Dun Laoghaire to pick up passengers, and also charged 1 3/4 pence per ton on their registered tonnage. Cruise ships were now charged £1.10 per trip if between two hundred and fifty and five hundred tons, £3.00 between five hundred and one thousand tons, £6.00 between one thousand and one thousand, five hundred, £9.00 between one thousand, five hundred and two thousand and £12.00 to £15.00 over two thousand tons.

In the 1930s mail steamers sometimes ran excursions from Dun Laoghaire before their next crossing to Holyhead. They had permission to cruise anywhere within forty five miles of the East Pier Lighthouse.

The stark shortages and deep changes of attitudes and customs that followed the end of the 1939–45 war meant that pleasure, or tourist cruising in Dublin Bay, with its many decades of happy history, was going to have problems re-establishing itself – much more than in many continental ports; and it must be said that several of the ventures launched were unable to receive encouragement from a harbour authority which was not a body geared to enterprise so much as to preservation of what had been. The new cruise proposers themselves, in some cases, unconventional to say the least, were profoundly dissimilar from what the eager tourists can regularly expect if they embark on a tourist cruise in the ports of Antwerp say, or Marseille.

The cruise urge was fairly quick returning to Dun Laoghaire. In July 1948 a seventy two foot motor vessel "Marlene Dolores" had permission sought for her to run "summer trips" but the project was soon dropped. However, in the same week the Dublin Cruising Club requested the right to run cruises with the M.V. "Larsen", of which a good deal was to be heard. A leaflet was issued advising that this vessel would make three cruises daily, morning and evening, for two hours in afternoons at 5/- if for three hours at 7/6, "with light refreshments, bar and music."

On July 22nd Captain C. O'Connor, Assistant Harbour Master to Lieutenant Commander R. Shiel R.N.R., reported that twelve trips had been made in the week ending on July 15th. One Smythe, "Larsen's" owner, a distinct character, who assured acquaintances that his daughter (who was mildly stunning) was going to make a fine marriage "through the Embassy at Constantinople(!)" applied to the Harbour Office for help to get the £12,000 mortage on his ship transferred from a British to an Irish bank ("Larsen" had been M.L. (motor launch) No. 346 in the British Navy and had taken a quite notable part in the celebrated raid by the British on German held Dieppe in summer 1942.) He got permission to berth "Larsen" alongside "The Old Quay", and then laid her up in Arklow for the winter.

Back in Dun Laoghaire in March 1949 Smyth (as he now spelled his name) wanted "Larsen" to lie this year at the dolphin on the East Pier. A Harbour Constable's report for July 2nd disclosed that, on that evening, the vessel's bar was used in port and she did not start her last cruise until 8.20 p.m.

A leaflet for July 9th announced cruises at 11.15 (2/6), 3.30 (4/-), 8.00 p.m. (2/6) and a midnight cruise at 7/6. Smyth(e) sent the Harbour Office a letter guaranteeing that the bar would not be open again in port and that the last cruise would normally terminate at 11.30 p.m.

In August, "Captain Smyth" complained to Clann na Poblachta, the political party recently and rather sensationally formed by Sean MacBride, that his midnight cruise had been prohibited though nearly all the leadership of the new party was booked to travel on it.

On August 13th the Office of Public Works wrote complaining that despite the ban, the midnight cruise had taken place. Meanwhile a Dalkey man had applied for a licence to run cruises in a twenty eight foot motor vessel "Oceanic".

On August 18th a J.A. Metcalf, Master of the "Merrie Golden Hind" (ninety five point fifty one tons, one hundred and twelve foot by eighteen foot, with a six hundred h.p. engine and a crew of five), sent a request for permission to deliver this ex-submarine chaser from Guernsey to Dun Laoghaire into the ownership of one Harold and under the management of "Smyth".

There was another plan by a British naval party in Harwich to come to run cruises but it came to nothing. Captain O'Connor then told "Larsen's" owner that she might return to the East Pier providing her dues were paid.

On 27 April 1951 the new Harbour Master, Captain Reginald Kearon of Arklow, received his first application for a licence to cruise; of which nothing apparently came. But on 9 November "Merrie Golden Hind" sank alongside the East Pier dolphin, according to Smythe because the seacocks had been removed. Smythe announced that he would sue Dun Laoghaire Corporation, and Captain Kearon reminded him his dues had still not been paid.

On 4th March 1954, Smythe wrote to the Office of Public Works to say that "from a malicious act" he was out of business. He requested a loan so as to enable him to meet the more than £500 he owed in dues and so as "to restore the amenity of cruises to Dun Laoghaire". This was refused, and in due course Smythe wrote to say he was dropping his case as he could not prove "Merrie Golden Hind's" accident had occurred in the Corporation's jurisdiction. He was last heard of acting as a footman in a large mansion in inland west Dun Laoghaire. In the following decade a German ex-frogman arrived with a converted trawler and offered tours round the Bay, at a very reasonable rate, from St. Michael's Wharf. His venture did not end in disaster. He made, as he had intended from the first, enough profit out of the amenity he provided to be able to equip his vessel as a base for extensive diving operations which he had long been planning in the Red Sea.

A few years later a rather sumptuous diesel pleasure ship ran trips round Howth Head from the East Pier and seemed to be doing well enough, but failed to appear when the next season came. Then much more recently a very comfortably converted small motor tug, "Ingot", under Captain McCann came on the scene from Cork. He also sailed from the base of the East Pier, usually off into Killiney Bay, with a tape recorder on board broadcasting for the passengers the history of the coast along which the vessel sailed. Her failure to return after the 1994 season when she had built up much popularity and a considerable clientele is attributed to an opportunity to make more profit cruising down the Lee and around the lower reaches of Cork harbour. But Captain McCann is still interested in restarting coastal cruises from Dun Laoghaire at the time of writing.

It is greatly hoped by many that cruising from Dun Laoghaire harbour will soon at last become a permanent feature of the asylum port's expected prosperous future. Meanwhile the memory of vessels like "Dodder" and "Larsen" and "Ingot" remains along with that of the little fleet of the port's miniature steam dredgers ("Saxifrage's" machinery is preserved in the National Maritime Museum), not so long ago discarded, and of a miniature salvage ship "Clearwater", a neat and finely kept twin-screw motor-vessel, owner-skippered by a Dutch North Sea seaman of the very old school. She did briefly run cruises, but eventually found it more profitable to operate from the Isle of Man. Her owner has very recently returned from the Isle of Man with a new "Clearwater", but this one is a very up to date fishing vessel.

All are part of the long story of a port made famous by the fine passenger ships that have graced it but also the home of numerous smaller power-driven vessels, in their day as familiar to the port's devotees as the celebrated "mail-boats" and yachts and lighthouse tenders.

Meanwhile, a new prospect was opened by the arrival, unfortunately before the establishment of the new Harbour Board, of the celebrated English pleasure paddle-steamer "Waverley" to run a weekend of trips of varying lengths. The trips were extremely popular and very many who went on them expected "Waverley" to return the following year. Her owners, however, were said to have complained that she had received so much obstruction at Dun Laoghaire that they would never let her back there. However, the new Harbour Board has a specific policy of encouraging cruise ships to visit Dun Laoghaire regularly, and it is greatly hoped that one day "Waverley" will be tempted back.

There were, indeed, a few cases since the Second World War when large passenger ships on long cruises paid a visit to Dublin Bay, where they anchored for some hours, disgorging passengers to pay a short visit to Dun Laoghaire. Some of these ships were very well known, such as the Swedish "Kungsholm", and the British "Canberra", Irish-built by Harland and Wolff. The new Harbour Board hopes to attract such cruise vessels, and as they are becoming more numerous every year in every sea, they can be expected to turn up regularly off, or in the case of smaller vessels, into Dun Laoghaire, where special visits of interest for instance to the Maritime and Joyce Museums or other entertainments would be ready for them to enjoy. The celebrated Cunard cruise ship "Queen Elizabeth II (QE2) came to Dublin Bay in July 1997, with two scheduled further visits in 1998.

## SHIP AND BOAT BUILDING

It was expected by experts in the early years of the harbour, particularly by a number of the officers of the British Navy who were asked or who offered advice about its future, that it would become a quite important ship-repairing centre. This never happened, the shipbuilding firms that from time to time flourished in Dublin were near enough to provide necessary repair facilities and though they no longer exist, up to a point the repair facilities still do. What Kingstown did, for a period, become celebrated for was the building of yachts.

The most celebrated Kingstown/Dun Laoghaire yacht builders were the Mahony family. Their yard was in operation for over a hundred years from the middle of the 19th century, and its closure was a great loss. The yard, it is true, was away up Patrick Street in the town, but the vessels designed and built there were always brought down to Dun Laoghaire harbour for the initial trials, and very many of them were kept in the harbour, and sailed from it, by their purchasers.

There are still stories circulating about the problems posed by having to trundle new Mahony boats for launching and old ones for overhaul down or up Patrick Street and Marine Road, and about regular differences of opinion between the Mahonys escorting a yacht and unfortunate bus men trying to pass them along one of the town's steep streets.

Dublin Bay Water Wags, 17s, 21s, 24s and 25s, all celebrated in their time, were products of the Mahonys. They also built boats of the long-celebrated Mermaid class, and some larger vessels, five tonnes and over.

Of all the Mahony boats, the twenty five footers seem to have been the most successful and left the longest memory. Other local builders of 25s, and of the also long celebrated Dublin Bay Water Wags, were Macken and Clancy.

Mahonys built their boats upside down, for which they were much discussed, and were adept also at designing and constructing currachs. The last two Mahonys in the business, Christy and Ned, were virtual worshippers of the wood with which they built their products – it had to be the best. They lived to see the arrival of plastic in boat-building, and deplored it. The new types of yacht coming in at the end of the Mahony era were, Ned said, "built for cheating the rules". Among the best-known Dublin 25s was "Windward", built by Clancy for one of the leading Dublin business men of the Sean Lemass era, J.J. O'Leary. One of the largest yachts the Mahonys built was a twenty eight footer, "Cushla", constructed for John McCormack, the singer, who was to lose her later off Sandycove Point.

The Mahonys lived to see the rise, success and ruination of a large small-ship or large-boat yard, behind the West Pier. It opened in the late 1940s and lasted nearly ten years, reaching the point when it had forty five persons in steady employment, including nine indentured apprentices. Its greatest achievement was with the last order completed, for two dozen harbour tugs for Turkey, five at least of which were still visible and busy at Izmir twenty years later. Unfortunately the Turkish Government was slow producing payment for its fleet of tugs, but an order was received from the Polish Government for a batch of tugs of the same design.

The yard was anxious to start at once on the Polish order, but needed cash to keep going till the money came from Turkey. It applied for a loan, to be repaid by some of this money, to the Government in Dublin, which was the second Inter-Party Government, of 1954–1957. The United States Government, which considered anything going on anywhere in the world to be its business, as leader of one side in the notorious, extravagant and, as we now realise, fake "Cold War", then in progress, heard of the order to Dun Laoghaire from Poland for a set of diminutive harbour tugs.

The Minister for Industry and Commerce was informed that the receipt of these tugs by Poland would alter the strategic balance of power in the Cold War. Though he was a representative of the Labour Party, which claimed origin from the ideas of the lion-hearted James Larkin, the Minister was a poltroon, genuflected to Washington and refused the loan. That was the end of small-ship, large-boat building in Dun Laoghaire, an industry which had really taken root in the harbour, and of which the local population was proud. Nearly all the employees got jobs in Scottish shipyards, still flourishing in the 1950s. Mr. Joe Green, a carpenter aboard the Commissioner of Irish Lights' "Granuaile" served his time at that yard.

## A MINOR NAVAL BASE

The British Admiralty had its eye on the new Royal Asylum Harbour at Kingstown from the first, as can be judged by the copies of numerous letters therefrom to the Harbour Commissioners about its potential value, the need for watering facilities there, the proper width of the entrance and other matters.

Various fractions of what was then the world's largest navy visited Kingstown fairly frequently, sometimes on manoeuvres, sometimes accompanying royalty, sometimes for some official occasion. In the Great War, particularly after U-boats became very active in the Irish Sea late in 1917, Kingstown showed its potential as a minor naval base.

During the 1939–45 war vessels of the tiny Irish Marine Service visited Dun Laoghaire from time to time, particularly the gunboat, once fishery research and protection ship and later British gunboat H.M.S. "Helga", the Marine Service's largest vessel, the "Muirchu". Dun Laoghaire was that ship's base during most of her career. Sometimes one or more of the Service's motor torpedo-boats paid a visit, they were its most dangerous component.

Since the establishment of a permanent Naval Service in 1946, and particularly following that Service's expansion in the 1970s and 1980s, Irish warships have been to Dun Laoghaire more and more frequently. One or other of the corvettes "Macha", "Maev" and "Cliona" paid an occasional visit, and since their replacement all the ships of the Service have paid at least one visit, normally berthing at the East Pier. The Service's flagship "Eithne" has visited on a number of occasions, one of which will be mentioned below. French fishery patrol ships were fairly frequent visitors in the 1950s and 1960s, and more recently groups of French, German, Spanish and Belgian naval ships have come in, chiefly to honour Dun Laoghaire's Annual Festival, and a small unit of the U.S. Navy, U.S.S. "Sorocco" visited during summer 1995. In July 1996, the aircraft carrier USS "John F. Kennedy", lay in Dublin Bay, off Dun Laoghaire, attracting many visitors, and a number of protestors, and disgorging hundreds of crew members to visit the town.

A letter of 31st July, 1952 from the Department of Defence to the Harbour Authority is interestingly worded, noting that the "corvettes were frequently using Dun Laoghaire when on patrol", and "berthage accommodation must always be available". The Department suggested "a mooring buoy in the harbour purely for naval use ... as in former years", i.e. a renewal of the system operative through the famous H.M.S. "Melampus" buoy. Buoys were removed during the construction work for St. Michael's Pier (1965–70), and the naval service was then given use of the disused temporary car ferry berth at the East Pier. Yacht moorings increased from the 1960s onwards.

The British Navy kept a Guard ship on alert at Kingstown almost throughout the Royal Asylum Harbour's existence under this name. Some of these ships were famous in their day. One of these was H.M.S. "Ajax", commanded by the luckless Captain Boyd. Her predecessor "was like Ajax" one of Britain's former "Wooden Walls", a "battleship of the line", which had a primitive steam-engine put in her during the 1840s.

"Ajax" was built at Blackwall, London, in 1809, rated as a third rate seventy four gun ship-of-the-line. She was one hundred and seventy six feet three inches long, her tonnage was one thousand seven hundred and sixty one, with a crew of five hundred and ninety men. She served in the Mediterranean from 1809–1814, and then transported troops to North America to take part in the Anglo-US war of 1812–1814. Back in Europe she was based from 1818 to 1850 at Portsmouth, where she was fitted between 1845 and 1846 with screw steam machinery and re-armed with fifty six, more modern, guns. In 1850, now classified as a "steam guard ship", she was stationed at Cork under Michael Quin as captain, and stayed there until 1853. In 1854–55 she was in the Baltic, participating in the Crimean War, more particularly in the celebrated bombardment of the fortified Russian port of Bomarsund (in Finland, then Russian), during which the first Victoria Cross was won – by an Irish seaman.

In 1858, after spells at Portsmouth and Devonport, "Ajax" came under Boyd to Kingstown. Here she remained until she sailed away in 1864 under Captain

HMS Melampus

Michael de Courcy, her third Irish captain, to be broken up. An official note on her career from the British National Maritime Museum gives a hint of problems her three Irish and seven other captains must have had with her: H.M.S. "Ajax" was noted for her "poor performance under steam or sail".

A ship well known in her day, stationed at Kingstown before "Ajax", was a sloop H.M.S. "Wolf", built in 1826, relegated to the role of coal hulk and lent to the Board of Works in Dublin from 1851–6.

"Ajax's" successor from 1864 to 1869 was one of the last "wooden walls", built by the British Navy in 1826 when far-sighted British naval officers like Beaufort of Navan, to whom Harbour Master Hutchison owed so much, were already foreseeing steam-driven fleets. This "Royal George" was flush-decked, unlike her predecessors in the period of the French Wars. She was classified as Coast Guard Ship First Rate when transferred to Kingstown. She was originally one of many British Navy ships called H.M.S. "Neptune". A previous "Royal George", flagship of Admiral Kempenfelt, a pioneer expert in naval signalling, was the subject of a well-known poem, *The Loss of The "Royal George"*, when, in 1782, she capsized and sank with "twice four hundred men", when at anchor at Spithead. During "Royal George's" spell the Admiralty also stationed the brig "Ranger" at Kingstown from 1865–7, with the unusual designation as a "church ship".

After the "Neptune" came the recently commissioned steam corvette H.M.S. "Pallas", built in 1865, but she was soon replaced by the newly built Coast Guard Depot Ship H.M.S. "Audacious", replaced in her turn in 1871 by a very important vessel, one of the first group of iron-clad battleships built by the British as an answer to the French "Gloire", Europe's first battleship constructed with protective iron sides. This was H.M.S. "Vanguard", a celebrated British Navy name, which was sunk in a collision during fleet manoeuvres in fog off Bray Head. She was a ship of six thousand and ten tons, designed by E. J. Reece, chief constructor of the British Navy from 1863–70, and built at Birkenhead at a cost of £355,000. Her three thousand, five hundred h.p. reciprocating engines and twin screws, gave her a speed of thirteen point six knots. She carried nine inch guns and had a complement of four hundred and fifty men. She took fifty six minutes to sink after collision with her sister ship "Iron Duke". Plans to salvage her were never carried out, and it is hoped that diving vandals do not break the law by interfering with her still intact hull. The only casualty when she sank was Captain Dawkin's dog, which speaks well for the quality of the seamen stationed at Kingstown at that time. The very similar "Iron Duke" replaced her from 1875–7. These two were perhaps the most interesting and, for their time, most modern Kingstown guardships. "Iron Duke" gave way to the steam frigate "Topaze" (1877–8), after which the custom built Coast Defence Ship "Bellisle", predecessor of the long remembered guardship cruiser "Melampus", came on station.

The cruiser "Melampus", built at Barrow on the opposite side of the Irish Sea between 1889 and 1892, spent nearly half of her career as Kingstown Guard ship, 1893–1905. She was commanded for some time by the Duke of York, who was to become, in 1910, King George V, and under whom she took part in extensive fleet manoeuvres in 1905. She was classified as a Second Class Cruiser, four thousand, three hundred and sixty tons, three hundred and twenty feet long, speed nineteen knots. Her complement was three hundred and eighteen men, she had a two inch armoured steel deck and a conning tower with three inch steel armour. Her armament was eight four point seven inch guns, ten six-pounder and thirteen one-pounder guns, and four torpedo tubes. She never fired a shot in anger and was sold for scrap in 1910. The "Melampus" buoy was the special navy buoy to which she was moored in Kingstown/Dun Laoghaire harbour: a vicious storm more than sixty years after "Melampus's" demise uprooted her buoy and it became no longer a local seamark. Later, interesting vessels stationed at Kingstown were armed yachts "Ilex" and "Boadicea".

The light cruiser "Dublin", built in Scotland 1911–13 was briefly at some stage near the end of British rule at Kingstown, and her battle ensign was presented to Christ Church Cathedral, from whence, some seventy years later, it was transferred to the National Maritime Museum in Dun Laoghaire. A five thousand, four hundred ton cruiser four hundred and thirty feet long, with eight six inch and four smaller guns and two torpedo tubes, she had a speed of twenty five knots. She had a dramatic career in the 1914 war, serving in the Dardanelles campaign and then as Admiral Kelly's flagship in the Adriatic, where she was damaged by a torpedo from an Austrian submarine. In May 1916 she took part in the war's biggest naval battle, Jutland or Skager Rak.

During the 1914 war Kingstown harbour as a naval base was chiefly concerned with anti-submarine work and mine-sweeping. The vessels stationed there were

HMS Adventure

chiefly destroyers, patrol craft of various kinds, and armed trawlers equipped as minesweepers. In fact, though they did a great deal of damage, only two U-boats were sunk, "U87" on Christmas Day 1917 by patrol boat "P56" and sloop "Buttercup", both of which frequented Kingstown, about halfway across the Irish Sea, and "UB 85", sunk by the drifter "Ereopis" off Larne in April 1918. Numerous other U-boats were reported, in good faith, as sunk, for instance by H.M.S. "Lively" between Kingstown and Holyhead on October 12th 1918, believed to have been the U-boat that had sunk the "Leinster" two days earlier (but she was destroyed by the British mine-barrage between Scotland and Norway) and two by "Helga", both proved false later. Several other submarines were sunk off other parts of the Irish coast, with warships familiar in Kingstown taking part.

Kingstown/Dun Laoghaire harbour was made decisive use of by the British Navy during the Easter Rising, 1916. Telephone and telegraphic communication was broken between the area of the rebel operations and other strategic areas notably the Imperial capital and seat of government, London. The break in communications was ominous for the Imperial Government, but the essential reconnection was made by the main Irish naval base of the British Navy, Haulbowline, Co. Cork, despatching at full speed to Dun Laoghaire the modern six inch gun light-cruiser "Adventure", which kept her radio at the disposal of the British Government in Ireland and its military authorities engaged in combating the insurgents. When this author published a small book, *The Sea and the Easter Rising*, on the occasion of the jubilee of the Rising, President de Valera asked to see it. After perusing it, the President, in discussion with the author, admitted that the rebel leaders had never once thought of in some way obstructing Dun

Laoghaire harbour or the mouth of the Liffey as part of their preparations which members of the Maritime Institute of Ireland had long thought one of the most sensible things they might have considered doing.

## YACHTING

Perhaps to the surprise of Harbour Master Hutchison, with his constant anxiety about the fate of cargo sailing ships in or approaching from Dublin Bay, and about the unexpected growth of his charge as a significant commercial and major mail and passenger port, and about problems concerned with H.M. ships in his harbour, blinded in one eye when giving help to a ship in trouble in stormy conditions in 1844 and surely proving himself worthy of his £1,000 p.a. salary – (quite big then) – the Royal Asylum Harbour, quite early in its career, began to be a yachting centre. By the time Hutchison retired there were three yacht clubs operative at Kingstown and in 1872 there had been the first yachting fatality in a Kingstown boat. Daniel O'Connell's grandson Daniel was drowned when his yacht "Peri" sank near the North Burford Buoy. This was in the first recognised single-handed yacht race. Its disastrous outcome led the Dublin press to criticise at length the rash folly of yachtsmen daring to tempt the sea by challenging it single-handed.

The Royal Irish and Royal St. George yacht clubs each claim to have been Kingstown Harbour's first club. The facts seem to be that plans for establishing a yacht club were first made by what became the Royal Irish, but owing to delays, another group, the "George", got active first. The Royal Irish Club's attractive club-house, believed to be Europe's first custom-built yacht club, opened in 1848. This club in its early years was very democratic. It opened its ranks to such abnormal beings as foreigners and Jews, and it went out of its way to encourage the local fishing community. It organised an annual fishermen's regatta with handsome prizes for the winners of rowing races. It instructed all its members to watch out for innovations in gear, or improved gear, in other fishing ports that they might visit, and to be sure to report them on their return to Kingstown for relay to the Kingstown fishermen.

The Royal St. George Yacht Club was exclusive, its members were drawn chiefly from what there was of an aristocracy in Victorian Ireland. It succeeded in due course in making its regattas celebrated throughout the yachting world, attracting the most famous yachts in the world in Kingstown's headiest days as a world yachting centre, during the last thirty years or so before the outbreak of the Great War.

The Royal Alfred was also a somewhat exclusive club, whose members competed in all the port's big yachting events but did not provide themselves with a permanent headquarters.

What is now the National Yacht Club began as a rowing club. It did not achieve the same reputation for high living and high quality yachts and yachting until after the establishment of the separate Irish State. It won a national reputation as a centre for almost everything that was important during the Lemass era, several members of the family being members. When the author as Hon. Secretary took over the Dun Laoghaire Lifeboat Station in 1956, Mr. John Jenkins, the coxswain told him, by way of advice, that "one of these three clubs sees a lot of drinking, another a lot of gambling and I would not like to say what you would see in the third".

The Motor Yacht Club was founded thirty years ago as a more democratic counterpart to the more expensive and supposedly more exclusive Royal St. George, National and Royal Irish Clubs. It was an immediate success in its corner at the base of the West Pier facing the Coal Harbour. It was remarked that while members of the port's lifeboat crew were boatmen in the older clubs, in the Motor Yacht Club they were members.

In recent years the problems of insufficient yacht moorings in the harbour, and of where a marina or marinas could be built without making it impossible for the small boat owner not a member of any club to operate any more at Dun Laoghaire, have tended to draw the clubs together in a more realistic and generally co-operative mood than heretofore.

It would be wrong to omit from this section the laudable efforts of the Sailing Centre, at the base of the West Pier opposite the Motor Yacht Club in the building that once housed the Irish Nautical College, training centre for aspiring merchant navy officers, the transfer to Cork of which was a blow to Dun Laoghaire. The Sailing Centre has great achievements to its credit in teaching young people seamanship and how to learn to sail a boat without fleecing them, and is also a valuable centre for discussion and further education for more experienced leisure sailors.

Nor should the St. Michael's Rowing Club be forgotten, which valiantly, year after year, trains youngsters from the economically deprived areas of Dun Laoghaire in boatmanship, elementary seamanship and racing rowing. All these activities would no doubt impress the shade of Captain Toutcher, and satisfy that of Hutchison that he had presided over developments in his harbour that made it possible for them all to carry on and enhance aspirations of his more than a century after his death. An invaluable facility that was also available in the harbour for generations for boat lovers unable to afford their own boat has gone, part of the steady drift towards making leisure use of the harbour more "classy". This was the availability of rowing boats for hire at a modest fee. Some of the happiest of the countless hours of my life spent on the waters of Dublin Bay were spent in hired Dun Laoghaire rowing boats. Sadly it now seems too late to revive this facility.

At this stage it is just to recall some of the splendid pleasure craft not locally built that have in their day graced the waters of Kingstown Harbour, and mention those who sailed some of them. First for mention must be the magnificent

J Class yachts

J. Class monsters, with a crew of up to fifty, like King Edward VII's and his son's "Britannia", and Thomas Lipton's "Shamrocks". (When Lipton was seized with an ambition to win the America's Cup, which he never fulfilled, he had built for him no fewer than five "Shamrocks").

Other great yachts of the early years of the century were "Flora" and "Avalanche", then "Maureen" and "Candida", of all of which illustrations still abound, and "fast-gliding" "Iverna", whose skipper was a well known local man, Reilly O'Neill. Then there was the 25 "Fodhla", which was a "local", built by John Doyle of Kingstown and owned by one of the last Lord-Lieutenants, Lord Dudley.

The Mahonys characterised the heyday of the J. Class yachts as "the time when a centre-board was built down twenty nine feet through the keel of a yacht".

Of course not all great yachts were big yachts, anymore than the converse is true. One of the more picturesque and memorable events of the not so distant past, for instance, was the Royal Irish Club's annual Firefly race, an exciting small boat affair.

The passionate enthusiast about the history of yachting from Dun Laoghaire and Dun Laoghaire as a yachting centre should consult the words of W. M. Nixon (even though a Howth man with a Northern accent!) and his colleague in the management of Ireland's leading yachting periodical "Afloat", authentic Dun Laoghaire man David O'Brien. Each of these is among the most accomplished of

'Saoirse'. Homecoming of Conor O'Brien,
first Irish yachtsman to circumnavigate the globe

contemporary yachtsmen.

David O'Brien and John Lavery, in their Dun Laoghaire based Fireball, scored a notable triumph in September, 1995 by winning the World Fireball Championship in Dublin Bay, after a hundred hours of rigorous training in local waters. Earlier in that summer the locality's reputation as an ideal centre from which to run international sailing events was reinforced, as it is year by year, with the staging of the Carlsberg J24 European Championships, a contest that rose high in the news through the disqualification of no fewer than seventeen of the competitors in the fourth race.

David O'Brien, incidentally, contributed a provocative article to the *Irish Times* on 10th November, 1995, deploring and analysing the decline in recent years of dinghy racing in Dublin Bay. This particular skill has for generations been one for which Dun Laoghaire harbour and the Dublin Bay Sailing Club operating from it have had an exceptionally high reputation. Anyone interested in maintaining that reputation would do well to look up the *Irish Times* article mentioned. Many dinghy sailors look to the new port authority that has arisen out of the implementation of the 1996 Harbour Act to use its position to help the organisations and individuals concerned with a serious revival of dinghy racing to get together in a constructive spirit to work out the best methods to accomplish that end.

Two sailing men who placed Dun Laoghaire in the headlines by their skills were men of singularly different backgrounds and outlook. One was Conor O'Brien who came back by way of Dun Laoghaire in 1931 in his yacht "Saoirse", the first individual to sail round the world under the Irish tricolour, adding to the world's oceanographic knowledge by a discovery he made in the South Atlantic. The other was Charlie Gilmore, brother of the celebrated Republican Socialist George Gilmore, one of the founders of the Republican Congress which gathered a fair amount of support in the country in the mid-1930s, and whose views he shared. Charlie was a Dun Laoghaire Harbour Constable, and was the first to turn a discarded turf-carrying Galway Hooker into a neat and successful pleasure yacht. In due course Dun Laoghaire Harbour became a centre for converted hookers. Charlie was also in his day celebrated for his differences of opinion (professional as well as political) with Harbour Master from 1938–49, Lieutenant Commander Shiel. It was one of the local events to go walking on the East Pier and listen, at a discreet distance, to the Commander and his Constable arguing with equally abundant courtesy and conviction.

Another local expert with a converted hooker is Paddy Barry of Monkstown, who in 1991 completed a remarkable five thousand, five hundred mile cruise, that saw him well into the Arctic Circle in his hooker "St. Patrick". Paddy like Charlie Gilmore, could make the vision of his hooker brought into port with a stiff breeze blowing one of those visions of which great poets can make great verse. Paddy is quite recently back from a daring "South Aris" expedition (not in his hooker!) in Antarctic waters in the wake of the epic open boat voyage, early last century, by Irish Antarctic explorer, Ernest Shackleton.

John Ryan, broadcaster, restaurateur, one-time editor of the much missed "Dublin Magazine", member of Dun Laoghaire Lifeboat Committee, was also an accomplished painter as well as yet another Dun Laoghaire hooker expert. As a painter he re-pioneered the art, for many years abandoned, of serious marine painting in this country. A successor with an international reputation in this sphere is another local amateur sailor, an accomplished author and a doughty environmentalist, one more native of Dun Laoghaire though since recently resident in the capital, Peter Pearson, already mentioned.

Concluding this section it is only right to recall a class of Kingstown/Dun Laoghaire sailing boat owner, sometimes truly skilled, often rash, nearly always poor, who rowed and sailed his boat not for pleasure but to earn a paltry living. These people were the "hobblers" who, until even into the second quarter of the last century, would race out from Dun Laoghaire even in the most filthy weather hoping to be the first to accost and board a ship seen to be approaching the harbour, with the offer to its Master to act as linesman and so facilitate the berthing process. There are too many cases for comfort recorded when hobblers set out from the harbour in high hopes and never returned alive. The "hobblers" of his day were the "pilots" mentioned by Harbour Master Hutchison in an official report to the Harbour Commissioners cited above.

Detail of Duncan's Martello Tower and Kingstown

# 10
# SCIENTIFIC & TECHNOLOGICAL EXPERIMENTS

The dream that fires man's heart to break.
To build, to do, to sing or say
A beauty Death can never take,
An Adam from the crumbling clay.

JOHN MASEFIELD

Masefield, who became Poet Laureate in Britain, had served at sea in hard driven sailing cargo ships towards the end of the 19th century. He was a perfectionist who admired the remarkable efforts of designers and builders of the last generation of cargo sailing ships that, for many years, were able to compete successfully with the ever-improving and proliferating steamships. He welcomed every new invention to improve safety at sea and educate public opinion about the importance of the sea for mankind.

MENTION HAS ALREADY BEEN MADE of the remarkable, and successful, experiment which the London Post Office and the City of Dublin Steam Packet Company made of ensuring that every place in the island of Ireland, not too far from a railway station, would every day have the possibility of keeping all its clocks and watches on accurate time.

That experiment, which turned into a daily routine, was not the first time that the Royal Asylum Harbour had been the scene of a scientific experiment. Already back in 1852 the first anenometer, an instrument designed and built by Professor Robinson of Trinity College, Dublin, had been erected on the East Pier Wall. Anemometers are now common throughout the globe, but the science of measuring the strength of the wind at a given spot, so important to meteorologists, navigators and many others, was first developed here with the help of the instrument erected on the East Pier Wall. It fell into disuse in the early 1980s after the special waxed paper for its recordings was no longer available, but is still mechanically sound and a replacement was inaugurated on the East Pier recently.

The use of a word made up of the Greek words "wind" and "to measure" to designate the new instrument recalls how deeply rooted all learning (of European origin) was, for centuries, in the classics of ancient Greece and Rome.

It is worth noting that for a number of years in the later part of the 19th century, John Wigham, by many considered the greatest lighthouse engineer of the century, was one of the Office of Public Works Commissioners for Kingstown Harbour. A Scot who resided most of his life at Booterstown on Dublin Bay, he kept his fellow Commissioners abreast with if not ahead of the most important marine scientific developments of the time.

Still, in many ways the most sensational scientific experiment with which the harbour was associated in its Kingstown period, dates from 1898. The brilliant young half-Italian half-Irish scientist, Guglielmo Marconi, had first transmitted a message through the air, without wires to travel upon, in Italy in 1895. That achieved, he quickly improved his primitive radio equipment till it was capable of broadcasting a coherent and uninterrupted message over a considerable distance, in most weather conditions, from a moving platform, using the Morse Code.

Marconi then in 1898 hit on the idea of broadcasting the description and result of a sporting event. The prelude to countless broadcasts of sporting events to innumerable enthralled listeners took place in Dublin Bay. The Royal Saint George Yacht Club's prestigious annual regatta was accompanied by a steam tug with Marconi on board, with broadcasting equipment. In an upper room in the Kingstown Harbour Office of those days, now the Heritage Centre in Moran Park, was an assistant of Marconi's, with a journalist from the Dublin Daily Express, since defunct.

It happened to be a foggy day, and spectators along the front trying to see over the harbour into the Bay, and people at the north-facing upper windows of the Harbour Office, could make out nothing of what was going on. Marconi, however, was able to get his steam tug to take note of the position of each yacht, as it moved westward towards the finishing line, and of every change of position in the array of yachts. The mesmerized journalist took down in shorthand Marconi's assistant's translation from the Morse messages he was receiving, and eventually found himself with a clear description of the race, and the name of the winner, which by a coincidence was an Italian yacht, and his paper was able to provide the public with deails of an event denied to anyone else. A plaque recalling this achievement of Marconi off the port of Dun Laoghaire was unveiled in Moran Park on the centenary of what accurately, for once, may be termed an epoch making event. One of the inventor's daughters was present.

Not long after Marconi's experiment, Irish scientists used Kingstown Harbour as a base for pioneer experiments in a technique that has proved to be of very great value for several important activities in most of the world's seas and oceans. They sortied from the harbour and between Scotsman's Bay and Dalkey Island set off a series of undersea explosions, calculating the time that the sound of each took to travel between two points and, more important, what was revealed of the composition of the seabed between the two points. The technique is now used daily in scores of different places and has revealed information of priceless value.

An older contemporary of Marconi, who is customarily listed as one of the most important scientists who opened the way for Marconi and several other outstanding scientific geniuses, was the Irish professor of Huguenot French descent, Professor Joly of Trinity College Dublin. A number of his researches concerned sea water and many took place in the sea in and near Dun Laoghaire Harbour. Joly (1857–1933) was Professor of Geology and Mineralogy at Trinity College, Dublin from 1897–1933. He invented the thalometer and meltometer to determine the melting point of minerals. He saw the importance of radio activity in the earth's history and was a pioneer of colour photography. He introduced radioactive methods to date geological formations, was famous for inventing new apparatus to further various researches, and from the strictly maritime viewpoint is above all celebrated for having introduced estimation of the earth's age by the length of time taken by salt to accumulate in the sea. One of the greatest scientists of his age, he was for a time the Kingstown Harbour Commission's Special Scientific Adviser.

In 1946 Dun Laoghaire Harbour was chosen for a very widely publicised demonstration of the latest Schermuly Rocket Life-Saving apparatus, then becoming compulsory equipment in many merchant fleets, coast guards and life-saving services.

Sixty five years after Marconi's first broadcast of a sporting event, a start was made in Dun Laoghaire Harbour on an experiment that was to prove a lasting success and greatly enhance the Harbour's reputation: and the safety of its approaches.

The Commissioners of Irish Lights decided, despite the warning fingers of a number of self-styled and some real experts, to build in the harbour a huge concrete tower as a lighthouse, of a kind used by the Swedish lighthouse service in the tideless waters of the Baltic, to take the place of the lightships which had now for a century and a half lit the approaches to the Kish Bank. The various phases of the construction of this phenomenon were followed, with a keenness rarely if ever before given to maritime affairs, by the Dublin press. Photographs proliferated of the tower in all its stages and diagrams demonstrating what would be in it, and how, after being secured on a firm base created on the sandbank to which it had been towed, its higher portion would telescope upwards.

The lighthouse was built in its early stages in two locations in the harbour. The two separate structures were then assembled at St. Michael's Wharf. The whole procedure was delayed by storm damage to the base section, which was sunk deliberately to shelter it, before being raised and towed from the Coal Harbour to St. Michael's Wharf. It was then discovered to be so much harmed that it had to be abandoned and a new one started. Shades of Rennie and Hutchison saying "I told you so" to those of the obstructors in London who had refused permission for the originally planned narrower harbour entry with the inward turning pier ends. (The abandoned original base is now a feature of Greystones Harbour).

At last on May 21 1965, in their Notice No. 12 (1965), the Lights Commissioners announced that on May 29 or as soon afterwards as circumstances would permit (the event actually occurred on June 30) "a reinforced concrete lighthouse will be towed out from Dun Laoghaire Harbour and placed on the seabed in a position 123 (T) 5.5 miles from the Baily Lighthouse". The tower, the Notice continued, has a base with one hundred and four feet diameter which would be totally submerged when placed on the seabed, after which the tower would rise in three sections with diameters sixty four feet, thirty six feet and eighteen feet surmounted by a helicopter platform thirty three feet in diameter. Lights to be placed on the helicopter platform would be at a height of one hundred and one feet. The total weight of the structure is twenty five thousand tons, and its light has a strength of two million candlepower, capable of being raised to three million in fog, more than twice the power of the light in the last Kish lightship.

The lighthouse was officially inaugurated on November 9 1965, by E. F. Benson, Chairman of the Lights Commissioners, and has been in operation ever since (recently automatized), a lasting tribute to those who built it in Dun Laoghaire harbour.

At the time of the construction of the Kish Light a very well attended demonstration was held in the Coal Harbour of the use and usefulness of inflatable liferafts, the incalculable value of which was beginning to be recognized in the seafaring community. That demonstration hastened a much more widespread installation of this device, and a Department of Transport Marine Notice (No. 11 of 1969) some years later bears witness to the fact that by then, by the Merchant Shipping (Life-Saving Appliances) Rules, 1967, many types of vessels were now obliged to be equipped with it.

Another important marine development with the inauguration of which Dun Laoghaire Harbour was involved, was a systematic wave-data investigation at the Kish, the Barrels and the Daunt Rock, published by the Institution of Engineers of Ireland in April 1971. The information published had been systematically gathered over a long period (a wave recorder was in operation throughout the twelve months till the new Kish light was inaugurated, on board the last Kish lightship, and contemporaneously seventeen years of wind velocity recordings at Dublin Airport were minutely studied).

The data for each station covered:

Wave heights – Spring
Wave heights – Summer
Wave heights – Autumn
Wave heights – Winter

Zero crossing periods – Four seasons
Spectral width parameter – Four seasons
Spectral width parameter – Whole year
Persistence diagram
Scatter diagram
Ten and hundred year waves

Among facts discovered was that the highest wave at the Kish lightship in 1964 was on November 29, with wind NNE force six, reaching twenty six point nine feet. Among various calculations it was judged that every ten years the Kish tower would once experience a forty seven foot wave, and every hundred years one of sixty four feet, as already noted.

The World Fisheries Exhibition of 1971 of which mention has been made above was an occasion when some aspects of the latest fishing technology first became public knowledge, once again making the name of the port of Dun Laoghaire more familiar to seafarers. Soon after the completion of the revolutionary Kish Light Tower, the lifeboat at Dun Laoghaire, the first steel-hulled fourteen knotter in the RNLI's service, was involved in technical experiments new to Ireland. This new lifeboat, "John F. Kennedy", ON 1002, was the first Irish lifeboat equipped with radar, and she inaugurated the now regular practice at every Irish station of joint exercising with helicopters of the Air Corps in air-sea rescue work. Twenty years later Dun Laoghaire became the operational centre for the first of regular cross-channel air-sea rescue exercises, involving passenger ferries and naval vessels from both Ireland and Britain, specially preparing for dealing with a possible emergency to a passenger ferry. Dun Laoghaire lifeboat in the late 1970s also held an exercise necessarily less elaborate but no less vital in view of the possibility of a descent of a commercial aircraft into Dublin Bay over which area eight hundred fly daily.

# 11
# A FEW PARTICULAR EVENTS

The ancient rune of the venturer man,
Builder of ships since the world began,
To brave the perils and dare the ways
Of the sea that serves him, the sea that slays.

C. FOX SMITH

Ships are no longer built in Dun Laoghaire, but who knows what lies in the future? In the past, our harbour has witnessed the keel-laying, the launching, and the first crucial trials of a variety of craft, including some of the finest yachts of their day. It would be pessimistic to assert that, in an ambience so rich with boat and ship-building traditions, those skills have died beyond hope of revival.

As in every busy harbour, the routine of the Asylum Harbour is interrupted daily by incidents – some serious, some humorous, some farcical – as if the harbour felt the need, like the Roman poet and philosopher, Terence, to emphasize that *nihil humani a me alienum puto.* Some of the, fortunately not very numerous, truly disastrous incidents in the port's history, like the hurricane of February 1861, have already been described. Here are a few more that emphasize that the Asylum Harbour's history has been neither drab nor monotonous.

In 1860 six unfortunates with connections with the port found themselves in court charged with offences. Five prisoners got three months' hard labour for having "signed ship's articles to sail in the barque "Aden" to Batavia and elsewhere for three years and then in the Irish Channel refused to touch another rope unless to work the ship in Kingstown", and Michael Doyle (46), gardener from Ballycarrick, Co. Wicklow got one month for the charge that "he shouted to Her Majesty's ship "Ajax" and jumped from the East Pier, Kingstown into the harbour and said he dreamed that if he swam to the ship he would be made a Baronet or a Bishop".[19]

In 1858 fines of 10/- each were introduced by the Commissioners for "any member of the public intruding into the ship passenger's area".

19 Information in a letter from Officer of the O.P.W. in charge of Kilmainham Gaol, May 25th 1996, headed "Kilmainham Gaol: Maritime Crime".

On Novemer 15th, 1865, Sarah Baxter was fined £12.10s (a heavy fine for then) on each of two counts of selling liquor without a licence from a shed at the end of the East Pier (where she had the right to sell confectionery).

1870 – Henceforth official currency transactions were to be in English, not the then (as now) lower value Irish currency.

1870 – The first club-house of the Rowing Club which was to become the National Yacht Club, since extended, then seriously damaged by fire, then rebuilt, was completed, at a cost of £4,000.

October 16 1878 – The Commissioners received legal advice that from now on they were entitled to levy the same charges as those authorised by the Dublin Port and Docks Act 1869. This was a triumphant if long delayed acknowledgement of the now sixty two years old Kingstown Harbour's right to greater financial freedom.

In July 1880 the port had differences with certain shipowners who came to Kingstown to export horses. Harbour Commissioners decreed that horses to the number of not above fifteen could be handled between 10 a.m. and 4 p.m. only and only on condition that they made up less than twenty five percent of the ship's total cargo. The ships were to be charged at 5/- (passenger steamer's) rate for each day spent in port and $6.^{1}/_{2}$d tonnage sale if going to home ports and $10.^{1}/_{4}$d. if foreign. When the Anchor liners "Castalia" and "Mercury" began regular visits, the Harbour Secretary suggested counting each horse as one ton of freight, but Harbour Master Crofton feared that a higher charge would stop the Anchor ships calling ("Mercury" took eighteen horses that July). Few citizens of present day Dun Laoghaire realize that, for a short period, their local port was engaged in a transatlantic passenger service.

On 16 November 1886 the steamer "Solway" of Glasgow, seven hundred tons, with a crew of nineteen and fourteen passengers, left Belfast at 4 p.m. on her way to Dublin with a cargo including whiskey, oils, rum, and flour. At about 6.30 a.m. a very severe explosion occurred on board. A number of people were blown into the sea, others were frightfully burned. Captain Fry sent the ship's boat under his son to the Isle of Man to seek aid and set the remaining crew to patch up some of the damage, eventually getting a tow from another ship through rough weather which greatly hindered efforts to extinguish the fire. The hull of the "Solway" was towed into Kingstown, where Harbour Master Crofton quickly organised help and had the fire put out and casualties taken to St. Michael's Hospital. The ship's boat was never seen again. The *Irish Times* of 17 November wrote: "No equally melancholy event has perhaps ever occurred in our coast".

This was indeed an occasion when Kingstown/Dun Laoghaire proved to be a very genuine port of refuge. The *Irish Times* account of the incident follows:-

"EXPLOSION IN THE CHANNEL – NINE PERSONS KILLED"

"Last night about ten o'clock a small steamer named the "Solway", trading between Bristol and Glasgow, was towed into Kingstown in a sadly crippled condition. It appears from the particulars which have reached us that while passing down the Channel yesterday midday a terrific explosion took place on board the steamer blowing the decks and bulwarks into atoms, killing no less than nine of the crew, and inflicting what it is feared will prove fatal injuries on a large number of persons who, on the arrival of the disabled steamer in the harbour, were at once taken to hospital. The origin of the explosion is not as yet definitely known, but it is attributed to either of two causes – one is, that the boiler gave way and the other is that it arose from some dynamite. It is of course, impossible to say, with any degree of accuracy, to which, if indeed, to either, of these causes the disastrous occurrence is attributable, but beyond doubt, the work of destruction has been most complete, and the appearance presented by the ill-fated steamer is one of the most deplorable that it is possible to imagine. Most of the wounded were taken to St. Michael's Hospital where, it is unnecessary to add, they received prompt and skilful attention from the staff of that institution, which was quickly in attendance augmented, we understand, by several professional gentlemen not officially connected with the hospital. The sad calamity, notwithstanding the late hour at which it became known, created widespread consternation throughout the town and district and sincere and deep sympathy for the numerous sufferers. In addition to those who were killed by the immediate effects of the explosion a great many persons – members of the crew and passengers – were blown into the water and drowned. The cargo was principally composed of oil, which, according to one account exploded. The wounded are in such a deplorable state that it would be cruelty to ask them to give a narrative of the details of the catastrophe, even if their condition did not render it all but impossible for them to do so.

On the steerage deck at the time of the explosion passengers were literally enveloped by flames, and before the unfortunate people could escape from the fire that surrounded them their shrieks of terror and screams of agony were silenced in a terrible death. The rest of the passengers and crew – some fearfully burned – fled to the stern of the vessel. There terror and confusion prevailed. So believing that in a few minutes the flames would reach the rest of the highly inflammable cargo with which the vessel was laden, the Captain launched a boat and, its crew's terror at a worse impending fate, put off towards shore, but whether they succeeded in reaching it or were drowned in the storm is not known. The flames continued to spread, the scene on board, as described by the survivors, was one of the most awful horrors ever witnessed. The fire, fed by the oil and the timber, raged fiercely, rising high in the air and rendering the portion of the ship in which it burned a blazing, crackling mass of flames.

The Captain at once ordered the crew to the buckets to throw water upon the fire, and by this means, and with the aid of donkey-engine and hose, and unyielding effort, the crew succeeded in keeping the flames somewhat in check, at least as far as prevented them extending further. In the midst of the dire distress which prevailed, a steamer came in sight of the burning vessel, the crew exploded rockets and burned blue lights as tokens of extremity, but the steamer, it is sad to say, passed on unheeding the signals, leaving the unfortunate people on board the "Solway" to their fate. All that time till evening the ship lay in the midst of a heavy sea, exposed to the storm and with its crew manfully fighting the flames which threatened to burn the vessel down to the waters. Between five and six o'clock a pilot attracted by the signals of distress came from shore to the assistance of the "Solway". A pilot went on board, and the vessel was steered for Kingstown Harbour."

March 29, 1886, the troop transport "Resolute" ran down and sank in the harbour the brigantine "Virtue". The prestigious *Illustrated London News* thought the incident (an extremely rare blemish on the harbour's excellent safety record) was worthy of a dramatic black and white drawing.

December 24, 1895, as the Christmas crowds were gathered in the shopping streets word spread that the lifeboat "Civil Service No. 7" a modern boat capable of sailing as well as being rowed, as almost exclusively lifeboats had been till a few years before, had been called out. The crew of fifteen were quickly assembled under Coxswain Williams, including Williams' father, former coxswain, who in 1891, won the Lifeboat Institution's rarely awarded Silver Medal for a particularly perilous service in a redoubtable November storm. The "Palme", that belonged to the last great commercial sailing ship owner the Swedish Erikson, from the Finnish-inhabited but then Russian ruled Åland Islands, had tried to get into Kingstown but was driven past the entrance by the severity of the easterly gale. She had a crew of nineteen and the Captain's wife and child on board.

On receipt of news that the "Palme" was driven aground off Blackrock, first the lifeboat "Civil Service No. 7" then the second lifeboat, "Hannah Pickard", left the harbour under the supervision of Captain Crofton, Hutchison's successor as Harbour Master, to give help. The first was capsized by freak seas and the whole

Memorial to lifeboat crew

fifteen crew drowned. "Hannah Pickard" under Coxswain Horner was unable to reach the wreck and was driven ashore at Vance's Harbour, Blackrock. Horner had six volunteers from H.M.S. "Melampus" in his crew. This was the worst lifeboat disaster in Irish history. The crew of the "Palme" survived on their slowly disintegrating ship till 27 December, when the boat of the lighthouse tender "Teraght" rescued them. A memorial to the dead lifeboatmen is on the promenade overlooking Carlisle Pier near the George IV Monument. Every Christmas Eve, Dun Laoghaire Lifeboat puts to sea. A member of its crew casts a wreath into the sea where their predecessors drowned. On the hundreth anniversary a big memorial meeting and service took place in the Maritime Museum, formerly the church where Hutchison as well as some of the 1895 men worshipped, and where Hutchison's gold medal was on display. The Finnish Ambassador, Eamon Gilmore T.D., Minister of State at the Department of the Marine, and other notabilities were present.

A map made by the Harbour Engineer in 1909 shows that the Harbour Commissioners' Office then was just inshore of St. Michael's Wharf, just past the Sailors' Rest, one time refuge for shipwrecked seamen. For its last seven years it was the National Maritime Museum's first home.

In 1911 the veteran lifeboat "Hannah Pickard" went on her last exercise before withdrawal from service, but the exercise occasioned "a row with the honorary secretary",[20] with the result that Coxswain Brennan[21] and the second coxswain, his brother, both resigned. (But it was soon all patched up, and both got a lump sum in compensation when "Hannah Pickard" was withdrawn).

In November 1915 a hurricane force storm reminiscent of that of February 1861, drove the one thousand, four hundred and fifteen ton steel Aberdeen barque "Inveresk" ashore at Sandycove and smashed the top of the monument commemorating the heroic John McNeill Boyd, which had been placed over the spot on the East Pier where he had been drowned.

In September 1921 the reed foghorn which had recently replaced the gun fog signal at the East Pier was transferred to the West Pier Light. The L.N.W.R., now owners of the "mail boats", had to pay £10 a year for this amenity.

On October 29, 1925, the recently acquired first motor lifeboat at Dun Laoghaire went out on her finest service, the last by a local lifeboat to a commercial sailing ship, to the one thousand, nine hundred and eighty five ton German steel barque "Hamburg" aground on the Burford Bank, and brought in all forty six of her crew. She was one hundred and thirty days out of Melbourne with a cargo of three thousand, five hundred tons of wheat for Cork. Coxswain Dan Murphy was highly commended for this feat. This was the year when maroons were introduced for summoning the lifeboat crew to a service.

20 Dun Laoghaire Lifeboat Station Archives.

21 There was a succession of Brennans in the Kingstown/Dun Laoghaire Lifeboat Station's crews, all related, from at least as far back as the early 1870s, to Jack Brennan, whose retirement in 1980 was much lamented by his colleagues.

In 1926 Harbour Master Holmes had purchased for £30 a redundant RNLI double ended lifeboat from the rowing and sailing era. Her dimensions were thirty feet by eight point six feet by three point six feet. She was converted in the harbour to a divers' barge. In 1936 Captain Cassidy, Holmes's successor, decided to get rid of her. She was sold for £10 to a P. Tyrrell of Ringsend, but the new owner was not able to take her for two years "owing to poor health and bad salmon fishing". It would be interesting to have details of this boat's career in her glory as an official lifeboat, and of how she fared under Mr. Tyrrell. Meanwhile R. Shortall of Dun Laoghaire bought two old sails originally from Hutchison's time for £1.

On 11 October 1944 Harbour Constable Doyle, in impeccable handwriting, put in a report about how the motor schooner "Windermere" of Arklow[22] had damaged M. V. "Capella" and the neat little much missed port dredger "Sisyphus" when entering the harbour. A fortnight later Lieutenant Commander Shiel, Cassidy's successor as Harbour Master, wrote to Kevin Tyrrell at Arklow announcing that a bill of £6/7/10 for repair to "Sisyphus" was on its way.

Autumn 1939. A serious note in the Harbour's archives at the National Archives in Bishop Street, Dublin, conveyed that an unprecedented world crisis was in progress and reports correspondence from the Saint John's Ambulance Brigade about the urgency of having personnel and material on the spot in case the port should have to deal with a torpedoed ship or survivors from one.

On 12 February 1940 arrangements were demanded from the Department of Defence for accommodation to be made available for two soldiers "guarding certain boats property of the Department of Defence". These, it is now known, were the two motor torpedo boats acquired at the last minute to form the nucleus of the naval force without which our declaration of neutrality would be invalid under international law. They were in charge of Lieutenant Basil Peterson, of the Air Corps, a Dun Laoghaire man who became one of the first leaders of the Maritime Institute of Ireland and author of *The Turn of the Tide*, one of the very rare maritime books published in Ireland between 1948 and 1981 which called on the people of Ireland to urge the building of a strong maritime economy and an adequate naval defence force.

In December 1943, with the reputation of his harbour very properly at heart, Harbour Master Shiel got directly in touch with the offices of the Taoiseach and the Minister for Coordination of Defensive Measures (Frank Aiken) requesting permission to allow the team filming a very popular series of actualities programmes in our censor-controlled country to film Dun Laoghaire Harbour. Permission was refused, but Major (later Colonel) Dan Bryan, our wartime Director of Military Intelligence and a real intellectual giant, appears then to have acquired Aiken's leave. But the Chairman of the Harbour Commissioners checked with a Mr. Moynihan, who seems to have spoken for the Taoiseach's

22 Once an elegant topsail schooner, built at Connah's Quay in 1890, "cut down" and motorised in 1927, one hundred and seventy tons, in trouble at Dun Laoghaire before, and one of the last of Arklow's picturesque schooner fleet.

office, and he gave a peremptory NO to publicity filming of the port of Dun Laoghaire in war time!

On March 4 1947 the twin screw diesel lifeboat "Dunleary II" carried out her greatest service, under acting coxswain Sam Blackmore, to the Norwegian motor passenger-cargo ship "Bolivar" breaking up in a powerful north-easterly on the Kish Bank. "Dunleary II", quite severely damaged, brought in forty five survivors including the Antarctic explorer Admiral Evans (of the "Broke"), one of "Bolivar's" passengers.

In 1954 the beautiful ninety five years old schooner "Brooklands", the last Irish commercial purely sailing vessel, called at the Coal Harbour for the last time before her loss on the Saltees shortly after.

In 1959 the last of the once large fleet of Arklow auxiliary schooners, the "De Wadden", called into the Coal Harbour just before being erased from the fleet. She is now a show-piece museum ship at the Merseyside Maritime Museum.

On November 7 1956, Captain Reginald Kearon, who had succeeded Captain Shiel as Harbour Master in 1951, went out on an evening fishing expedition in severe weather in spite of urgent advice, and was drowned near the Poolbeg lighthouse with two companions. He had recently become honorary secretary of the lifeboat station, and had unfortunately strictly forbidden the coxswain ever to put to sea without his permission. When the alarm came that a launch was in trouble in the Bay, the coxswain began a long and fruitless search ashore for Kearon. The result was that when the boat did put out it was too late. Commander Harvey, Irish District inspector of the RNLI, held an enquiry, and proposed closing the Dun Laoghaire Lifeboat Station and leaving rescue in Dublin Bay to the Poolbeg Lifeboat Station. When this writer protested against Harvey's proposal to close Ireland's oldest lifeboat station, Harvey said he would drop the proposal if the writer would agree to take over the secretaryship, which he felt it obligatory to do, remaining in the office for twenty six years. As a result of Captain Kearon's death, Captain Thompson, who had once had a long spell commanding the famous "Muirchu" (based in Dun Laoghaire), became Harbour Master.

On July 9, 1968, a new optic was fitted in the East Pier light, which has been converted to electricity from incandescent paraffin vapour.

In June 1969 late at night in stormy conditions in the Coal Harbour, Eric Offer, Dun Laoghaire Lifeboat Coxswain, won the Lifeboat Institution's Bronze Medal, the first of that body's rarely awarded medals won by a local lifeboatman since Henry Williams in 1881, for a most courageous and highly skilled rescue of a drowning man of some eighteen stone weight.

In 1967 the Dun Laoghaire Harbour Sea Scout Group was established, and took over the former Arklow lightship "Albatross", built in Leith in 1926, and now decommissioned, as its headquarters, over by the West Pier where Irish Lights keeps any lightship not on station. She was transferred to the Grand Canal

Basin in summer 1995 and still retained for use by the Sea Scouts.

The Dublin *Irish Press* of May 12th 1970 published "sensational" news about Dun Laoghaire port, namely that on the previous day hundreds of tons of ammunition and arms had been loaded behind a cordon of "heavily armed troops" and with a large crowd of spectators kept at a very respectable distance, on board "a British Naval vessel at Dun Laoghaire Pier". The whole transaction had been kept strictly secret partly from fear of hostile demonstrations against a British warship, partly from anxiety that residents near the port would start a barrage of complaints against the transport of live ammunition too close to their homes. In fact the ammunition was chiefly heavy nine point two inch shells, that had been left behind by the British Navy when it evacuated the "Treaty Ports" at the mouth of Cork Harbour and at Lough Swilly in 1938. The big nine point two inch guns (standard armament of the British Navy on its armoured cruisers, already obsolete in 1914) were shipped away too, and the whole event was soon forgotten. No such quantity of ammunition has passed through our harbour since.

On November 24 1988, following several years of strong public pressure by local opinion, particularly through a widely representative body known as the Harbour Watch, and a well-attended conference of all interested bodies called by the Department of Marine, the Dun Laoghaire Harbour Planning Review Group, chaired by Professor Mac Aleese and set up by the Department of Marine the previous June, published its report. This outlined a plan for full development of the harbour as a passenger port, yachting and leisure centre, minor commercial port and general local amenity.

In 1991 an interim Dun Laoghaire Harbour Authority was set up, advising the Department of the Marine, which had taken over the port from the Board of Works in 1989. In April 1992 the Harbour Development Plan was put before the public. It was an amalgam of the ideas in the Report of the Planning Review Group and subsequent suggestions put forward particularly by Dun Laoghaire Sailing School, Harbour Watch, Dun Laoghaire Corporation, Dun Laoghaire Chamber of Commerce and on behalf of the lifeboat station.

In Spring 1993 site investigations for new development of the harbour were started, with core samples being taken over the entire harbour area.

In August 1994 work on the new ferry terminal complex was commenced. Also in 1994 a group of German minesweepers visited the harbour for the commemoration held in the Maritime Museum of the rescue by the small Irish coaster M.V. "Kerlogue" in December 1943 of one hundred and sixty eight German seamen whose ships had been sunk by a British task force. Some members of the British task force and more than fifty survivors of the German ships were received by the President of Ireland, Mary Robinson, and heard speeches by her, the German Ambassador and David Sheehy, President of the Maritime Institute of Ireland, and were later entertained on board the Naval Service's flagship L.E. "Eithne", berthed along the East Pier.

Then on May 10, 1997, at a moving ceremony on board "L.E. Emer" in Dun Laoghaire harbour, recognition in full was at last given, as the Maritime Institute had long been urging, of the unique services to our nation provided during the period of the Second World War by Commander Seamus O Muiris, Director of the Marine Service, predecessor of the Naval Service, which he largely had to improvise. A portrait of this former Royal Navy officer from Galway who had been at the terrible Battle of Jutland in 1916, and who had resigned his commission in protest against the behaviour of the Black and Tans in 1920, was presented to the Minister for Defence Barrett, who gave it to Naval Service Director Commodore Kavanagh to have it permanently hung, with the portraits of each Naval Services Director, in Naval Headquarters, Haulbowline, Cork. Members of O Muiris's family were at the presentation.

Anyone seriously interested in the bitter, and at times acrimonious enough to be called ferocious, controversy that stirred Dun Laoghaire and neighbourhood ceaselessly from early in the 1980s to past the middle of the 1990s about the future of our harbour might be interested to know that in the National Maritime Museum the Maritime Institute of Ireland has a large number of indexed press cuttings relating to the port of Dun Laoghaire going back indeed as far as 1957. These can be examined in the Museum by arrangement with the Museum's librarian.

From these it can be seen that as early as the 1960s Councillor Jack Fitzgerald of Dun Laoghaire Corporation and a group of lovers of the harbour began pressure for modernization and development of the harbour, seeking improved amenities for the small boat-owner, more commercial traffic so as to develop local employment, plans for serious development of boat building around the harbour, and the encouragement of tourist cruising. Another demand was the restoration of boat hiring in the harbour. Voices were heard intermittently questioning the wisdom of allowing much profit to be lost to the port with the sale by coal importers, for generations the local merchant princes, of property that in a balanced community, it was thought, could have been in some way or other useful to the harbour. In the years roughly from 1960 to 1980 there was always a hope that Dun Laoghaire Corporation would put pressure on whatever Government was in office to get the Board of Works, as the owner of the port, to consider itself under an obligation also to develop it, not simply to preserve it (which on the whole it did very efficiently, if hardly hurriedly). As has been noted, also, for a number of years there was movement to make sure that Dun Laoghaire (the country's sixth fishing port in 1969) would grow as a fishing port.

In the 80s controversy raged chiefly around the need for a marina or marinas at Dun Laoghaire, as there were insufficient moorings for pleasure craft which were believed to be seeking berths here in large numbers and which would bring wealth to the locality. When a serious proposal for a marina was tabled it was seen that it would take over the Old Harbour and deprive small boat owners of essential space. That part of the controversy was ended when Mr. Charles Haughey, the then Taoiseach and alleged sponsor of this scheme, graciously received the Harbour Watch, the small boat owners' champion, and gently let the plan expire.

A period followed when a number of big yacht owners, ignoring two facts, that Dun Laoghaire grew out of and depends upon its passenger traffic, and that it is the harbour dues paid by the passenger vessels that keep the port financially viable, opened a campaign to move the passenger traffic out of Dun Laoghaire and give Dublin (despite several evident advantages of Dun Laoghaire such as its short but vital closer situation to Holyhead) the monopoly of passenger traffic across the central Irish Sea (an ambition frustrated many times by past history). The growing interest of local public opinion, reflected in renewed pressure by local politicians at national level, torpedoed this piece of what appeared to many to be selfish local treachery.

1994 saw the start and 1995 the remarkably rapid completion of the new Dun Laoghaire Passenger Terminal, the greatest advance made in the equipment of the port since Hutchison and the construction of the Carlisle Pier. Very soon, the new terminal won an international award for its functional excellence and aesthetic attraction. In great part this achievement was due to the pioneer imagination of the Department of Marine's First Secretary, Ó Muircheartaigh.

At the time of writing a new optimism and a refreshing wish for harmony, without sacrifice of constructive criticism, seemed to permeate the atmosphere around the port. Much of this, at least accordng to one observer, is the result of the conciliatory, efficient and imaginative attitude of members of the interim harbour board, the Minister of State at the Department of the Marine (no doubt with his Senior's approval), Deputy Eamon Gilmore, the self-effacing but immensely industrious Harbour Manager, Mr. Tom Vaughan, and, not least, Hutchison's worthy successor, Harbour Master Captain Carter. It is fervently to be hoped that this atmosphere and attitude will be fostered and intensified now that the port has got a permanent governing authority, established by the 1996 Maritime Act as a semi-state commercial company, on March 3rd, 1997.

# 12
# THE FUTURE

Ye true relations of such rank and station,
With clear observation pray list awhile;
Our work surpasses the flood of Jordan,
Strong Baalbec's works on the river Nile;
For Hector, Caesar, or great Alexander,
Who made nations with tear and frown,
Were they existing they would land with pleasure,
And spend their leisure in sweet Kingstown.

It is strongly to be hoped that the future management of Dun Laoghaire harbour will be inspired with the same spirit of pride and unbounded optimism as moved the learned balladeer of the premises of Kingstown Harbour in far-off 1821.

THE STORY OF THE CREATION in a wilderness of a harbour that had to be man-made as it has none of the attributes of a natural harbour, specifically to fulfil a function that quietly stopped being more than a minor function, a harbour that was never quite finished but within fifty years of commencement had won an international reputation, a harbour that begat behind and around it a quite picturesque, populous and economically thriving town, is really quite an epic.

What view can one have of the future for the port? The locals have for generations taken it for granted, forgetting that a harbour, like any other facility, has to keep up with the times or go into decay. The harbour, by adding a long-overdue new ferry terminal and linking its future as it did in the 1860s and 1890s with the most advanced type of sea-transport hitherto conceived, is capitalizing on its situation four miles closer to Holyhead than Dublin with an attractive town and alluring uplands visible from the deck of an approaching ship and a long-proven high reputation for safety. Among the tens of thousands who have sailed to or from this port in the past have not only been persons of importance in many spheres, politicians like Parnell, thinkers like Tom Kettle, poets like Ledwidge, scientists like Walton, monarchs like George IV, Victoria (twice) and Edward VII, Habsburg princes and Indian rajahs, national heroes like James

Larkin, Michael Collins, Arthur Griffith and Erskine Childers, and businessmen like Thomas Lipton (many of whom wrote about the harbour and their voyages from and to it), but myriads of the anonymous citizens without whom the great would have nobody to practice their greatness upon nor the important to prove their importance. Without the passage to and fro, in the best types of vessels available, of continuing anonymous myriads the port has no future.

Thus it is essential to have port management as wise and up-to-date as in Hutchison's day, and ships as up-to-date now and in the future as the City of Dublin Company's were in the past. We have for the moment, thanks to the Stena Company, the ships. It is to be hoped that the legislation recently introduced about the harbour's future provides the machinery guaranteeing that the port will always have an authority truly representative of all that is best and most far sighted in the Dun Laoghaire community. To be sure to have such an authority assisting the economy and the morale of the local community, that community must learn to interest itself more closely than it has in the past in its harbour. The more the community understands its harbour and its needs, and expresses its opinion on them the safer and more productive will the harbour's future be.

Among steps that must be demanded, and among the principal, is ongoing development of the port as a flourishing passenger port, the following seem reasonable to hope for as well:–

> Development to the limit possible, not forgetting possibilities behind the West Pier, of facilities for the leisure boat user of limited means, whether as a private individual or as a member of a club, or some sort of association, such as, for instance, trade unions promote in some ports on the Continent.
>
> Help to the traditional clubs to develop (in harmony) their full potential, hoping to keep alive and improve Dun Laoghaire's reputation as a national and international yachting centre.
>
> Encouragement of a cooperative project or projects to re-establish a boat building industry at Dun Laoghaire, again not forgetting the area behind the West Pier.
>
> Encouragement of the maintenance and development of the other existing facilities in the harbour, the work of Irish Lights and the lifeboat station, the Sea Scouts, the Sailing School, the St. Michael's Rowing Club, and, not least, the vital thoroughly up to date facilities for discharging and loading with regularity a sizeable volume of freight. Dun Laoghaire must also be able to welcome ships of the country's hard working Naval Service and an occasional foreign naval visitor, and might find it possible to encourage in and around the port progress in vitally important areas of marine research.
>
> Finally, both piers and the shoreline between their bases and of course the new Ferry Terminal and a refurbished Carlisle Pier, must be

maintained as attractive centres both for the scores of strollers who are surely likely to continue the strolling tradition that dates from the port's very first years, and for visitors looking for sources of entertainment or education.

In the summer of 2000, with Dun Laoghaire port not yet two hundred years old, there is still argument and there are still doubts about its future. It was built after many years of ever-growing demand as the result of a final effort of unrelenting pressure on the authorities in London by the ever sparse, but closely united, population living around Dublin Bay. Also by the shipping comunity in the capital, native shipowners of every designation and representatives of foreign shipowners trading to Dublin. It was looked upon as a hard-earned amenity for the citizens living around the Bay and the shipping community in the capital. It was administered first by commissioners appointed by the Viceroy, then for most of its existence, by the Board of Works, whose administration for most of the time can be summed up as honest and efficient but unimaginative, particularly in its later decades. It is now administered by a Board meant to represent the various interests using the harbour in their different ways. Many had hoped that a carefully elaborated system of selection of membership of the Board would manage to guarantee a strong element of the elusive ingredient, supposed to inspire every form of government of Irish life, called democracy. In fact the application of democracy in the administration of the port of Dun Laoghaire is left, in practice, to the members of the Board and, in a measure, their employees.

## CONCLUSION

The harbour's final years of management by the Board of Works were turbulent. In the words of a life-long lover and user of the port and upholder of our country's too long ignored maritime traditions, Tim Magennis, "an attempt at a commercial take-over of the coal harbour of Dun Laoghaire for a privately-owned marina" took place. It was foiled by the energetic activities of an organisation thrown up by the harbour-using public, called the *Harbour Watch.* Among those most active in this body were Deputy Eamon Gilmore, Councillor Jane Dillon-Byrne, the late Matt Byrne and myself, whose opposition to the prospect of big money dictating the future of the harbour was evidently approved by the public who re-elected them in style when they next faced the voters.

Then in 1997 a coalition government in Dublin consisting chiefly of the Fine Gael and Labour Parties, got a new Harbour Act passed by Dáil Eireann, which abolished the harbour boards which had for decades managed most of the State's ports, withdrew from the management of the Board of Works those ports controlled by it, and arranged that all these ports should henceforth be managed by commercial companies, the members of which would be chosen somewhat complicatedly and not unaffectedly democratically. Such a Harbour Company has now for more than two years been managing the Asylum Harbour of Kingstown, now Dun Laoghaire.

Among recent developments in the port of Dun Laoghaire, some of them set in motion under the previous régime, are: the handling of all passenger traffic for the foreseeable future to fast jet-propelled ferries (an expert's description of which, written by Dun Laoghaire's present Harbour Master, is printed in Appendix XI in this book); the handling henceforth of the greater part of the port's imports and exports by the ferries, the entry into operation of the "airport style" new Dun Laoghaire passenger terminal – very popular according to continued soundings by the author of this book; continuation of regular use of Dun Laoghaire harbour by the Commissioners of Irish Lights and the nation's Naval Service; an increase in use of the harbour for sea-angling but an end of its long career as a major fishing port on the Irish sea; a steady increase in the use of the harbour for leisure sailing, but how exactly the different elements of the leisure sailing users will, or can, mutually accommodate their interests is by no means clear; the restoration to the Dun Laoghaire lifeboat station (which it is worth re-emphasising, is the country's oldest and in some years its busiest) of a proper Lifeboat House, opened early in 2000 at a ceremony by the author of this book, some forty years after the demolition of the handsome previous Lifeboat House, a long delay which was scandalous, arbitrary and an insult from authority to the memory of the twenty-three Dun Laoghaire lifeboatmen who have given their lives trying to save others and the scores of other volunteers who have kept this essential service operative for now nearly two centuries.

If the details of why Dun Laoghaire Harbour was built are less well-known than they should be (which is why the book was written) the people of Dun Laoghaire have never ceased to look upon the port as their own, of which they are proud, it having been built as the result of public demand before officialdom eventually decreed it, and from instinctive realisation that without Dun Laoghaire Harbour there would be no sizeable, handsome Dun Laoghaire town, only a small village.

The way the harbour will be managed in the next few years will decide how the public of Dun Laoghaire in the third century of its existence (due to be celebrated in less than two decades) will feel about what has for almost two centuries been their pride.

In a few years time it will be possible for the citizens of Dun Laoghaire to pronounce judgement on whether recent or present developments of the Harbour have enhanced its value as a precious asset for the pleasure and profit of the citizens of Dun Laoghaire inherited from their ancestors, or if it has become too much an instrument for the pleasure and profit of a selfish minority.

# APPENDIX I

CERTAIN STAGES OF GROWTH

a) Numbers of ships shown by port registers in the Board of Works archives as visiting the port exclusive of warships, mail steamers or ships sheltering or waiting for the tide.

1842 – 129;
1847 – 184;
1852 – 247;
1857 – 302 including 38 ships which had called in "for orders";
1867 – 741. The *Irish Times* of 3rd June 1866 reported that the Board of Works (the port's owner's) 1865 report showed that in 1864 238,025 tons and in 1865 308,827 tons of shipping called at Kingstown.

b) Information in a letter to the author from Harbour Master Lieutenant Commander Thompson dated May 22 1972, in reply to some queries:

Number of commercial vessels excluding lighthouse tenders and the regular ferries visiting Dun Laoghaire in 1971: 14
Number of trawlers regularly visiting Dun Laoghaire in 1971: 15 (one called more than 30 times)
Number of moorings for pleasure craft: 419 (in 1995: 560) increase largely as result of introduction in 1995 of a fore and aft mooring régime).
Final sentence: "No improvement works in progress and none immediately contemplated".

c) Freight movement by volume through Dun Laoghaire:

| | | |
|---|---|---|
| 1976 | Exports 17 000 tons<br>Imports 17 000 tons | total 34 000 tons |
| 1977 | Exports 63 000 tons<br>Imports 51 000 tons | total 114 000 tons |
| 1978 | Exports 83 000 tons<br>Imports 88 000 tons | total 171 000 tons |

from a document entitled: Dun Laoghaire Harbour Development Project, written for the Irish Overseas Transport Association by George P. McVitty, Secretary, dated February 15, 1982.

These figures were an important factor later in that decade in getting the Department of Marine, newly set up, to start the process leading to the 1991 harbour development plan.

d) Figures published by the Dun Laoghaire office of Dublin Tourism for tourist numbers arriving in the Dublin area from Britain, Dun Laoghaire port being the route by which the majority of those coming by sea came each year; and the estimated annual revenue therefrom

| | | |
|---|---|---|
| 1989 | 329 000 | £59.5 million |
| 1990 | 547 000 | £56.8 million |
| 1991 | 620 000 | £66.0 million |
| 1992 | 606 000 | £65.7 million |
| 1993 | 630 000 | £76.6 million |

e) The throughput of cargo tonnage at the port of Dun Laoghaire in 1998 was:

| | |
|---|---|
| Inward | 150,000 tonnes |
| Outward | 90,000 tonnes |

# APPENDIX II

## CONTAINER TRAFFIC

In 1956 one of the rather rare proposals for a new kind of operation in the harbour came up for discussion, warmly welcomed by Harbour Master Reginald Kearon who in his short term of office showed himself to be a determined innovator. A memorandum signed by him dated October 15 1956 outlined his suggestions for implementing a proposal from CIE for bringing container traffic, then comparatively new but about to revolutionise the entire management of maritime cargo transport world wide, was put before the Board of Works as owner of Dun Laoghaire Harbour. Kearon showed how the marked fall in the importation of coal, which had been the ports basic import since its earliest days, had affected employment and revenue. In less than a month Kearon was dead in circumstances described in the text of this book. The new proposal refused to die, and in April 1959 was publicised at length in the newspaper *The Evening Press* which reported that CIE had sent an engineer to Larne to train in the handling of container traffic, which had become well established there, and how a plan to test the feasibility of container-handling at Dun Laoghaire had collapsed temporarily when the British government had commandeered, for its abortive campaign to prevent Egypt nationalizing the Suez Canal, the ship which had been specially chartered to discharge the first container cargo at Dun Laoghaire. But after this hesitant start the port began in the 1960s to develop the expertise in container management for which it is now well known.

# APPENDIX III

## CAPTAIN MALCOLM

The statement in favour of building an asylum harbour at Dunleary, in which Malcolm described the terrible reputation of Dublin Bay for shipwrecks and loss of life, has been widely and frequently quoted. A summary of the career of this distinguished seaman who spent many months in the harbour in King George IV's yacht "William and Mary", of which he was captain, here follows:

Sir Charles Malcolm, made Vice-Admiral of the Blue in 1847 and of the White two years later, was born in Scotland in 1782. His maternal grandfather and one brother were Admirals, another brother was a Colonel of Marines. He went to sea as a Midshipman at the age of thirteen and spent the next eight years in the Far East in a squadron operating against the Spaniards in the Philippines. He won rapid promotion, becoming in 1801 captain of a sloop and in 1803 of a frigate. Back in Europe he captained frigates in the North Sea, the English Channel and the Bay of Biscay always with distinction and was in charge of the "William and Mary" at Kingstown and also a second royal yacht, the "Royal Charlotte", from 1822 to 1827 on special service to the Lord Lieutenant of Ireland, the Marquess of Wetherbey, who made him a Knight. The rest of his active career was in India, where he transformed the East India Company's Bombay Marine into the (formerly Royal) Indian Navy of today. He was celebrated as the first mariner to introduce steam navigation to the Red Sea. He died on June 14 1851.

# APPENDIX IV

## BRITISH NAVAL VESSELS THAT SPENT LONGISH PERIODS ATTACHED TO KINGSTOWN HARBOUR EITHER AS THE OFFICIAL GUARDSHIP OR IN SOME OTHER CAPACITY

As noted in the text, the British Admiralty from the moment of the conception of the idea of building an asylum harbour in Dublin Bay said that it could be of considerable importance in its plans and activities. Several ships belonging to the British that were stationed in the new harbour are mentioned in the text. Here we list as far as has been possible the British guardships from H.M.S. "Ajax" which arrived in 1853 and other British naval vessels stationed here for more or less lengthy periods.

As early as 1822 it was decided, as shown in Section 6, to station the hulk "Essex" at Kingstown, as a convict ship. This vessel had been a unit of the navy of the recently founded USA, which had been captured by the British navy in the war of 1812 to 1814 between Britain and USA.

In 1848 H.M.S. "Wolf", a sloop built in 1826, was sent to Kingstown as a coal hulk (the British navy was in the process of changing to the steam engine instead of sails as the means of moving its ships.) From 1851 to 1856 "Wolf" was lent by the navy to the Board of Works in Dublin, but she returned to Kingstown in 1856 where she remained till 1865 when she was transferred to Cobh, where the creation of a major naval base was being arranged.

H.M.S. "Ajax", categorized as a Third Rater, details of which are in the text, came as Guardship in 1853, and stayed till 1864.

H.M.S. "Royal George", formerly "Neptune", built in 1827, classed as First Rate, replaced "Ajax" in 1864 as Guardship and remained till the last day of 1869.

The corvette H.M.S. "Pallas" took the place of "Royal George" on the first day of 1870 and remained on duty till October that year when the Coast Defence ship H.M.S. "Audacious" took her place till July 1871. She was a brand new ship having been completed in 1869.

Kingstown was still further honoured when "Audacious" was replaced by H.M.S. "Vanguard" one of the then new fangled iron-clad battleships rushed into production by Britain in reply to France's "Gloire", Europe's first steam iron-clad battleship.

Unfortunately, as noted in the text, "Vanguard" was sunk in collision during naval manoeuvres (as a base for which the Admiralty used Kingstown) by a sister-ship H.M.S. "Iron Duke" (the British Navy's next "Iron Duke" was its Grand Fleet's flagship in the 1914–18 war).

Iron Duke

H.M.S. "Iron Duke" acted as Guardship from October 1875, just after "Vanguard"'s loss, to September 1877.

The Coast Defence ship H.M.S. "Topaze" followed "Iron Duke" as Guardship till July 1878.

"Topaze"s successor was H.M.S. "Belleisle", again a brand new ship, which gained a considerable reputation during her career.

The cruiser H.M.S. "Melampus" about which there is more in the text and which left many memories, was the successor to "Belleisle". She was taken out of service in 1900, and research has not discovered her immediate successor.

But when the 1914 war began a whole division of ships under wartime organization was operative out of our harbour, between September 1914 and July 1915, an armed yacht H.M.S. "Ilax", and then till 1919 another armed yacht H.M.S. "Boadicea II" (which actually also served in the Second World war), played the harbour policeman and were known as guardships.

Only one other long termer came to light, the 1825 – built brig (a late sailing warship) H.M.S. "Ranger" was moored from 1835 to 1860 in Kingstown, first as a Hulk, then as a "Church Ship", function not defined.

Ghost of Three Sailors

# APPENDIX V

## THE HARBOUR MASTERS

Everybody acquainted with the everyday activities of a port is aware that the smooth-running and cumulative success of these activities depend on the efficiency, imagination and tact of the port's harbour master. Curiously, when I began this investigation there was no list of the harbour masters who have held that office down at the harbour, nor was there an easily visible list of them among two thousand, two hundred and seventy two documents so well preserved in the National Archives. It was only by hazard at quite widely separated intervals that gradually the roll-call of these distinguished public servants with the dates of their assumption and departure from office, became clear. Here they are.

| | |
|---|---|
| Lieutenant (later entitled in official documents Captain) William Hutchison | 1816–1874 |
| Captain F.G. Crofton<br>(Veteran of the Crimean War in 1854 and of the British war of China, 1857). | 1874–1900 |
| Captain P. Tudor | 1900–1909 |

| | |
|---|---|
| Captain A. F. Holmes | 1909–1931 |
| (his assistant harbour master C. Cassidy became Acting Harbour Master in 1931) | |
| Captain C. Cassidy | 1933–1938 |
| Captain L. Sheil (Lieut-Cdr. R.N.R.) | 1938–1949 |
| Captain R. Kearon | 1951–1956 |
| Captain A. Thompson | 1957–1975 |
| Captain J. Carter | 1975 to date |

Some of these, such as Hutchison, managed to remain immortal even through the fog of official documents, others do not. Hutchison has had a whole section of this work devoted to his critical period of harbour-mastership. Had he not consistently acted with outstanding moral as well as physical courage, with decisiveness, foresight, efficiency and imagination, the asylum harbour could well never have achieved much eminence. It remains a blot on the reputations of successive local authorities of Kingstown/Dun Laoghaire that no one of them to date has had the chivalry or gratitude to have any public building, street, square or park named after the man to whom they, as well as all other citizens of Kingstown/Dun Laoghaire, owed or still owe so much. It is to the credit of the independent harbur authority set up after 1989 that it named the first official vessel it ordered after the port's great first harbour master.

Crofton must have had, or at least appeared to have had, good publicly-recognizable qualities as the local authority named a fine major street along the edge of the western area of the port and a shorter street adjoining it and leading towards St. Michael's Hospital after him. He appears to have been conscientious and on occasion capable of resolute action but his official documentation does not always, and at once, bear the mark of an exceptional personality like his predecessor.

It is worth quoting two of the numerous everyday problems which Harbour Master Captain Crofton had to tackle from the earliest days of his appointment. On October 24, 1881 he reported, no doubt with considerable relief, that the schooner *Annie Cowley* out of Rotterdam was now fit to resume her voyage. She had put in owing to severe weather having lost her main boom – evidence of the permanent value of Kingstown/Dun Laoghaire as a harbour of refuge or asylum. Her cargo was dynamite.

This problem arose hard upon the outbreak of a controversy about charges levied by the port when "a small number of horses" (i.e. under twenty five percent of the full cargo) was embarked by any vessel at Kingstown. Meanwhile the master Giuseppe Bougigiovanni of the Italian barque *Italo*, had put in on September 8 in order to lighten ship before proceeding to Drogheda to discharge the bulk of his cargo. He had stayed at anchor in the harbour while transferring a portion of his cargo by arrangement to a schooner called *Agnes* which had already paid harbour dues. As his ship had not made use of or in any way encumbered any of the harbour's quays or other instalments, he saw no reason why he should be charged harbour dues. His correspondence was carried on in meticulous English which might not have been his own but his signature was in the same excellent handwriting as the text of his letter. Crofton was not moved.

Captain Tudor seems to have left many if not most of the problems of his short period of office to his assistant Commander Drury, for example mediation in the very delicate problem of the almighty squabble between the City of Dublin Steam Packet Co. and the L.N.W.R.

Captain Holmes must have had a great deal of favourable opinion crying out to be expressed on his behalf. The very fact that this man, a Captain (since 1908) of the British Navy (a high-ranking office equivalent to a Colonel in an army) managed to stay in office both through the Great War, when his port became a British naval base, and when he must have had tricky sharings of authority to negotiate and then through the complicated and sometimes explosive first nine years of the first Irish State, his allegiance to which must have been questioned by more than a few, must indicate a good deal more than a noteworthy instinct for survival. A diary of his years of office, if he wrote one, would be a rich source of information not only about Dun Laoghaire's history but about Irish history in general during the period. Even without a personal diary or papers it ought to be possible to glean quite a lot from British Admiralty official papers for 1909–1931. From the authoritative Lean's Royal Navy List it appears that he died in 1934 when his name ceased to figure in the list of retired naval officers.

Of Captain Cassidy it does not seem easy to say much beyond the fact that during his short spell as harbour master he seems to have carried on the same style of administration as Captain Holmes.

Captain Shiel was educated at Clongowes and then in the famous British merchant navy cadet officer's training ship "Conway" at Liverpool before joining the Ulster Steamship Company. After a few months he went off to complete his training in big cargo sailing ships. He had twice sailed round the world before he was twenty. He then served in the Elder Dampster, Bibby and Royal Mail lines, earning close acquaintance of ports in Africa and South America. He gained his Master's certificate in 1912. He joined the Royal Naval Reserve before the Great War and in its earlier stages saw service in the East Mediterranean and the South Atlantic, before passing the last two years of the war under Admiral Keyes in the particularly dangerous Dover Patrol (like Evans of the "Broke" saved by Dun Laoghaire lifeboat off the Kish Bank by Sam Blackmore and his crew in 1947), as First Lieutenant in H.M.S. "Hazard". Before becoming Harbour Master he lived in Corrig Avenue, Dun Laoghaire.

Captain Kearon was unquestionably a very fine seaman, with a splendid reputation with the Shaw, Savill and Albion shipping company on whose celebrated liner service to Australia he served. He also had imaginative ideas about improving Dun Laoghaire harbour which have been mentioned, and the prohibition placed by the Office of Public Works' Port Commissioner on his intention to follow one of them up greatly upset him, as he explained at great length to this author. He was also convivial and good company. He had however two qualities that proved fatal to him. His version of discipline I heard described as quite brutal by at least one person who knew him a great deal more closely than I. The fact that Dun Laoghaire lifeboat crew, who were not exactly kindergarten pupils, were so professionally impressed by his repeated command – and the way it was issued – NEVER to take the lifeboat to sea without his express order, led to the delay in getting the lifeboat to sea on the fatal 7th November night, 1956, which resulted in her arriving too late at the spot where the launch he was in had capsized.

Unfortunately, he could be rash to a degree unsafe for a man in his position. I know I was not the only person who drew his attention to the appalling weather forecast for that evening nor, I suggest, to the actual visible and tangible conditions. And he knew he was foolish to go, admitting it after a long discussion, and promising not to. Had there been, as there ought to be, a system of warning by flag at points around the coast, where swimmers or persons sailing for pleasure set out, Reginald Kearon could well be alive to this day as I do not believe he would have had the face, especially in the company of friends, to disobey a warning put up under his own authority.

Commander Thompson was a meticulous, patently honest and truthful public servant who was always dependable and more or less universally respected but not loved. He was probably chosen as someone exactly the opposite of Kearon, one who had been in state service through most of his career, took pride in his function but seemed to have few ideas outside the strict performance of what seemed to be his duty precisely according to the rules. Many will remember his regular appearance in an immaculate uniform, the golden braid on which appeared to be new every day, at the arrival and departure of each passenger vessel. If there was very little sign of the improvement the port so clearly needed and an acceptance of steps so deservedly unpopular as the first car ferry terminal at the base of the East Pier during his harbour-mastership there was during that time no scandal or disaster to stain the record of his administration.

Captain Shiel has been mentioned for among other things, his imaginative special recording of wartime passenger arrivals and departures, for his praiseworthy attempt to thwart one of the absurdities of our essentially absurd wartime censorship and for his vigorous and unending differences of opinion, chiefly on political matters, with the popular Harbour Constable Charlie Gilmore. These differences were carried on quite publicly, but never appeared to impair a proper mutual respect on both sides.

But what Sheil deserves eternal memory for I came across in a report from November 1941, unsigned but evidently written by one of the lifeboatmen, which emphasises that these (three colleagues of the writer of the report and

Sheil) were told by all present that they were risking their lives by crossing in the circumstances the bridge to Carlisle Pier, and begged not to do so.

The lifeboatmen involved in this affair, who were still attached to the station in 1956, and whose names appear on the document attached to Sheil's (clearly draft) report were Bert Smith (mechanic) H. Shortall, John Jenkins (later coxswain) and J. McDonald. MacDonald was a posthumous son of one of the lifeboatmen drowned in the "Palme" incident on Christmas Eve 1895. By a grim coincidence he was later drowned himself one stormy Christmas Eve when boarding a coaster in the Coal Harbour in which he was night watchman.

I think the Office of Public Works should (as I gather it did not) seek from the state some form of recognition for Shiel's behaviour. It should, I think, here be noted that since 1956 the secretary in charge at Dun Laoghaire lifeboat station, or his deputy in his absence, automatically hastens to the lifeboat station on receipt of an alarm and takes charge of direction of the rescue. This direction is subject to the final judgement of the lifeboat's coxswain and any such person as the Harbour Master or the person put in charge, now that it exists, by the Marine Rescue Centre.

It is only in paragraph thirteen of his report that Shiel, who obviously had to provide as objective an estimate as possible of the incident, was obliged to note his decisive act in running a seven inch manilla rope to the SS "Saint Kenneth" on the night of the incident, which his modesty had made him erase from paragraph four. In his paragraph eleven he virtually conceals the fact that he personally went to the point of peril on Carlisle Pier. Another account in the archives, one of model clarity, unspoiled by one unnecessary word, generous in its praise for the other heroes of the event, and praiseworthy because it is only after a very careful scrutiny of the report what suddenly vaults out is the irrefutable fact that Sheil himself was the true hero of the episode. Without his direction the port would almost surely have seen its worst catastrophe since the disasters of February 1861.

I was the more impressed by this report, as the report in the local lifeboat records, normally very full and admirably accurate, is truncated, and fails to give, as I read it, the praise to lifeboatmen who were still in the crew when I took charge of the lifeboat station fifteen years later (I was patrolling the banks of Lough Foyle for the LDF/LSF in 1941). I think the RNLI should have been asked by its local committee to give some special recognition to those who helped Sheil on this occasion, and the state should probably have congratulated him.

One of a number of ways in which Captain Carter has impressed this author and many others by attention to what he considers his duty, beyond any obligation of necessity, is his very regular attendance at meetings of Dun Laoghaire Lifeboat Committee. It is normal for that Committee to elect the local Harbour Master a member at every annual meeting. There are many matters going on in the harbour (or rumoured as being about to go on) which vitally affect the lifeboat service. This is particularly so with many changes taking place and with the lifeboat station waiting more than thirty years for a satisfactory new station to replace the fine Boat House demolished after nearly sixty years at the entry to Carlisle Pier. There was a period too, not so long ago, when all and sundry were submitting new plans for the harbour's future, and one group charmingly planned a future for our port without room in it for a lifeboat station at all. More serious has been the trouble the station has had to get the harbour authority to remove the slipway, down which till far off 1938 lifeboats used to glide (to the joy of beholders), from the long demolished boathouse into the water of the eastern part of the harbour.

Big, long term and immediate, problems cannot be solved by the Lifeboat Station without consulting the Harbour Authority through its proper agent the Harbour Master. Captain Carter's attentiveness to the lifeboat's needs, by regular attendance at the lifeboat station's committee meeting, as neither Captain Thompson nor apparently Captain Sheil did with any frequency has earned much gratitude from the lifeboat service. Other groups active in the harbour have also (not all!) found reason to be grateful to Captain Carter who, if by way of being outspoken which it is right he should be, is also courteous. He has the gift which some of his predecessors certainly had not, of making fascinating conversation and he has shown himself to be a Harbour Master ready to risk his own life, notwithstanding the high office he holds, which would have made it very easy for him to order somebody else to take the risk.

It was on 29 November 1990 M.V. "Fisko" had loaded a full cargo of frozen fish which was quite frequently exported to distant destinations from Dun Laoghaire often in ships with what still seemed rather exotic ports of registry like Valletta. She had the pilot already aboard and was now facing seaward in the act of casting off from No. 4 Berth when one of the harbour constables fell off the quay into the harbour. Without a moment's hesitation Captain Carter threw off his overclothes (remember this was November), swam to the man in peril and performed a classic rescue of an individual in danger of drowning. The man rescued had fallen into the water with his glasses on and Captain Carter noticed that he had them still on when brought ashore, to the man's amazement when he lifted his hand to the bridge of his nose. It took no little effort by this author to extract from Captain Carter the details of an event which proved him to be a worthy successor to men like Hutchison and Shiel.

Before becoming Harbour Master at Dun Laoghaire Captain Carter went through a long and varied set of experiences chiefly when serving in the tanker fleet of the British Petroleum Company.

# APPENDIX VI

## HOURS OF OBSCURITY

The hours of obscurity recorded by the Commissioners of Irish Lights at the East Pier Dun Laoghaire Fog Signal over a period of ten years are here noted as are the comparative figures at Baily Head Fog Station – one of very many factors, particularly in the days before modern navigational improvements became customary: – which would have been carefully watched by shipowners having a choice to make between sending their ships with passengers to Dun Laoghaire or to Dublin.

STATIONS

| | JAN | FEB | MAR | APR | MAY | JUNE | JULY | AUG | SEPT | OCT | NOV | DEC |
|---|---|---|---|---|---|---|---|---|---|---|---|---|
| | Hrs Mins | Hrs Mins | Hrs Mins | Hrs Mins | Hrs Mins | Hrs Mins | Hrs Mins | Hrs Mins | Hrs Mins | Hrs Mins | Hrs Mins | Hrs Mins |
| **1958** | | | | | | | | | | | | |
| DUN LAOGHAIRE EAST | 39 40 | 28 20 | 134 00 | 33 05 | 23 50 | 64 30 | 76 15 | 48 10 | 69 35 | 14 10 | 118 40 | 79 35 |
| TOTAL 729 Hrs 50 Mins | | | | | | | | | | | | |
| BAILY | 77 55 | 21 40 | 149 45 | 32 30 | 52 10 | 81 55 | 105 45 | 64 50 | 79 50 | 13 15 | 106 25 | 81 15 |
| TOTAL 868 Hrs 15 Mins | | | | | | | | | | | | |
| **1959** | | | | | | | | | | | | |
| DUN LAOGHAIRE EAST | 68 20 | 112 55 | 32 50 | 04 05 | 29 35 | 35 00 | 02 50 | 11 15 | 80 40 | 48 55 | 57 55 | — |
| TOTAL 454 Hrs 20 Mins | | | | | | | | | | | | |
| BAILY | 113 05 | 104 40 | 57 05 | 10 35 | 56 40 | 58 40 | 10 15 | 35 00 | 105 10 | 55 45 | 29 55 | |
| TOTAL 691 Hrs 00 Mins | | | | | | | | | | | | |

STATIONS

**1960**

DUN LAOGHAIRE EAST

| JAN | FEB | MAR | APR | MAY | JUNE | JULY | AUG | SEPT | OCT | NOV | DEC |
|---|---|---|---|---|---|---|---|---|---|---|---|
| Hrs Mins | Hrs Mins | Hrs Mins | Hrs Mins | Hrs Mins | Hrs Mins | Hrs Mins | Hrs Mins | Hrs Mins | Hrs Mins | Hrs Mins | Hrs Mins |
| 26 30 | 33 20 | 112 15 | 03 05 | 29 25 | 42 56 | 25 14 | 30 11 | 13 50 | 05 21 | 35 15 | |

TOTAL 435 Hrs 50 Mins

BAILY

| JAN | FEB | MAR | APR | MAY | JUNE | JULY | AUG | SEPT | OCT | NOV | DEC |
|---|---|---|---|---|---|---|---|---|---|---|---|
| Hrs Mins | Hrs Mins | Hrs Mins | Hrs Mins | Hrs Mins | Hrs Mins | Hrs Mins | Hrs Mins | Hrs Mins | Hrs Mins | Hrs Mins | Hrs Mins |
| 39 35 | 42 30 | 166 15 | 16 05 | 68 25 | 70 10 | 953 16 | 10 15 | 05 56 | 45 39 | 55 | 122 33 |

TOTAL 664 Hrs 25 Mins

**1961**

DUN LAOGHAIRE EAST

| JAN | FEB | MAR | APR | MAY | JUNE | JULY | AUG | SEPT | OCT | NOV | DEC |
|---|---|---|---|---|---|---|---|---|---|---|---|
| Hrs Mins | Hrs Mins | Hrs Mins | Hrs Mins | Hrs Mins | Hrs Mins | Hrs Mins | Hrs Mins | Hrs Mins | Hrs Mins | Hrs Mins | Hrs Mins |
| 31 35 | 20 30 | 26 30 | 96 35 | 21 25 | — 06 | 00 — | 46 50 | 17 20 | 20 55 | 67 35 | |

TOTAL 333 Hrs 15 Mins

BAILY

| JAN | FEB | MAR | APR | MAY | JUNE | JULY | AUG | SEPT | OCT | NOV | DEC |
|---|---|---|---|---|---|---|---|---|---|---|---|
| Hrs Mins | Hrs Mins | Hrs Mins | Hrs Mins | Hrs Mins | Hrs Mins | Hrs Mins | Hrs Mins | Hrs Mins | Hrs Mins | Hrs Mins | Hrs Mins |
| 45 40 | 44 45 | 54 00 | 137 45 | 23 40 | 2 30 | 11 45 | — 64 | 20 34 | 15 45 | 20 58 | 30 |

TOTAL 517 Hrs 35 Mins

**1962**

DUN LAOGHAIRE EAST

| JAN | FEB | MAR | APR | MAY | JUNE | JULY | AUG | SEPT | OCT | NOV | DEC |
|---|---|---|---|---|---|---|---|---|---|---|---|
| Hrs Mins | Hrs Mins | Hrs Mins | Hrs Mins | Hrs Mins | Hrs Mins | Hrs Mins | Hrs Mins | Hrs Mins | Hrs Mins | Hrs Mins | Hrs Mins |
| 35 15 | — 58 | 05 08 | 30 05 | 45 — | 26 55 | 535 6 | 40 61 | 50 10 | 30 04 | — 00 | |

TOTAL 243 Hrs 05 Mins

BAILY

| JAN | FEB | MAR | APR | MAY | JUNE | JULY | AUG | SEPT | OCT | NOV | DEC |
|---|---|---|---|---|---|---|---|---|---|---|---|
| Hrs Mins | Hrs Mins | Hrs Mins | Hrs Mins | Hrs Mins | Hrs Mins | Hrs Mins | Hrs Mins | Hrs Mins | Hrs Mins | Hrs Mins | Hrs Mins |
| 45 25 | 07 10 | 96 40 | 181 05 | 25 10 | 02 40 | 68 25 | 21 10 | 31 30 | 144 40 | 62 10 | 33 10 |

TOTAL 556 Hrs 25 Mins

**1963**

DUN LAOGHAIRE EAST

| JAN | FEB | MAR | APR | MAY | JUNE | JULY | AUG | SEPT | OCT | NOV | DEC |
|---|---|---|---|---|---|---|---|---|---|---|---|
| Hrs Mins | Hrs Mins | Hrs Mins | Hrs Mins | Hrs Mins | Hrs Mins | Hrs Mins | Hrs Mins | Hrs Mins | Hrs Mins | Hrs Mins | Hrs Mins |
| 38 40 | — 08 | 35 11 | 00 02 | 20 11 | — 15 | 14 05 | 17 15 | 10 15 | 13 55 | 26 05 | 16 00 |

TOTAL 169 Hrs 25 Mins

BAILY

| JAN | FEB | MAR | APR | MAY | JUNE | JULY | AUG | SEPT | OCT | NOV | DEC |
|---|---|---|---|---|---|---|---|---|---|---|---|
| Hrs Mins | Hrs Mins | Hrs Mins | Hrs Mins | Hrs Mins | Hrs Mins | Hrs Mins | Hrs Mins | Hrs Mins | Hrs Mins | Hrs Mins | Hrs Mins |
| 72 40 | 09 55 | 44 15 | 41 25 | 09 55 | 48 30 | 41 10 | 47 00 | 38 15 | 29 25 | 30 10 | 22 00 |

TOTAL 435 Hrs 40 Mins

STATIONS

| | JAN | FEB | MAR | APR | MAY | JUNE | JULY | AUG | SEPT | OCT | NOV | DEC |
|---|---|---|---|---|---|---|---|---|---|---|---|---|
| | Hrs Mins | Hrs Mins | Hrs Mins | Hrs Mins | Hrs Mins | Hrs Mins | Hrs Mins | Hrs Mins | Hrs Mins | Hrs Mins | Hrs Mins | Hrs Mins |
| **1964** | | | | | | | | | | | | |
| DUN LAOGHAIRE EAST | 53 16 | 36 25 | 84 00 | 00 40 | 37 10 | 09 15 | 24 15 | 07 20 | 31 15 | 12 25 | 37 20 | 18 00 |
| TOTAL 351 Hrs 25 Mins | | | | | | | | | | | | |
| BAILY | 74 40 | 59 50 | 00 15 | 31 00 | 51 20 | 31 25 | 21 15 | 14 30 | 17 10 | 31 20 | 35 45 | 26 45 |
| TOTAL 485 Hrs 15 Mins | | | | | | | | | | | | |
| **1965** | | | | | | | | | | | | |
| DUN LAOGHAIRE EAST | 32 00 | 42 50 | 25 40 | 21 05 | — 02 | 40 21 | 50 — | 05 00 | 40 55 | 02 30 | 12 00 | — |
| TOTAL 187 Hrs 40 Mins | | | | | | | | | | | | |
| BAILY | 29 55 | 36 10 | 74 00 | 07 30 | 18 45 | 25 25 | 56 25 | 15 35 | 09 50 | 78 56 | 11 55 | 29 35 |
| TOTAL 394 Hrs 00 Mins | | | | | | | | | | | | |
| **1966** | | | | | | | | | | | | |
| DUN LAOGHAIRE EAST | 35 00 | 28 05 | — 48 | 50 10 | 05 37 | 25 — | 08 40 | 42 45 | 06 30 | 23 55 | 00 30 | — |
| TOTAL 241 Hrs 45 Mins | | | | | | | | | | | | |
| BAILY | 41 35 | 46 50 | — | 88 05 | 9 55 | 43 00 | 2 00 | 20 30 | 48 25 | 10 25 | 20 45 | 30 05 |
| TOTAL 334 Hrs 35 Mins | | | | | | | | | | | | |
| **1967** | | | | | | | | | | | | |
| DUN LAOGHAIRE EAST | — 01 | 40 — | 06 00 | 03 30 | 6 55 | 13 00 | 17 20 | 43 35 | 00 50 | 49 00 | 57 55 | |
| TOTAL 199 Hrs 45 Mins | | | | | | | | | | | | |
| BAILY | 03 40 | 02 25 | 00 50 | 06 40 | 05 05 | 17 05 | 12 25 | 26 35 | 31 30 | 02 15 | 94 30 | 39 02 |
| TOTAL 242 Hrs 20 Mins | | | | | | | | | | | | |

These figures were useful in weakening the case of those in the early 1990s who wanted all passenger traffic across the middle Irish Sea to go through Dublin, leaving Dun Laoghaire as an outsize yachting centre.

# APPENDIX VII

## CAPTAIN SHIEL'S FIGURES OF PASSENGERS THROUGH DUN LAOGHAIRE IN THE LAST YEARS OF THE 1939–45 WAR AND THE FIRST POST WAR YEARS

This meticulous recording in a Harbour Office notebook was inaugurated by Harbour Master Lt. Cdr. Sheil in August 1943 and continued till January 1950 when he died. Acting Harbour Master O'Connor for some reason abandoned the practice. The total number of passengers arriving and departing each month at the port of Dun Laoghaire is interesting both to make possible a quick contrast between the number of passengers passing between Dun Laoghaire and Holyhead at the height of and in the early years after the the 1939–45 war, and as a fascinating exposition of the month-by-month fluctuations of travel in wartime, and of the periods when the inflow was greater than the outflow (some in critical war months). When the opposite was the case some of the early post-war figures vividly recall to long-time citizens of Dun Laoghaire the hordes of malnourished British citizens, still severely rationed, who poured over here to enjoy (above all!) a good beef steak.
The passenger numbers follow:

Arrival & Departure of mail steamers from 2nd to 21st Aug 1943 showing number of passengers carried to & from Dun Laoghaire. (both dates inclusive)

| DATE | TIME OF DEPARTURE | No OF PASSENGERS | TIME OF ARRIVAL | No OF PASSENGERS | TIME LAST TRAIN LEFT PIER |
|---|---|---|---|---|---|
| August 2nd | $7^{50}$ am. | 387 | $7^{37}$ P.M. | 751 | 9 P.M. |
| " 3rd | $7^{56}$ am. | 777 | $8^{03}$ P.M. | 760 | $9^{30}$ P.M. |
| " 4th | $8^{13}$ am. | 1,108 | $10^{25}$ P.M. | 975 | $12^{30}$ am. 5th aug |
| " 5th | $8^{11}$ am | 1,009 | $9^{06}$ P.M. | 1,048 | $10^{45}$ P.M. |
| " 6th | $8^{21}$ am. | 1,095 | $9^{32}$ P.M | 1,073 | $11^{30}$ P.M. |
| " 7th | $8^{28}$ am | 1,139 | $9^{12}$ P.M | 965 | $11^{15}$ P.M. |
| " 9th | $8^{11}$ am. | 946 | $9^{35}$ P.M. | 1,030 | $11^{30}$ P.M. |
| " 10th | $8^{18}$ am. | 1,081 | $9^{17}$ P.M. | 1,003 | $11^{15}$ P.M. |
| " 11th | $8^{12}$ am. | 1,045 | $9^{15}$ P.M. | 952 | $11^{15}$ P.M. |
| " 12th | $8^{11}$ am. | 1,049 | $9^{09}$ P.M. | 972 | $10^{45}$ P.M. |
| " 13th | $8^{16}$ am | 1,084 | $9^{35}$ P.M | 1,019 | 11 P.M. |
| " 14th | $8^{27}$ am | 1,186 | $9^{19}$ P.M. | 899 | 11 P.M. |
| " 16th | $8^{23}$ am. | 906 | $9^{30}$ P.M. | 1,002 | $11^{20}$ P.M. |
| " 17th | $8^{25}$ am | 1,021 | $9^{25}$ P.M. | 990 | $11^{15}$ P.M. |
| " 18th | $8^{27}$ am | 987 | 9 P.M. | 891 | $10^{45}$ P.M. |
| " 19th | $8^{20}$ am. | 927 | $8^{45}$ P.M. | 900 | $10^{30}$ P.M. |
| " 20th | $8^{28}$ am | 1,017 | $9^{28}$ P.M. | 1,008 | $11^{15}$ P.M. |
| " 21st | $8^{38}$ am. | 1,238 | 9 P.M. | 818 | $10^{30}$ P.M. |
| TOTAL | OUT – 18,002 | | IN – 17,056 | | |

| MONTH | No of PASSENGERS DEPARTED | No of PASSENGERS ARRIVED | REMARKS |
|---|---|---|---|
| MAY 1943 | 16,236 | 11,014 | from 26th April to 15th May (both dates inclusive) Pier was closed to non travelling public for Morning Departure Steamer. |
| JUNE " | 16,910 | 15,529 | Sailing Tickets in use all the month |
| JULY " | 18,917 | 23,923 | Sailing tickets in use all the month |
| AUGUST " | 26,180 | 24,199 | Pier closed to non travelling public from Aug 9th to Sept 4th (both dates inclusive for departure Steamers) Sailing tickets in use all the month |
| SEPTEMBER " | 26,781 | 16,668 | Sailing tickets in use all the month |
| OCTOBER | 17,679 | 9,412 | Sailing tickets in use all the month |
| NOVEMBER | 10,312 | 9,982 | Sailing tickets in use all the month |
| DECEMBER. | 10,015. | 24,420 | Pier closed to non travelling Public from 27th Dec '43 (to 31/1/44) |
| JANUARY '44 | 24,834. | 10,991 | Pier closed to non-travelling Public to 31.1.44 |
| FEBRUARY '44 | 11,723 | 9,484 | |
| MARCH " | 10355 | 9,815. | |
| APRIL. | 5,782 | 2,561. | on 25th April Sailing reduced to 3 days per week. |
| MAY | 3,270 | 1,290 | |
| JUNE | 2817 | 1569 | |
| JULY | 2,354 | 4,935 | |
| August. | 5,959. | 15,128. | Daily Sailings (except Sundays) resumed on 21st |
| | 210,1[illegible]4 | 190,[illegible]20 | |

| MONTH. | No OF PASSENGERS DEPARTED | ARRIVED. | REMARKS. |
|---|---|---|---|
| 1944 | | | |
| SEPTEMBER | 19,827 | 22,955 | One sailing each way daily, except Sundays. |
| OCTOBER | 19,262 | 14,573. | |
| NOVEMBER | 11,207 | 9,370 | |
| DECEMBER | 10,355 | 24,877 | Pier closed for Outward sailing 26/12/44<br>Pier closed to public for outward steamers 27.12.44 to 27.1.45 |
| 1945. | | | |
| JANUARY | 24,093 | 12,650 | |
| FEBRUARY | 10,141 | 8,317 | |
| MARCH | 11,049 | 14,958 | (Easter Sunday – 1/4/45) |
| APRIL | 16,635 | 12,408 | |
| MAY | 17,151 | 15,202. | |
| JUNE | 21,306 | 24,873 | |
| JULY | 26,770 | 28,502 | Sat 21st JULY, "HIBERNIA" developed leak, NO SAILING.<br>EXTRA SAILING on SUNDAY 29th JULY, BY CAMBRIA. |
| AUGUST | 29,451 | 28,075. | |
| SEPTEMBER | 28,872 | 25,969. | |
| OCTOBER | 27,023 | 18,790. | ✓ |
| NOVEMBER | 15809 | 14302 | ✓ |
| '45 DECEMBER. | 15,191 | 32,201. | Year ending 31·12·46 Dept 243,491<br>✓ Arr. 229 247 |
| | 243,491 | 229,247 | 14,244 |

No. of Passengers arriving and departing, D.R. Hbr
(Cont'd. from p. 11)

| MONTH | No Passengers Departed | Arrived | Remarks. |
|---|---|---|---|
| 1946. JANUARY | 29,501. | 13,481. | |
| FEBRUARY | 12,715. | 13,063. | |
| MARCH | 14.429. | 15.928. | |
| APRIL. | 19,232 | 22,004 | |
| MAY. | 23852. | 21168. | |
| JUNE. | 23985 | 29223 | |
| JULY | 34,162. | 48,637. | |
| AUGUST. | 57,383 | 54,898. | |
| SEPTEMBER | 54,484 | 36,514 | |
| OCTOBER | 28,417 | 19,413 | |
| NOVEMBER | 15.935 | 13451. | |
| DECEMBER | 17,080 | 35.976. | Year ending 31.12.46 Dep'td ~~314,095~~ 331,175<br>Arrd. = ~~307,756~~ 323,756<br>~~6,339~~ 7,419 |
| 1947. JANUARY | 30192 | 11706 | |
| FEBRUARY | 10102 | 10489. | |
| MARCH | 12295 | 13701 | |

Continued from page 21

| Month | Departing. | Arrival. | Remarks |
|---|---|---|---|
| 1947 May. | 19901. | 21637. | |
| June | 26569. | 28954. | |
| July. | 34747 ~~44 110~~ [illegible] | 44 110 | |
| Aug. | 52023 | 50.105. | |
| Sept. | 39217 ~~28 289~~ | 28289. | |
| Oct. | 24777 | 16943 | |
| Nov. | 11,360 | 12,314 | |
| Dec. | 13627 | 30,972 | |
| 1948 January. | 24904. | 12184. | |
| Feb | 11,722 | 10,078 | 244,161 103,154 347,815 |
| March | 15.630 | 18.950 | |
| April | 21181 | 16.225 | |
| May. | 24.228 | 24521 | 23915 9848 337,68 |
| June | 30712 | 32.655. | |
| July | 45925 | 65384 | |

Continued from page 32.

| Month | Departing | Arrival | Remarks |
|---|---|---|---|
| 1948 | | | |
| September. | 51,801. | 36,702. | |
| October. | 25,630 | 18,792. | |
| November. | 12,739. | 12,009. | |
| December. | 14,484. | 30,977. | |
| 1949. | | | |
| January. | 25036. | 10,885. | |
| February. | 11605 | 9,200 | |
| March. | 12401. | 11,458 | |
| April. | 17449. | 17,085. | |
| May. | 19061 | 18,610. | |
| June. | 28347 | 31,680. | |
| July. | 46,286 | 79,153 | |
| August. | 71381. | 56,103 | |
| September. | 53,584. | 37,949. | |
| October. | 22,129 | 19,898 | |
| November. | 11267 | 11,174. | |

No. of passengers arriving & Departing at Dun-Laoghaire.

Continued from page 43.

| Month. | Departing. | Arrival. | Remarks. |
|---|---|---|---|
| 1949 December | 15.650 | 32,493 | |
| January. | 26264, | 12150, | |

**BEACHING OF THE S/S SAINT KENNETH IN DUN LAOGHAIRE HARBOUR ON THE NIGHT OF SUNDAY 19th JANUARY 1941.**

| | | |
|---|---|---|
| 1. Length 185.5 feet. | Net Tonnage 287 | Built at Bowling in 1924 |
| Breadth 28.6 " | Gross " 681 | Registered at Dublin 1924 |
| Depth 10.7 " | Horse Power Engines 85 | |

Owned by Messrs. Thos. Heiton & Co. Dublin.

2. Captain Murphy was in charge of the vessel when she arrived in Dun Laoghaire Harbour on Sunday 19th January 1941 whilst on a vayage from Cardiff to Dublin with a Cargo of Coal (approximately 730 tons).

3. The vessel arrived in the Harbour in a sinking condition, having sustained damage at sea, and dropped her starboard anchor at $7^{05}$ p.m. between the inner Dolphin and the Mail Pier with the vessels head towards the Mail Pier. She grounded at 7.30 p.m. about 140 feet N.E. from the National Yacht Club. The ship was deliberately beached to prevent her sinking in deep water.

4. Immediately afterwards a rope was run from the port bow of the Saint Kenneth to the Mail Pier, and then a rope was run from the starboard quarter of the vessel to the East Breakwater. A wire from the starboard bow was run to the inner Dolphin, and ~~at 3 p.m. the Harbour Master who had already supervised the running of all the ropes went down to the Master of the Mail Steamer "Hibernia" and got~~ a 7" inch Manilla rope ~~This~~ was placed on a truck and taken round to the Eastbreakwater and run by boat to the starboard quarter of the St Kenneth.

5. All these ropes were hove tight and made fast on board, and in addition a rope was run from the starboard bow to the Mail Pier and hove tight on the windlass. All this work was completed at 10.20 p.m. Fires were drawn from the boilers as [it] could not be got to the feed pump.

~~Captain~~ Mr Wallace and a mechanic arrived immediately after the ropes were run, and went on board to make arrangements for the pumping out of water in the holds. The wind which was blowing a Mod.Gale (Force 7) at the time of the vessels arrival had now increased in force, but the vessel was resting comfortably on the bottom and in no further danger.

7. At $2^{50}$ ~~p~~a.m. in strong Ely Gale and driving rain, the vessel either dragged her anchor or parted her Cable.

At $3^{10}$ a.m. the vessel carried away the port bow rope. (H.W. 5.18 a.m.)

" $3.^{18}$ a.m. the starboard bow rope carried away.

" $3.^{33}$ a.m. the rope on starboard quarter (belonging to vessel), carried away.

The vessel was now working heavily fore and aft in the heavy swell and high wind blowing, and at 3.40 a.m. the wire on the starboard bow carried away.

The only rope holding the vessel now was the seven inch on the starboard quarter.

Another rope was run to the Mail Pier from the Saint Kenneth bow and made fast on board but it carried away and the vessel now grounded at the foot of the Lifeboat Slip her stern towards the East Breakwater.

8. Monday 20th At 6.30 a.m. a rocket was fired ashore and a four inch rope was set up between the lifeboat slip and the ship and by this means the ships lifeboat was ferried backwards and forwards and the Crew landed three at a time. At 7.30 a.m. the Master of the vessel, who was last to leave, was landed.

6. At 12.30. a.m. on Monday in consultation with Mr. Wallace, Marine Supt., for Messrs. Heiton, Owners of the vessel, we agreed that the best thing to do was not to pump the vessel out, although the Motor pump was then working, but to allow the vessel to settle upon the bottom, and thus prevent any further damage to the ship, and Mr. Wallace undertook to carry this out; had he done so all the subsequent damage to the ship and the Pier would not have occurred.

9. At 7.15 a.m. when the crew had left the ship, unknown to me the Motor Pump was left running, and apparently worked for some hours by itself; with the result that the vessel was partly pumped out at low water and when the tide rose she floated again.

10. The gale was then at its height, and the vessel proceeded to range fore and aft and did considerable damage to the Mail Boat Pier.

11. About 2 p.m. on Monday, at considerable risk, three men boarded the ship on her forecastle head and we succeeded in getting four parts of a 5" (five inch) Manilla rope from the ship to the Mail Boat Pier with the object of keeping the vessel off the slipway and the large boulders inshore.

12. At 4.15 p.m. the vessel listed heavily to port, filled through the fore hatch, and sank. The motor pump must have stopped working some hours before this, because the vessel was settling down from 1.30 p.m. until she sank. The vessel now lies upon an even keel, and a divers report discloses considerable damage to her bottom, and her rudder post and rudder have been carried away.

13. In my opinion, had it not been for the seven inch hawser which I ran out from the East Pier on Sunday ~~evening~~ night, the vessel would have grounded upon the Lifeboat Slip, and with the weight of cargo (730 tons Coal) would have either broken her back, or listed to starboard and sunk upon her side.

At Low ~~water~~ tide there is only 5 feet of water at the end of the Life Boat Slip and 9 feet where the vessel now lies. ~~R. Steel~~

~~Harbour Master.~~

14. Salvage work on the St. Kenneth commenced on the 22nd Jan^y about 260 tons of coal have been discharged into lighters. ~~Should the present favourable weather continue it is expected~~. Temporary external repairs to the hull have been carried out by a Diver, and if the present favourable weather continues it is expected that the vessel will be refloated in the course of the next few days. -----

Harbour Master.

# APPENDIX IX

## MAIL BOATS – CAR FERRIES – HIGH SPEED VESSELS 1964–1995

The Mailboats started to carry passenger vehicles from July, 1959 (loaded into their forward hatch by shore crane) and were followed by the Car Ferries in 1965. These first ferries operated from a temporary berth at the East Pier, ran during holiday peak periods and were designed only to carry passenger vehicles.

The car ferries transferred over to the, then newly built, Car Ferry (St. Michael's) Pier in 1969/70 and gradually increased in frequency until they finally replaced the Mailboats by Autumn, 1976. Freight Ro-Ro, i.e. commercial vehicles, was introduced in March 1975 as second generation car ferries were in service and able to take the larger vehicles. The Carlisle Pier West side was converted into a ro-ro berth by having a ramp installed and a causeway built to connect it to the existing Car Ferry Terminal. This new berth was designed for the next generation of multipurpose car ferries which were introduced from May 1977.

Both piers remained in use by the ferries up to Summer 1994 – as St Michael's Pier was adapted for use by the larger ferries. One berth of St Michael's Pier was converted for use by catamarans (by means of a pontoon) from 1993 and the remaining berth, along with shoreside buildings, started being redeveloped in Summer, 1994 for the H.S.S. From Autumn, 1994 only the Carlisle Pier berth was handling ferries and ro-ro freight traffic – as the catamarans (like the first ferries) were designed only to carry passenger vehicles.

The H.S.S. entered service 1st October 1995 and all ferry traffic is eventually planned to be operated from the redeveloped St. Michael's Pier. The H.S.S.carries freight and passenger vehicles can be accompanied (if required) by back-up services of a ferry and/or catamaran.

## NOTES ON RO-RO TRAFFIC FIGURES

Private caravans and trailers not included in the given figures, generally two to three thousand per annum, increased to four thousand five hundred for 1993 and also 1994.

Trade Caravans and Trailers (e.g. horseboxes) not included in given figures, generally remain within four to eight hundred per annum range.

Trade vehicles not included in given figures, throughput peaked at three thousand in 1986, since then has varied two to nine hundred per annum.

Motorbikes remained between one to two thousand per annum up to 1987, since then gradually increased; four thousand, two hundred and twenty four in 1994.

For the first two years of ro-ro freight cargo dues were calculated on the appropriate commodity rate x tonnage. This was tedious and cumbersome and was then altered to the current system of charging by vehicle length x empty/loaded mode.

INWARDS OUTWARDS

THROUGHPUT OF RO-RO

| YEAR | LOADED % | EMPTY % | LOADED % | EMPTY % | FREIGHT |
|---|---|---|---|---|---|
| 1975 | 85.9 | 14.1 | 64.0 | 36.0 | 3474 |
| 1976 | 80.7 | 19.3 | 62.8 | 37.2 | 6608 |
| 1977 | | Not Available | | | 15196 |
| 1978 | 88.1 | 11.9 | 78.8 | 21.2 | 22274 |
| 1979 | 91.5 | 8.5 | 76.9 | 23.1 | 28530 |
| 1980 | 87.2 | 12.8 | 80.5 | 19.5 | 23156 |
| 1981 | 88.9 | 11.1 | 82.6 | 17.4 | 24006 |
| 1982 | 89.5 | 10.5 | 85.1 | 14.9 | 22757 |
| 1983 | 90.0 | 10.0 | 84.3 | 15.7 | 22794 |
| 1984 | 91.0 | 9.0 | 86.7 | 13.3 | 23129 |
| 1985 | 91.3 | 8.7 | 88.1 | 11.9 | 21898 |
| 1986 | 94.1 | 5.9 | 85.5 | 14.5 | 18824 |
| 1987 | 96.8 | 3.2 | 86.6 | 13.4 | 25166 |
| 1988 | 96.6 | 3.4 | 85.1 | 14.4 | 22420 |
| 1989 | 95.8 | 4.2 | 84.9 | 15.1 | 26876 |
| 1990 | 95.6 | 4.4 | 83.9 | 16.1 | 23813 |
| 1991 | 95.5 | 4.5 | 84.9 | 15.1 | 25283 |
| 1992 | 95.0 | 5.0 | 83.1 | 16.9 | 34278 |
| 1993 | 94.3 | 5.7 | 83.0 | 17.0 | 33391 |
| 1994 | 94.2 | 5.8 | 85.8 | 14.2 | 40418 |

| YEAR | PRIVATE CARS & BUSES 000's | PASSENGERS 000,000's |
|---|---|---|
| 1964 | 7457 | 0.81 |
| 1965 | 30652 | 0.89 |
| 1966 | 36219 | 0.74 |
| 1967 | 62661 | 0.87 |
| 1968 | 77406 | 1.04 |
| 1969 | 83543 | 1.04 |
| 1970 | 82160 | 0.76 |
| 1971 | 81573 | 0.66 |
| 1972 | 57566 | 0.91 |
| 1973 | 72843 | 0.79 |
| 1974 | 84514 | 0.82 |
| 1975 | 83746 | 0.79 |
| 1976 | 81820 | 0.72 |
| 1977 | 112695 | 0.94 |
| 1978 | 136638 | 1.12 |
| 1979 | 124223 | 1.09 |
| 1980 | 135084 | 1.14 |
| 1981 | 121438 | 1.05 |
| 1982 | 107441 | 1.09 |
| 1983 | 116402 | 1.16 |
| 1984 | 111354 | 1.19 |
| 1985 | 103895 | 1.22 |
| 1986 | 100275 | 1.03 |
| 1987 | 121019 | 1.08 |
| 1988 | 152392 | 1.03 |
| 1989 | 194741 | 1.16 |
| 1990 | 183437 | 1.08 |
| 1991 | 210808 | 1.11 |
| 1992 | 199091 | 1.16 |
| 1993 | 246177 | 1.38 |
| 1994 | 254363 | 1.44 |

# APPENDIX X

## VARIOUS EVENTS WHICH WILL HAVE AFFECTED FIGURES

| | |
|---|---|
| 1965 | Commencement of Car Ferry Service. |
| 1966 | British Seamens' Strike. |
| 1969 | Troubles started in Northern Ireland. |
| 1971 | Bridge at Menai Straits, Wales out of service (fire), traffic to Dun Laoghaire via the longer Heysham route. |
| 1975 | Ro-Ro commenced in March. |
| 1976 | Mailboats redundant by Autumn. |
| 1977 | Multipurpose ferry introduced. |
| 1978 | Duty free introduced in March, Ro-Ro freight vessels operating along with passenger ferries on a feasability study (for a second multi-purpose vessel) for three years. |
| 1979 | P & T strike for five months; petrol shortage in summer as also in 1980. |
| 1981 | 'St David' a second multi purpose ferry introduced on route. |
| 1982 | B & I operations at Holyhead hindered by shoreside staff and retaliation by B & I vessels blockade of Dun Laoghaire. |
| 1985/86 | Only one vessel on route, 'multipurpose' ferry; joined by a ro-ro freight vessel from 1987. |
| 1987 | Cheap air fares introduced and '48 hour' duty free sales. |
| 1988/89 | Dun Laoghaire to Liverpool service in operation (Ceased Jan. 1990). |
| 1990 | Re-introduction of second passenger ferry on Dun Laoghaire/Holyhead route; two passenger ferries and one freight retained on route in 1991 and 1992. |
| 1992 | Two passenger ro-ro ferries on route; introduction of catamaran service from July. |
| 1994 | Two passenger ferries and catamaran throughout year, original catamaran replaced by larger vessel from June. |
| 1995 | New 'freight only' route Holyhead – Dublin due to operate from Nov. 1995, thus reducing ro-ro freight through Dun Laoghaire – but preparing for the modern era of catamaran use in Dun Laoghaire by phasing out the unaccompanied ro-ro freight traffic. |
| 1996 | H.S.S. arrives on the service from Easter, 1996. |
| 1998 | End of 'duty free' is expected to cause a drop in day trip passengers. |

# APPENDIX XI

## THE HIGH SPEED PASSENGER FERRY

### OBSERVATIONS AND HARBOUR EXPERIENCES REGARDING CATAMARANS, WAVEPIERCERS AND HSS

CAPTAIN J. P. CARTER, HARBOUR MASTER
DUN LAOGHAIRE HARBOUR COMPANY
IRELAND
MAY 1998

PREFACE

My original paper was issued in March, 1997. In the intervening period of time, whilst the harbour information held true, the progression of fast ferry had somewhat dated the remaining sections of the paper. Hopefully this revised edition covers the new developments, is relevant to the present time and does not date as quickly as the original.

CAPTAIN J. P. CARTER
DECEMBER, 1997

### SUMMARY

At present we are in the throes of a change in sea transportation which has been compared, in many articles, to the introduction of the aero engine in the aviation industry.

There is a bewildering assortment of fast ferries now in existence; beyond the earlier hydrofoils and ageing hovercraft are the modern catamarans and monohulls. These are waterjet driven, hulls of high tensile steel or aluminium and with superstructures of aluminium or a composite mix.

The possible overall combinations of types and sizes, or a specific choice, of these fast craft require thorough analysis to correctly determine which craft is required for operational use. Many routes are "site specific" and the judged suitability of a chosen craft is the result of many interacting variables; weather conditions; carrying capacity; distances/speed – the passage time dictating layout of passenger accommodation and on-ship sales; propulsion units; fuel consumption; crew manning levels; capital costs; depreciation; etc.

Some general trends are starting to appear:–

- Where fast ferries have been introduced on established routes they are, in some instances, backed by a "conventional" ro-ro vessel. Besides providing an alternative service in adverse weather (i.e. above the permitted operating limits of the smaller fast craft) they, most importantly, provide immediate alternate shipping in the event of damage to what is, in some specific cases, a specialised and dedicated fast craft linkspan.
- Where conventional ro-ro ferries are being retained in service their replacement vessels are evolving to be ro-pax conventional vessels – preparing for the future, to work in a tandem service with small fast craft.
- Dual-role fast ferries are being built; to cater for passenger traffic during the tourist season or operate as a fast freight vessel outside of it.
- Finally, it is noted that fast ferries can operate at slower speeds if the high speed element is not required. This obviously gives flexibility to the operator and presents another variable in the adaptation to seasonal fluctuations.

## HISTORY OF FAST CRAFT

Catamarans, as is well known, originated with the Polynesians and for centuries the Europeans experimented to adapt the concept to large sailing vessels, but without lasting success.

The first catamaran steamer operated on the River Neva, Russia, in the early 1830s. The mid-Victorian era saw power-driven catamarans introduced on the English Channel: 1850 "Gemini", 1874 "Castalia" and 1877 "Calais-Douvres". Commercially they were not a success; the concept was more or less left in abeyance until modern times when they were able to be developed from further inventions and technological progress.

Although hydrofoils were first patented in 1897, one could reasonably argue that the 1950s marked the start of the modern, fast ferry era.

Early in the decade the first commercial hydrofoils made their appearance, ro-ro car ferries were developed and the "Hovercraft" was in service before it closed. The 1960s saw containerisation changing the shipping world and Space Age advances being passed on into industry in general. During the 1970s technology of the "Jumbo" jets was transferred to the water and created the "Jetfoil" – a hydrofoil driven by gas-turbine powered waterjets. In time these were followed by the ubiquitous "micro chip", compact computers and (now available) satellite navigation of the present time.

A bold commercial venture in 1986 introduced (Australian built) semi-fast, aluminium catamarans, on the Portsmouth-Isle of Wight route; these in turn led to the development of larger, faster catamarans. The first of these catamarans, a seventy four metres Wavepiercer type, claimed the "Blue Riband" of the Atlantic on its delivery run in June, 1990.

Like most prototypes these Wavepiercers encountered technical difficulties in their early years e.g. cracks in their aluminium welding, better ride control systems required to be fitted; but they continued to grow world-wide in size, numbers and routes. A ninety one metre version is due in service this month (May 1998) and a ninety six metre specimen, with freight capability, is due to be launched in August, 1998.

In this locality the Wavepiercers were introduced on the Belfast-Larne route in 1992, Dun Laoghaire-Holyhead 1993 and Dublin-Isle of Man 1996. (Hydrofoils and jetfoils have proved too susceptible to bad weather around our coasts – but continue to be built for routes suitable for their operation).

Meanwhile other countries, having experience of naval shipbuilding, were entering into the building of commercial fast craft – both catamarans and monohulls, resulting in a multitude of routes being developed throughout the world. The next major event was the introduction of the Finnish built "HSS 1500", a Swath type catamaran, on the Dun Laoghaire – Holyhead route in April, 1996. This was followed a few months later by a sister ship on the Belfast – Stranraer route, and the third vessel was introduced Harwich – Hook of Holland in June, 1997.

The success of the HSS design was further confirmed by a smaller "HSS 900" on the Gothenburg – Frederikshaven route in September 1997; there are now plans for a "HSS 760" version.

The HSS differs from the previous Wavepiercer's catamarans both in being of a Swath (Small Waterplane Twin Hull) design and being powered by "marinised" aero engines, as opposed to diesel engines in the smaller catamarans. Up to the introduction of the HSS 1500 the fast catamarans had not been capable of carrying freight. By virtue of its physical size and engine power the HSS 1500 (one hundred and twenty four metres l.o.a. x forty metres beam; sixty eight thousand kW) is capable of carrying a mix of passengers/cars/ro-ro similar to that of a conventional passenger ro-ro ferry – but at twice the speed.

Fast monohulls, their design primarily derived from naval ships, are fast following up on the catamaran, incorporating the catamaran-learnt ship technology and operating experience. Like the catamarans they started in small sizes, limited to carrying only passengers – one such "Destriero" winning the "Blue Riband" in 1992, and then evolving to passengers and cars. Their progress into the larger, ro-ro freight carrying capacity is currently taking place in an Italian shipyard; two "Jupiter" class vessels (one hundred and forty six metres l.o.a.) were being built for delivery in the 1998 season. These large vessels are powered by Combined Diesel And Gas turbine engines (CODAG) and of such a design that they may be operated as a tourist ferry in the Summer and a ro-ro freight vessel in the Winter. This dual role neatly overcomes the problem of the smaller European-based fast ferries – which lack full passenger markets in the Northern Winter with only a fraction of their number required for redeployment on routes during the Southern Summer.

In 1994 the IMO adopted a "Code of Safety for High Speed Craft" (regulating both the construction and operation of fast craft); compliance with the code was made mandatory in January, 1996. Prior to that fast craft had been operating a voluntary IMO code – which was based on the 1960 SOLAS convention and as such was inappropriate for the newly developed fast craft of the day.

Again, such advances have been made in technology (e.g. the seventy seven metre, B60-GT design catamaran "Luciano Fedrico L" with a service speed of fifty eight point seven knots) that this "new" code is already being revised, a new edition due in 1999!

## HULL SHAPES OF CATAMARANS

Hull forms, besides providing buoyancy, are designed for differing functions at high speeds:–

Wavepiercers initially float on their surface-showing side hulls, of three metre draft, whereas at around twenty one to twenty four knots they mount a self created wave and ride on its crest at the higher speeds, up to the full sea speed of thirty nine to forty knots.

Swaths have each of their (narrower) side hulls going down through the water surface to connect with a submerged, cigar shaped, form. A form runs fore-and-aft on each side, virtually the length of the vessel and remain submerged at all speeds, giving the HSS 1500 a permanent four point five metre draft. The Swath design provides a more stable ride in rough weather than Wavepiercers but has a higher fuel consumption for vessels if the vessels are of similar size and engine power.

Slice is a hull design that has evolved out of Swath, reducing the wavemaking drag by up to a further thirty five percent and so giving a faster vessel than a similar, size and engine powered, Swath vessel. This is achieved by altering the underwater forms into four short, separate pods. Each of the two forward pods have a controllable pitch propeller, powered by diesel engines. The propellers are in the amidship section of the vessel and are used for both power and steering; the after pair of pods set clear of the propeller flows. (The prototype vessel was launched in November, 1996, proved successful and the design is patented by the two companies which developed it).

Navafoil is an American built, thirty metre "catamaran hydrofoil" presently being developed, expecting to be launched in 1998.

It marries the technology of the Swath and Slice designs with those of previous, differing, hydrofoil designs, to provide two designs: a low flying, Mark 1 and a high flying (two metre hull clearance) Mark 2. These are being built to carry one hundred and fifty to two hundred and fifty passengers, operate to three metres significant wave height (Mark 2) and will be powered by either diesel or gas turbine main engines.

• Catamarans have massive stability (righting moments), fifteen to twenty times greater than a monohull, consequently rolling is virtually non-existent in a beam sea aboard a catamaran.
• Hull lengths of around one hundred and twenty four metres are sufficient to cut through three successive waves and so reduce vertical acceleration – the main cause of seasickness. The first Wavepiercers (seventy four metre l.o.a.) adjusted their courses, in a seaway, to ensure a reading of less than 0.2 on their bridge's vertical acceleration meter.
• It has been calculated that one fully flooded HSS hull would give the vessel an eight degree list; with two flooded side hulls the vessel would remain afloat, reserve buoyancy provided by the two metre deep "wet deck", which runs the length of the vessel.
• Modern fast ferries have no long service history to confirm their reliability. Although gas turbines are used on naval vessels they are not run continually at full working speeds; combined with hard running, day in day out. The aluminium hulled, fast ship's working life may not be the usual twenty to twenty five years. It may be more and it could be less – a possible forty years has been tentatively suggested for the HSS!

## PROPULSION

Waterjet propulsion has higher efficiency– giving lower fuel consumption, when operating at speeds in excess of twenty five knots, than propeller driven craft; it also gives better handling qualities:– ability to turn on its axis, move sideways and, when at full forty knot speed, the ability to stop in about four ship lengths.

Both HSS and Wavepiercer catamarans are driven and directed by water jets, having a pair of manoeuverable water jets (and their engines) in each side hull and are also fitted with bow thrusters, an exception being the earlier seventy four metre Wavepiercers which had no bowthrusters and a further variation of fixed innermost waterjets, their steering affected only by the outermost "wing" engines. Even so these smaller catamarans proved capable of berthing in force six to seven (twenty five knot wind) as, most importantly, they had the capability of first landing a line ashore and progressing from there.

The fore and aft component of the waterjet is controlled by adjustable buckets (which are externally fitted on each of the waterjets). It is the applied engine power, direction of waterjets and bucket setting which determine the harbour manoeuvring of the vessel. At sea speed the HSS is like any other vessel, with the waterjets set at full power and the steering on automatic pilot.

Generally speaking the direction of waterjets and bucket settings are combined into one control unit, a "Jetavator", on the ship's bridge; setting the required resultant simply activates the interacting components of the unit and it automatically adjusts the settings to provide the desired result. There is also a back-up manoeuvring system, beyond which is an additional, emergency system and a further system whereby an engineer in the machinery spaces, by radio contact with the bridge, can directly control the engines to their required settings.

HSS 1500s are powered by "marinised" aero engines of sixty thousand kW and have a fuel capacity of one hundred and sixty eight tonnes; by comparison the seventy eight mtr. length Wavepiercers are powered by diesel engines of seventeen thousand, two hundred and eighty kW and have a fuel capacity of thirty tonnes.

On the Dun Laoghaire – Holyhead round trip (fifty six miles x two) the HSS burns approximately forty eight tonnes and the seventy eight metre catamaran ten tonnes of fuel. A complete fuel load is never carried on this route in order to maximise freight deadweight. Bunkering is a continual "topping up operation", the ships operating with a prudent reserve, sailing with fuel for about two round trips.

Wavepiercers, with their diesel engines, shut down when made fast in the berth. By contrast the HSS, with jet turbine engines, shuts down only if the stop goes beyond an hour (port turnaround time thirty to forty minutes) as the fuel burnt would be less than the increased maintenance cost of the closing down and restarting procedures.

There is a spare (fourth) set of engines to service the three HSS 1500s; work being done ashore on the spare set and dry-docking vessels simply having their engines changed, aircraft style. Discussions are now taking place to increase the (present) dry-docking period to a two year cycle instead of an annual one.

## ENGINE EMISSIONS – POLLUTION CONTROLS

The implementation of Annex VI, Marpol 73/78 (Dealing with sulphur levels in ship bunkers and their consequential sulphur dioxide emissions in controlled areas) is due in the year 2002.

Diesels, by their very nature, have higher emission levels than gas turbines and, whilst their current sulphur dioxide levels are generally there or thereabouts with Annex VI, they may fall foul of levels set in special areas, especially the Baltic region.

The choice of gas turbines may thus become more attractive to the ship owner and that itself gives a further choice, "marinised" aero engine or the light industrial gas turbines? Some recent fast ferries have been fitted with modern, light industrial turbines – capable of burning either marine diesel oil or certain grades of heavy fuel. They are claimed to be more robust and, working at a lower operating temperature, to possess a longer working life than the aeroderivative gas turbines.

## COMPARISONS:
## EXAMPLES OF LARGER, MODERN FAST CRAFT

By early 1997 there was an estimated one thousand, two hundred fast ferries in existence; the vast majority being of the smaller "passenger only" type. The remainder, estimated at sixty vessels, carry passengers and motor cars, with only the very latest (larger) designs capable of carrying the additional freight or car/freight mix.

Dimensions in metres; Power in kW, D=Diesel, T=Turbine, C=CODAG.

| NAME | LOA | BEAM | DRAFT | PAX | CARS/ FREIGHT | ENGINE | SPEED | YEAR |
|---|---|---|---|---|---|---|---|---|
| CATAMARANS | | | | | | | | |
| Incat | 74 | 26 | 2.8 | 450 | 84/NIL | 1440D | 38 | 1990 |
| Increasing in capacity to: Incat (Devil Cat) | 91 | 26 | 3.7 | 900 | 240/NIL | 28800D | 43 | 1997 |
| HSS 1500 | 124 | 40 | 4.5 | 1500 | 375/NIL or 120/50 | 68000T | 40 | 1996 |
| HSS 900 | 88 | 30 | 3.7 | 900 | 210/NIL or 170/10 buses | 34000T | 40 | 1997 |
| B60-GT | 77 | 19.5 | 2.15 | 450 | 52/NIL | 32200T | 58.7 | 1997 |
| MONOHULLS | | | | | | | | |
| AQUASTRADA | 100 | | 2.0 | 450 | 150/NIL | 28000C | 20/40 | 1993 |
| Smaller and larger versions; the largest being: | 104 | | | | | | | 1997 |
| MDV 1200 | | | | | | | | |
| Pegasus 1 | 95 | | | 600 | 173/NIL + 6 buses | 24000D | 36 | 1996 |
| Supercat 1 | 100 | 17.1 | | 782 | 175/NIL | D | 40 | 1997 |
| Jupiter (MDV 3000) | 145 | 22 | | 1800 | 460/NIL or 150/30 | 70800C | 23/40 | 1998 |

## PRESSURE WAVES

The introduction of fast, aluminium ferries attracted immediate public attention. Wavepiercers, followed by the HSS 1500, had to be studied by the harbours to ensure their characteristics became known and, if found necessary, measures applied to ensure safe harbour use.

Obviously their high speeds and concentrated power (a seventy four metre catamaran having the same propulsion power as a conventional ro-ro ferry!) could not be used in harbours – where the vessels reduce speed and become for all intents and purposes the same as conventional vessels. It subsequently proved that it was out in harbour approaches that the problems occurred, and their solutions dealt with.

Three generations of ferry-design at Dun Laoghaire

WAVEPIERCERS

At the introductory period of the seventy four metre Wavepiercers in Belfast the Harbour Master and pilots observed the handling capabilites, intership reaction, wash effect and stern turbulence. This led to the usual harbour speed being *raised* to twelve knots, and full sea speed permitted when clear of the channel, well out in the Lough.

To great surprise no noticeable intership reaction was found when Wavepiercers, at full speed, overtook conventional ships out in Belfast Lough. The reasoned conclusion was that this was due to the very small displacement involved with the Wavepiercer whilst at high speed.

Wavepiercers behave as conventional craft up to the twelve knots, thereafter a greater wash is created until the vessel changes at around twenty two knots, to a "ride mode". At this speed the craft gives a slight surge and mounts to ride along its self-created wave up to full speed of forty knots – at which its jets are pumping out water at forty four tonnes (eleven tonnes x four engines) per second. This discharged water appears to quickly lose its energy, stern turbulence being perhaps the same as with a conventional vessel. In Loch Ryan, Scotland, the navigational buoys and a flock of eider duck were observed to gently bob in the outspreading ripples, well away from the fore-and-aft line of the wake; however, as with a conventional vessel, speed had to be reduced when passing Cairnryan in order to prevent a ferry from surging on its berth.

Later observations in Dun Laoghaire Harbour (speed limit of eight point seven knots) noted small harbour craft crossing the stern turbulence of HSS 1500, without any difficulty, shortly after the vessel departed. However by contrast large ro-ro freight vessels have reported pounding, minutes after the HSS has overtaken (at full speed) well clear, in deep water out at sea.

The HSS in dock

## HSS 1500

On its arrival in Dublin Bay the HSS was put through its paces by the Pilotage Authority and then underwent days of berthing trials at Dun Laoghaire before entering into service.

It was found to handle like the Wavepiercers and, like all other vessels created local turbulence when manoeuvring off its berth; the turbulence varying according to the engine power – which of course was weather related. Time proved this turbulence to differ from that of the conventional ferries. Its advance across the open harbour was indicated by rows of parallel, moored yachts starting to bob; one after the other. Then, up out of nowhere, a surge would well up from the depths and spend itself against the wall for about twenty seconds.

## SPEED/DEPTH LIMITATIONS

On the introduction of the Wavepiercers to Dun Laoghaire there were reports of sudden, unexpected waves breaking on the shoreline. The solution appeared to be re-routing the harbour approach down from the northwards, to the harbour mouth, instead of running along parallel to the coast.

The arrival of the HSS did not improve on matters; irrespective of what approach used, a wave could suddenly break on the harbour's sea wall or on the nearby coast. One line of thought was that perhaps a pressure wave was pushed ahead of the vessel owing to its Swath design, a more favoured one relating to the re-distribution of the fast vessels' stern power.

A further series of tests, combining speed reductions and approach tracks, was carried out; a favourite being to run towards a (North-South facing) sandbank, then reducing speed further as the HSS rounded the bank and headed south, direct to the harbour. (The sandbank absorbing and so preventing the pressure wave from running across Dublin Bay and onto its northside beaches). Reasonable success was met with in Dun Laoghaire Harbour approaches and the matter was kept under review. Meanwhile the Danish Maritime Authority had commissioned a study on the effects of fast craft waves in their own area.

Belfast Port followed with a HSS 1500 directly into their port a few months later. Due to its locality, lying at the head of a sea lough, the port had greater immediate problems: the pressure waves quickly going ashore along the beaches and ships surging on their berths and breaking lines.

The basic problem proved to be that vessels had a critical speed range – in which the excess energy created a sideways pressure wave at the stern. By slowing down, intending to reduce their speed and "pressure" wave, the vessels had unwittingly entered into their critical range and made matters worse! This created "pressure" wave then overtook the slowing down ship, spread out at an angle of seventy degrees each side of the bow and so creating an *apparent* bow "pressure" wave.

Practical application of ways to reduce the pressure wave was tried and tested, beyond the theoretical calculations, in Belfast over the Winter of 1996/7. This resulted in fast vessels now operating to a strict *water depth/ship speed* table. Results of the application of such an operating table was also monitored in Dublin Bay, by data-gathering buoys, during the Summer of 1997.

Such evolved control table has proved satisfactory in eliminating the "pressure wave". The HSS 1500 prevents creating it by avoiding quickly passing through its critical speed range of thirteen point eight to twenty six point seven knots when in shallow waters of eight to thirty metres and, additionally, using a slower "safe" speed when rounding sandbanks as it was found that the ship's momentum, when rounding a bank, also tended to create the wave; the ship increasing its "safe" speed once the turn was completed and it was on its new track.

## HARBOUR BERTHS

### WAVEPIERCERS:

Dun Laoghaire had a straightforward task in adapting a ro-ro ramp berth to accommodate the Wavepiercer catamarans. A specially fabricated floating pontoon, approximately twenty metres square, was moored directly in front of the shore linkspan ramp. It supports a raised deck (deck height being adjustable to cater for differing ship freeboards) on which both the shore and ship ramps land, and over which traffic passes.

Holyhead, with multi-user demands on the berth, adapted by mooring a differing design of pontoon; a straight decked pontoon fitted with a hinged and adjustable ramp on its seaward face, capable for use by forty-four tonne trucks. To prevent corrosion by electrolysis berth piles were faced with wood (to ensure aluminium hulls were kept clear of contact with differing metals) and furthered by having the ship's gangway and ramp landing areas insulated by rubber or the like.

HSS 1500:

A major civil engineering project was required to construct the specialised berth for the HSS. The vessel berths and locks, stern first, into the equivalent of a castle drawbridge. This linkspan, four hundred tonnes along with its (overhead) passenger walkways, is hinged on the shoreward end and supported by a buoyancy tank on its seaward end. The shore rampway (Bankseat) leading up to the linkspan is an enormous concrete construction, having to both hold the linkspan in place and absorb the berthing forces of the HSS.

The seaward face of the linkspan is raised higher for the approaching HSS – turned on its shore hinge by a pair of hydraulic rams; ultimately it is intended to have this mechanism activated from the approaching ship, at present it is shore operated. When the ship is in position the linkspan is lowered and its dagger pin (located in the centre of its sea face) goes home into its HSS housing. Once so held by the housed pin, a metal arm is driven out from each of the linkspan's seaward corners and lands over a small, stub post on the ship's quarters. These metal arm "locks" are drawn tight back into the linkspan, and then a further, hydraulic driven, lock goes over the dagger pin connection. The HSS is then firmly moored and no further moorings are necessary, regardless of weather conditions.

Various other ports were (1996) seeking berthing designs that could accommodate or be adapted to accommodate the HSS 1500, HSS 900 and other fast craft, as well as traditional ro-ro ferries.

Experience has shown that the catamarans are vulnerable to sudden sheers in strong beam winds, especially from "wind bursts". Dun Laoghaire is (retrospectively) fitting landing piles at the HSS berth. The two subsequent HSS routes had these landing piles fitted in their initial design in light of the experience, gained during adverse weather, on our initial route. The linkspan's overhead passenger walkways and (vehicle deck level) wing fenders dictate an almost fore-and-aft approach for the vessel; the HSS berthing at almost zero speed and at the same time ensuring both its stern end protusions (top-deck crane gantry and sea-level waterjets) are kept clear, no mean feat in bad weather.

## SHIP/SHORE: OPERATIONAL

Catamarans operate on the style of aircraft, there is no living accommodation aboard, no prolonged hours spent on the berth (except for the night stop) and speed on the sea is matched by quick port turnarounds.

The HSS has a capstan in each quarter and a windlass forward but normally does not make use of them, save for dry-docking (once the new fender piling, and their catwalks, are installed here in Dun Laoghaire the HSS will then also have the capability of putting a line ashore). In contrast the smaller Wavepiercers moor the same as conventional vessels and always have the comfort and reassurance of having "the first line ashore."

For this speed of operation there has to be good quality service and an adequate shore infrastructure as, using the HSS 1500 as an example, you are looking at up to three thousand passengers and seven hundred cars (or a car/freight mix) in a half hour turnaround:–

• All foot passenger heavy luggage is checked in at a departure desk, and subsequently collected off a carousel in the baggage hall of the next port – so no delays caused by individuals hauling baggage around, or using cabins. A lorry simply loads the baggage from the check-ins, rides over on the crossing and delivers to the baggage hall of the next port.
• Terminal building laid out to ensure that the flows of arriving and departing foot passengers do not impede each other and, likewise, any vehicle set-down/parking areas are kept clear of ferry vehicles.
• Sufficient vehicle areas, with services (ticket sales, refreshments, immigration, Customs, etc.), to simultaneously accommodate *both* the discharging and loading of vehicles to and from a vessel; plus allowances given for any other scheduled shipping.
• Connecting to the HSS, along the side of the linkspan, are fixed supply lines for fuel, fresh water and sewage, leading to shore installations.
• Wavepiercers are capable of taking a road tanker's load of diesel during a turnaround; the line connecting directly by flexible hose from the tanker. Otherwise these vessels do their main restoring during the overnight stop.
• By contrast to Wavepiercers the HSS takes its stores by containers, picked up at an overhanging stern gantry, run along the "roof" of the craft and then lowered down into the vessel!

• SAFETY SIGNALS

Dun Laoghaire lies within the Dublin Port Pilotage District and is formed by two huge outstretching breakwaters, which contain two finger-piers for ferries. Commissioners of Irish Lights, (depot in harbour) and Naval vessels also use the harbour, along with yachting interests and an assortment of smaller private craft.

The smaller, inner harbours cater for a dozen small, crab-pot fishermen and small yacht moorings, the majority of moorings being in the outer harbour. Dun Laoghaire, with four yacht clubs and an overall total of nearly six hundred moorings, is the major yachting centre on the East Coast of Ireland.

The ferry service to Holyhead from this port is currently provided by the HSS 1500 – which replaced two conventional ferries and the (introductory) Wavepiercer.

The foregoing set the position, traffic-wise, that had to be catered for with the arrival of the HSS 1500. It was really a natural progression from mailboats to ro-ro ferries and from there on to Wavepiercers and now the HSS, learning and adapting as we went. (Beyond the current use of VHF between the ferries and our two ports, Dublin Port is also scheduled to introduce a sophisticated VTS system in 1998 and before long will have its port radar at Howth Head.)

Warning/Safety signals had to be revised and updated for use with the introduction of the HSS in April, 1996. They consist of sound signals given by the vessel and visual signals given by the shore. Large power driven vessels are directed (by local Notice to Mariners) to use sound signals when manoeuvring off and/or departing berths and to sound a prolonged blast when approaching the harbour main pierheads from either direction (as per Collision Regulations).

The redeveloped HSS berth had a pair of Q.Y. signal lights installed, one mounted East and one mounted West – to ensure they can be seen throughout the harbour when the HSS (forty metre beam) is on the berth. These lights are activated by the harbour office and are fitted with a self adjusting intensity device (which varies according to available natural light), such giving a range which varies between one and two miles.

A well circulated, local Notice to Mariners explains the signals and fairway regulations; liaison being kept with local yacht clubs and other harbour users to ensure safety is kept to the fore; to date the combined safety signals have worked well.

Application has been lodged (October, 1997) for the construction of a large marina in the West side of the outer harbour. Such a project would add significantly to the harbour traffic by attracting more visitors/yachting events, increasing yacht capacity and extending the yachting season. It is planned to install a further (third) Q.Y. signal light, coupled to operate with the existing pair at the HSS berth, inside the breakwater arms of the proposed marina.

## SCOUR

In both their respective berths (sand/mud bottom) in this harbour the Wavepiercers and HSS have "dug" a twenty metre diameter, five metre deep hole, just off the linkspans where they manoeuvre with their engines. Approach tracks near to the berths have been deepened by around two metres but these lessen as one goes towards the centre of the harbour, these depths now appearing to have stabilised at these operational conditions.

By way of protection the shore wall of the HSS linkspan works was protected by two thousand tonnes of rock being placed directly there during its construction. Against this the Wavepiercer berth was an adapted ro-ro ferry berth and no ground protection was installed. The pier being a platform supported by concrete piles, with its wooden berth piling driven into the seabed and clenched to the pier at deck level, one of the wooden piles near the linkspan was found to be "dangling" i.e. clenched at deck level and its end sitting in a hole in the sea bed!

## BRIDGE TRAINING FOR CATAMARANS

Officers, after attending courses for the Wavepiercers, adjusted to manoeuvring with waterjets with "hands on experience". It was a relatively straightforward matter of adapting to the peculiar type of engine controls of the waterjets. They were still handling a vessel that moored with conventional ropes and whose, reasonably familiar looking, bridge gave the ability to go to the bridgewings and directly view their berth.

By contrast HSS ship handling was too far removed from the style of conventional ships. The "alien" nature of its operational procedures and bridge layout dictated a new philosophy, primarily a simulator course was used for training and this was followed by the practical training. In addition to the waterjet propulsion and the systems of the new vessel, *the* major adjustment (in my opinion) was having to berth, seated at a console – without an "eyeball" view of the berth or mooring lines.

- All the catamarans are fitted with a bow anchor, in reality a "fail safe" backing sysem and rarely, if ever, used.
- Prior to entering service the first HSS 1500 was uniquely fitted with a stern radar. This radar proved not to be required in operational use and has subsequently been removed.
- At present there is a project going ahead that will have a forward looking radar to view the head waves and, from the feed back information, adjust the vessel's ride control system to ensure a smoother sea passage.

## MARINE EVACUATION SYSTEM (MES)

Vessels only sail within their permitted operational weather limit, this limit was determined by the conditions in which the vessel's MES was tested. Present limits are three point five metres wave height for Wavepiercers and four metres for the HSS, intentions being to raise the HSS 1500 limit to four point five metres.

The Wavepiercers, which are much smaller and have lesser seakeeping qualities than Swath vessels, appear to be settled at their present limit; passenger comfort would dictate against vessels of their smaller size operating in more adverse weather.

The catamarans' MES has to function in lists of up to ten degrees. It comprises of stowed, compacted liferafts and slide chutes which are installed on the sides of the vessel.

Wavepiercers carry a bank of 100-capacity liferafts and, at the stern, a fast rescue boat. The HSS 1500 carries one hundred and thirty five-capacity liferafts, plus a fast rescue boat in each bow and quarter.

When activated the MES is deployed much in the same way as for aircraft, a major difference being that the catamarans have rescue boat(s) – which are used extensively in assisting their deployed liferafts.

An evacuation time of eighteen minutes has been set (and established in practice) for the evacuation, via twenty five metre long slide chutes, of the HSS's entire one thousand, five hundred passengers. Such time was determined by using a notional period of one hour, minus six minutes to assess the emergency and activate the MES, divided by a safety factor of three.

## HSS 1500:
## BRIDGE LAYOUT AND POWER CONTROLS

The bridge of the HSS 1500 is located right forward, sitting atop and in the centre of the vessel's superstructure. It houses the navigating console forward and, at a slightly lower level and further aft, a separate engineering console.

The Captain (sitting to port) and Navigating Officer sit as a pair at the navigating console, separated by the engine controls. Otherwise each has a duplicate array of controls, set on the panel of the console, along with a large visual display unit.

A TV display (where any of the ship's cameras can be called up) is mounted overhead of the navigating console. A clear sea view is given over the console top and the visual display units are capable of showing a variety of summoned information (e.g. radar, electronic charts, enlarged DGPS harbour positions – accurate to within a metre, stability/draft display).

The Chief Engineer attends the engineering console throughout and this is from where the engines are started and finally shut down, along with their auxiliary machinery and attendant systems. Transfer of engine power from one to the other (engineering/navigating) console is done by way of an established procedure, communicated directly by word of mouth.

A lookout is stationed aft during harbour manoeuvres to supplement the externally mounted TV cameras (the HSS bridge not extending the vessel's forty metre beam). So, from the seated navigating console, the Captain may directly gather information from personnel; TV cameras; the "real" outside view, a variety of console monitors and displays; radio traffic; etc. and so clearly assess and implement operational decisions on the operation of the vessel.

## POWER CONTROLS

All four HSS engines may be combined and directly controlled by a single "Jetavator", which is an azimuth-style disc with a power lever mounted upon it. The ship's computer system automatically adjusts the differing directional and bucket settings on all four engines to give the required resultant direction of the single Jetavator, the waterjets may be directed to a maximum of thirty degrees port/starboard. Engines are controlled from full ahead to full astern by the Jetavator's mounted power lever. A bowthruster joystick is set forward of the Jetavator and next to the Jetavator is a spring loaded "moment button" which, when activated, overrides the main control, further adjusts the setting on the waterjet buckets and produces a greater turning moment. Set immediately behind the main single Jetavator are a pair of smaller ones, these controlling the pairs of port and starboard engines respectively, and behind those a row of four individual levers, used to independently direct each engine.

Because of their smaller size the Wavepiercers have a combined bridge console, Chief Engineer sitting to port, Captain central and Navigating Watchkeeper to starboard. Neither have Wavepiercers the fingertip controls (set in the end of the chair arm rests) for course alterations at sea speed nor the "Jetavator" system of manoeuvring controls of the HSS. However they do have the advantages of remote, bridge wing controls which along with the ability to directly view their berth gives a more "natural" feel to their berthing operations.

When at sea both types of catamarans are on automatic pilot and their engines set at full power, the same as conventional ferries – which vessels the fast craft appears set to replace.

This has been my experience as Harbour Master in direct operations with fast craft. I sincerely hope that, coupled along with information gleaned from the "press", it presents a clear overview of an evolving situation, and I wish to thank you for your invitation to address this conference.

# APPENDIX XII

## STATEMENT BY HARBOUR WATCH TO DUN LAOGHAIRE HARBOUR CONFERENCE

1

Dun Laoghaire harbour was built as an Asylum Harbour at a time when Dublin was notoriously one of the most dangerous seaport cities in the world to approach. The long battle to get it built was fought largely by the seafaring community round Dublin Bay, appalled at the fact that annually several dozen lives were being lost by shipwreck in the vicinity. It was initiated by a master mariner resident in Dalkey with the safety of fellow seafarers alone in mind, who spent all his money in developing the campaign and died a poor man.

2

When completed, with its area of two hundred and fifty one acres, the harbour was the world's largest artificial harbur. More important, it provided as it still provides, the only considerable area of sheltered water on the east coast of Ireland south of Belfast Lough. It has never lost its original function as an asylum harbour or port of refuge. In our own time small trading vessels and fishing craft of this and other countries, as well as pleasure craft, have been thankful in heavy weather to take refuge in Dun Laoghaire, and this characteristic, known to grateful mariners of many lands, must not be allowed to be lost.

3

Quite quickly, Dun Laoghaire harbour began to be used not only as a port of refuge but also as a fishing port, as the major seaport in Ireland for the arrival and departure by sea of cross-Irish Sea passengers and mail, as a commercial port, as a depot for the Irish Light Service, and finally as a port for leisure craft. These varied activities gave it life and fame, and as a result of them a new and picturesque town grew up which is today the third in the state for population, outstripping famous and far older seaport towns like Waterford, Limerick and Galway.

4

Any hastily conceived project that would put an end to any one of the varied activities by which the importance of the harbour grew and that of the Borough with it, must be resisted.

5
The harbour, by reason of its ownership by the Office of Public Works is the public property of the Irish people. It is also morally the property of the citizenry of Dun Laoghaire, to whom it is not only an economic but an aesthetic, cultural and historic asset. Its future must not be decided without full opportunity, over a reasonable length of time, being given to the local citizens to discuss in detail propositions for its future development.

6
The present government of the harbour is unsatisfactory, as there is no properly defined machinery for consultation by interested individuals or organisations with the Office of Public Works.

7
The harbour must remain public property, with a responsible democratically chosen governing authority openly accountable to the people of the Borough in whose area the harbour operates.

8
A number of schemes have been or are alleged to have been put forward, all without any attempt to show the common courtesy of a desire to consult with the people of Dun Laoghaire, for the harbour's future use. A moratorium should be declared on the implementation of any such scheme until opportunities for ample public debate on all schemes so far tabled, and also on all other feasible possibilities, have been provided. A reasonable means of inaugurating such debate would be the publication of a Green Paper following the deliberations of the present conference.

9
After the full discussion, the Oireachtas, representing the public who presently, as noted above, own the harbour, should discuss and then enact a Dun Laoghaire Harbour Act, establishing a democratically constituted Dun Laoghaire Harbour Authority to legislate for the future of the harbour.

10
Development of the harbour is needed on many grounds, notably for the provision of better amenities for the local citizenry, to assist the growth of tourism, to enable the port to carry out more effectively the traditional functions performed by it, as outlined in paragraphs two and three above, and to give employment locally.

11
But development must not mean development in the interests only of a tiny minority, and at the expense of those of the great majority of Dun Laoghaire's population. These citizens are in the low and medium income brackets.

12
Development must mean a reversal of the steady process in recent decades – about which the people of Dun Laoghaire have never once been granted the politeness, let alone the right, of a discussion – which has largely removed access to their harbour from them. There must be development to facilitate in the harbour the hiring of rowing boats and other small craft (as once was possible) so as to make use of the harbour easy for the less well-off. There must be development to encourage the growth and activities of local rowing, canoe and angling clubs. There must be development to ensure that since, at long last, cheap local tours round the Bay and adjoining coast, run from Dun Laoghaire, are again available, the promoters of such tours are helped rather than hindered. The use of the harbour for longer coastal tours, such as made available briefly by P. S. Waverley two years ago, must be actively encouraged for the great benefits to tourism and to education which would ensue. Development must also mean much better access to the water for the boat owner not a member of a yacht club than exists at present, and much easier and more sightly access to the piers and other pathways round the harbour, which have always been a great attraction to tourists as well as to local citizens, but which in recent years even where not actually restricted, have been made ugly by unsightly barriers.

13
Dun Laoghaire harbour is very historic. Virtually no attempt has been made to develop tourist and local interest by properly publicizing by sign and plaque the very numerous spots around the harbour at which events of national and even international importance have occurred, and which a proper harbour authority would be proud to make known to visitors as well as locals, and in so doing would multiply the number of the former.

14
If, as is to be hoped, the regular passenger service out of Dun Laoghaire continues to operate and anyway in the very real hope of attracting regular coastal cruise operators, the present deplorable passenger-terminal must be humanized and beautified, since it is obvious from experience elsewhere in Europe that passengers disembarking or waiting to embark will in the great majority be ready to spend money at a local terminal if there is anything to spend it on and any comfort in which to spend it. It ought also to be obvious that arrivals well provided for at the point of entry are likely both to prolong their stay at that point and to encourage friends to use the same route. A really thorough policy of development for tourism would probably also need to include consideration of restoring railway access to Carlisle Pier.

15
While development for the local citizenry, for tourists, and for the traditional interests for which the port has long been catering, seems to be the first priority, development for the minority well enough off to be able to pay a substantial annual sum for moorings for a privately owned vessel is also important. Not only have such citizens rights which ought to be provided without their infringing the rights of the majority, but attention to their requirements would provide more local employment. The ideal area for a Yacht Marina (as has been emphasized to us in letters, by phone calls and in conversations indoors and outdoors) is west of the West Pier, where there is sheltered water and considerable vacant shore-space, some of it at present an eyesore to residents and visitors. At least one of the propositions for so-called development of Dun Laoghaire harbour recently publicized seems to have envisaged (apparently without any consideration of possible hydrographic consequences) the filling in of more than half the harbour, with consequent elimination of its use as an asylum harbour and as a fishing and commercial port as well as destruction of its beauty and an end to all possibility of use of the harbour by any but those in the high income bracket. If money to do all this in the harbour to the general detriment is available, can it not be diverted into carrying out a genuine marina development, with all the spin-off attributes publicized, in that area west of the West Pier?

16
Development in the area west of the West Pier, if undertaken, ought to include provision of facilities for boat repairing and if possible for boat building (an expanding industry in most European countries).

The administrative stupidity, or cowardice, responsible for the closing of the boat building yard which was flourishing in that area in the 1950s, and products of which are still afloat advertising the excellence of Dun Laoghaire boatbuilders, provides a lesson not to be overlooked. Another certain success in that area, if development is intelligently undertaken there, would be an aquarium. It is a disgrace that there is no public aquarium anywhere in Ireland. Aquaria are money-spinners in tourist seaside resorts in France, Yugoslavia, China, Scandinavia and South and North America.

## Kingstown Harbour, County Dublin.

*Imports.*—Coal and coke, 65,763 tons; stone, 1,150 tons; cement, 970 tons; sleepers, 1,170 tons; iron rails and chairs, 1,471 tons; bricks, 39 tons.

*Exports.*—Nil.

### Return of Fishing for year ended 31st March, 1914.

| Month | Herrings | | | Other Fish | |
|---|---|---|---|---|---|
| 1913 | Mease * | Hundred | Value £ s. d. | Cwts. | Value £ s. d. |
| April ... ... | — | — | — | 134¾ | 184 0 0 |
| May ... ... | — | — | — | 248¾ | 308 10 0 |
| June ... ... | 3 | — | 2 0 6 | 312¼ | 362 4 0 |
| July ... ... | 20 | — | 11 17 0 | 183 | 246 5 0 |
| August ... ... | 15 | — | 7 15 0 | 310 | 390 11 0 |
| September ... | — | — | — | 194 | 280 6 0 |
| October ... ... | — | — | — | 349½ | 425 12 0 |
| November ... | — | 2 | 0 15 0 | 283¾ | 388 0 0 |
| December ... | — | — | — | 308½ | 330 0 0 |
| 1914 | | | | | |
| January ... ... | — | — | — | 330 | 444 11 0 |
| February ... ... | — | — | — | 236½ | 330 3 0 |
| March ... ... | — | — | — | 180½ | 252 17 0 |
| Totals ... | 38 | 2 | 22 7 6 | 3,071½ | £3,542 19 0 |

* A mease represents 635 herrings.

### Return of tonnage and number of Vessels using Kingstown Harbour during the year ended 31st March, 1914.

| Month | Trading Vessels loading or discharging cargo. | | | | Vessels entering Harbour for shelter, bunker coal, orders, &c. | | | | Yachts visiting the Harbour. | | | | War Department Vessels. | |
|---|---|---|---|---|---|---|---|---|---|---|---|---|---|---|
| | Steam. | | Sailing. | | Steam. | | Sailing. | | Steam. | | Sailing. | | | |
| | No. | Tons. | No. | Tons. | No. | Tons. | No. | Tons. | No. | Tons. | No. | Tons. | No. | Tons. |
| 1913. | | | | | | | | | | | | | | |
| April, . . . . | 15 | 2,310 | — | — | 9 | 1,258 | 26 | 2,303 | — | — | 2 | 23 | 2 | 2,140 |
| May, . . . . | 15 | 2,030 | — | — | 3 | 164 | 25 | 2,070 | 2 | 361 | 12 | 541 | 6 | 10,577 |
| June, . . . . | 16 | 2,398 | — | — | 3 | 275 | 8 | 559 | 4 | 873 | 16 | 601 | 3 | 6,585 |
| July, . . . . | 10 | 1,248 | — | — | 6 | 1,411 | 1 | 52 | 9 | 1,365 | 9 | 301 | — | — |
| August, . . . . | 18 | 2,237 | — | — | 1 | 106 | 12 | 993 | 17 | 2,705 | 9 | 386 | — | — |
| September, . . | 19 | 2,615 | 1 | 52 | 6 | 555 | 18 | 1,336 | 13 | 410 | 2 | 172 | — | — |
| October, . . . | 15 | 2,998 | — | — | 17 | 4,252 | 24 | 1,852 | — | — | — | — | 1 | 805 |
| November, . . | 11 | 1,386 | — | — | 17 | 3,806 | 19 | 1,459 | 1 | 50 | — | — | 1 | 805 |
| December, . . | 18 | 2,418 | — | — | 12 | 5,061 | 15 | 1,100 | — | — | — | — | — | — |
| 1914. | | | | | | | | | | | | | | |
| January, . . | 18 | 2,738 | — | — | 9 | 1,476 | 20 | 1,640 | — | — | — | — | — | — |
| February, . . | 16 | 3,022 | — | — | 17 | 7,264 | 24 | 2,188 | 1 | 78 | — | — | 1 | 805 |
| March, . . . | 12 | 1,902 | 1 | 98 | 7 | 1,477 | 13 | 1,977 | — | — | — | — | 2 | 1,534 |
| Totals, . . | 183 | 27,302 | 2 | 150 | 107 | 27,105 | 205 | 17,529 | 47 | 5,842 | 50 | 2,024 | 16 | 23,251 |

Note.—In addition to the above the following vessels regularly use the Harbour, viz.:—
4 Mail steamers, 9 trawlers, 2 Irish Lights steamers, 120 smaller craft; 4 London and North Western steamers, 2 Pilot boats, 40 yachts and 1 Fishery Department Steamer.

# APPENDIX XIII

## TONNAGE AND NUMBER OF VESSELS USING KINGSTOWN HARBOUR

The two documents here demonstrate vividly the changes that have occurred in the operation of the harbour, the Royal Harbour of Kingstown, through the last century. Document 1 (opposite) is the official report of the Commissioners of Public Works, the harbour authority for the time of the activities in the harbour between April 1913 and March 1914, and Document 2 (below) provides the essential activities of the harbour in the year 1998, in which one thousand, one hundred and twenty one entries were recorded of the large HSS ferries and forty one of the smaller "Wavepiercer" catamarans, one thousand, three hundred and sixty two ferries in all. There would evidently have been more passenger ship entries in 1913–14 than in 1998, as there were two companies involved at the earlier date, but the ships of 1913–14 were not only slower but smaller.

DOCUMENT 2

**1998**

| | CARS/MBUS | OTHER | COACHES | PAX | FREIGHT | SHIP ENTRIES FERRIES |
|---|---|---|---|---|---|---|
| JAN | 8697 | 89 | 34 | 33810 | 906 | 67 |
| FEB | 12108 | 162 | 175 | 60907 | 1839 | 88 |
| MAR | 19563 | 338 | 620 | 121514 | 4020 | 118 |
| APR | 28230 | 344 | 765 | 162425 | 3465 | 118 |
| MAY | 31437 | 612 | 884 | 179073 | 3701 | 129 |
| JUN | 32945 | 651 | 800 | 178753 | 3713 | 127 |
| JUL | 39451 | 664 | 767 | 234684 | 4106 | 139 |
| AUG | 36834 | 496 | 754 | 251711 | 3843 | 139 |
| SEPT | 34210 | 489 | 781 | 174722 | 45190 | 126 |
| OCT | 28329 | 433 | 672 | 149014 | 4187 | 113 |
| NOV | 16902 | 246 | 368 | 93384 | 4192 | 108 |
| DEC | 14554 | 222 | 142 | 79856 | 3547 | 90 |
| | 303260 | 4746 | 6762 | 1719853 | 42038 | 1362 |

# PRIMARY DOCUMENTATION CONSULTED

1 Archives of the office of Public Works: section dealing with the Royal Asylum Harbour Kingstown.

2 Clery Pearson Memorial Institute Archives 1983 (for origins of Captain Toutcher of Stavanger).

3 British Admiralty Charts Nos. 1415, 1468.

4 Dun Laoghaire Harbour Watch, National and Royal St. George Yacht Clubs, Dun Laoghaire Sailing School, Stena Sealink Shipping Co. correspondence and documentation.

5 Dun Laoghaire Harbour: Report of Planning Review Group 1990.

6 Dun Laoghaire Harbour Development Plan, put forward by newly established Harbour Board 1992.

7 Dun Laoghaire Harbour Watch Archives and Minutes.

8 Dun Laoghaire Lifeboat Station Archives and Minutes.

9 Archives of the Maritime Institute of Ireland, especially classified newspaper cuttings 1956 to 1995.

10 Scout Association of Ireland: Lightship Albatross National Sea Training Centre, updated, c. 1968.

11 Speech of Joe Bermingham TD Minister in charge of Public Works, on future of harbour, 1984.

12 Paper of M.J. Tully to Old Dublin Society, October 1960.

13 Wexford Harbour Commissioners Minutes – January 15 1827.

## BIBLIOGRAPHY

a) Books

Catalogue of Maps and Charts in the Possession of Dublin Port and Docks Board, Dublin 1994.

M.E. Daly: *Dublin the Deposed Capital: A Social and Economic History 1860–1984*, Cork University Press 1985.

J. de Courcy Ireland: *Wreck and Rescue on the East Coast of Ireland*, Dublin 1981.

H.A. Gilligan: *A History of the Port of Dublin*, Dublin 1988.

B. Haresnape: *Sealink*, London 1991.

R. Lohan: *Guide to the Archives of the Office of Public Works.*

D.B. McNeill: *Irish Passenger Steamship Services*, Dublin 1994, Vol 2, South of Ireland, Newton Abbot, 1971.

J. O'Sullivan and S. Cannon: (Edition 2) *The Book of Dun Laoghaire* 1987.

P. Pearson: *Dun Laoghaire – Kingstown*, Dublin 1981.

B. Scott: *Sealink and its Predecessors in Dublin*, Dublin 1989.

H.P. Smyth: *The B + I Line*, Dublin 1984.

PERIODICALS

*Afloat* (*Dublin Monthly*) 1992–1998

Bulletin of Dun Laoghaire Harbour Board from No. 1 1991

46A (Dun Laoghaire) 1994 issues

*Journal of the Irish Railway Records Society* June 1994

*Sea Breezes* (Liverpool) Oct. 1952, July 1955, July 1961, Dec. 1961, Jan. 1967, Sept. 1975

# INDEX

THE FIRST SHEET OF AN ACTUAL SURVEY OF THE ENVIR
Clontarf Oyster Bed
THE HARBOUR
West Buoy
Light Ship
The Head of the Piles
Quarantine Sloop
The Pacquet Moorings
THE PILES
THE SOUTH BULL
THE SOUTH CHA
SOUTH LIBERTY
Cock Lake
The Line determins the Low Water of the Bounds of the Rt Hon the LORD MAYOR
Lord Merrions Brick Fields
The Strand of Cock Merrion
Sluice
Lake
High Water Mark
MERRION
Black Rock
BLACK ROCK TOWN
Road to Sillorgan
Counc. Cockley's House
Black Rock Avenue
Dunlary
EXPLANATION
Rivers
Hedges
Ditches
Buildings
Walls
Brooks
Roads
Orchards
Paths
Ponds
Hills
Pasture
The Sound taken at Lo the Figures